Women and Muslim Family

WOMEN AND MUSLIM FAMILY LAWS IN ARAB STATES

A COMPARATIVE OVERVIEW OF TEXTUAL DEVELOPMENT AND ADVOCACY

Lynn Welchman

ISIM SERIES ON CONTEMPORARY MUSLIM SOCIETIES

AMSTERDAM UNIVERSITY PRESS

Cover design and lay-out: De Kreeft, Amsterdam

ISBN 978 90 5356 974 0
NUR 741 / 717

© ISIM / Amsterdam University Press, 2007

to Akram al-Khatib

Contents

Preface

This book traces and compares the approaches of different Arab League member states to a set of issues in the family law codifications that apply to their majority Muslim populations as they appear in the early years of the twenty-first century ce. Looking at 'text' in this way has become rather unfashionable in at least some parts of the Western academy. This is mostly due to disciplinary developments in the specialist fields and in the profiles of scholars joining them – which, as elsewhere in scholarship, serve to locate and date earlier scholarship not only by years but by approach and perspective. Some well-deserved criticism has been made of the positivist, state-centric and 'Orientalist' approach of certain prominent Western scholars of Islamic law of previous generations. This foreword is not meant to be a double bluff; I'm not going to say that like others in my field I am aware of the limitations of state-law-focussed analysis of the legal field but having shown my awareness, will do it anyway. It is rather to affirm the continuing significance and interest of statutory codifications of Muslim family law in the Arab states of the Middle East and North Africa to an English-reading audience other than practising lawyers and 'experts'. It is abundantly clear that statutory law tells either only part of the story of 'the law', or only one story among many. That (part of the) story is still worth telling.

Following critiques of colonial-era academia, a recognition of the political contingency of scholarship has happily led to 'incentives to modesty' on the part of some scholars currently working in the area. Such modesty is all the more in order in light of the neo-imperial nature of political engagements with the Arab region at the current time; the discourses of post-colonial scholarship do not always recognise the full implications of this framework for the contemporary academic enterprise. However they are positioned, scholars in the Western academy need to be clear about the framework of 'the West's' current engagement with these issues. Humility and personal rigour about the different limits within which we each work, along with aspirations to push them, remain helpful guiding principles.

This small book was written mostly in Ramallah, over the period 2005-2006. I would like to thank all my friends from there, not only for the recent times, but for the years of memories and friendship, and in hope of better times for the people of Palestine. In particular: Salwa Du'aybis, Susan Rockwell, Zakariya Odeh, Mary McKone and Fateh Azzam, Rami and Haneen; Mahmoud and Helen Hawari, Tariq and Yara; Charles Shamas and Maha Abu Dayyeh, Raja and Diala; Majda Al-Saqqa, John Tordai, Raja Shehadah and Penny Johnson, Rema Hammami and Alex Pollock. Special thoughts for Samia Shibli, Richard Sexton and Sireen: Richard, you are much missed. I would also like to thank friends and colleagues at al-Haq (especially Sha'wan Jabarin, Ellen Saliba, Nina Atallah and Naser al-Rayes), Mizan (especially Essam Younis), PCHR (especially Raji Sourani) and WCLAC (especially Soraida Hussein). Evenings with Sami and Doha Ayyad and with Usama and Amal Halabi and their families considerably brightened the difficult summer of 2006 when the book was being finished.

I would like to acknowledge the Faculty of Law and Social Sciences at SOAS for the teaching leave that provided the opportunity to write this piece, and for a grant to have the index prepared. Annelies Moors is due particular thanks for encouraging the publication of the book; I value both her friendship and her scholarship. The same appreciation goes to Ziba Mir-Hosseini. At the School of Law, Ian Edge and Werner Menski both generously provided me with material for this piece; and my special thanks to Fareda Banda, Doreen Hinchcliffe and Cathy Jenkins. Among SOAS students I am grateful for particular material to Faten Abbar, Mohamed Keshavgee, Nahed Samour and Hesham Shawish. In Morocco I am indebted to Jamila Bargach, Fouzia Khan and Khalid al-Shaykh; in the UAE to Rana al-Khatib; in Jordan to Firas Bakr, Reem Abu Hassan and Nouf al-Rawwaf; in Palestine to Shaykh Taysir al-Tamimi; in London to Cassandra Balchin; in Egypt to Amal Abdel Hadi, Fateh Azzam, Abdullah Khalil, and Adel Omar Sherif; in the US to Farida Daif; in Syria to Fadi Sarkis; in Qatar to 'Alya al-Thani. My thanks also to the two anonymous reviewers, to the editors at ISIM, and to Sarah Hibbin for preparing the index.

Finally, as always, my thanks go to my family, given and chosen. Especially, this time, to Geoffrey Knights: Geoff, this is not only for Della, but for your love and laughter over the years as a father and a friend, and for taking me and Sian on as well as Elsie Jane, all those years ago.

1 Introduction

In the late twentieth century, a combination of geopolitical developments focussed particular attention on 'the Islamic shari‘a' and specifically on its role as an identity and legitimacy signifier for opposition movements in and the governments of Muslim majority states. Positivist approaches to legislative power concentrated on the statutory expression of rules in different areas of state law. After varying periods of independent statehood, a number of post-colonial states promulgated instruments of statutory law presented as reintroducing the rules and sanctions of Islamic criminal law into penal systems otherwise largely based on colonial legislation. Systems of Islamic banking and Islamic finance developed apace. Constitutional arguments focussed on the various formulations through which 'the shari‘a' or 'the principles of the shari‘a' are or should be established as a source (or the source) of statutory legislation. In different Muslim majority states, courts became a site for contestation of different perceptions of the requirements of the shari‘a and the extent to which statutory laws and the state-appointed judiciary would defend or concede to these different invocations of 'Islamic law'.[1]

Very much part of this context is the high degree of political attention currently paid to Muslim family law developments in Arab states and elsewhere, both in Muslim majority states and in countries where Muslims are a minority. At the same time, the particular focus on statutory expressions of the shari‘a governing family relations has been a more consistent feature in recent history than that on certain other areas of state law. Scholars in the Western academy have described family law variously as the 'last bastion' or 'last stronghold' of the shari‘a, evoking in such metaphors an image of the forces ranged against (secularist reformers, European colonial powers, encroaching state authorities, among others) and of the defenders of the fort (variously, the establishment shar‘i scholars and judiciary, and/or non-establishment constituencies).[2] The metaphors evoke ideas of siege and battle reinforced in current times by the forces of cultural globalisation, forces both insidious and rampaging. Historically, they relate to the processes of codification of laws and reorganisation of judicial systems which began in the Middle East in the nineteenth century under the Ottomans and the Egyptians and continued in the twentieth century under European colonial powers and in the independent states that emerged in the region. The wide-scale adoption or imposition of European-based statutory codifications excluded the area of family law – apart from the textual form of a 'code' – except in Turkey after the end of the Ottoman Empire. In Muslim family law, the claims of the state as the originator of authoritative norms were attenuated by a proclaimed subordination to the norms of the *shari'a* as extrapolated, mostly, from the established and diverse jurisprudence (*fiqh*) of Muslim jurists. This approach was not confined to Muslim family law; it was also how the Ottoman authorities had approached civil law, compiling selected rulings from the Hanafi school on civil law issues into the 'Majalla' in the late nineteenth century.[3] However, subsequent developments in the rules on contract and civil torts around the region have attracted considerably less public and political interest than those governing family law for the majority Muslim population.[4]

The process of codification of Muslim family law began in the Middle East with the Ottoman Law of Family Rights of 1917 and its accompanying Law of *Shar'i* Procedure for the *shari'a* courts. Prior to this, the uncodified jurisprudence of the schools of law, guided mostly by the prevailing opinions of the school of the particular *qadi* (judge), had been applied to questions of Muslim family law. Manuals, compilations and commentaries on the opinions of earlier prominent jurists guided the judges in the application of the law. Under the Ottomans the Hanafi school was the preferred or 'official' school of law. The Ottoman Law of Family Rights (OLFR) took Hanafi opinion as its basis while bringing in minority opinions from the school, and also drew on rules from the other Sunni schools, and on occasion from individual views of prominent jurists from the past, in order to implement and standardise legal approaches to issues of particular interest to the legislator at the start of the twentieth century, at the end of empire, and almost at the end of the encounter of the Ottoman Empire with the West.

The Ottoman law was abandoned shortly after its promulgation by the new Turkish state, which adapted a version of the Swiss civil code to govern family relations without formal or official reference to *shar'i* rules or assumptions. Recent research tracks the continuing application of *shari'a*-based family law among different sections of Turkish Muslim society, and how this application interacts with the state's formal legal system.[5] Elsewhere, the OLFR was applied to varying extents in different Ottoman successor states under the rule of Western powers established at the end of the 1914-1918 war. The British Mandate power in Palestine for example implemented those parts of the Ottoman law addressed only to Muslims, repealing the sections intended to apply to Christian and Jewish subjects in favour of requiring these communities to apply their own personal status laws. In Israel, parts of the original Ottoman law continue to apply to Muslim Palestinians, although modified by local legislation. Elsewhere, the OLFR provided a model drawn upon in form and in some of its substance by codifications of Muslim personal status laws for newly independent East Arab states in the 1950s. In Egypt, where the OLFR had not been applied, significant legislation was issued in the 1920s and 1940s which, while not constituting an overall 'code', addressed a number of areas of family law with approaches that were similarly incorporated into later national codifications elsewhere in the region. In the 1950s, in a second phase of Muslim family law reform, first codifications were issued in Jordan, Syria, Tunisia, Morocco and Iraq; since then, all these countries have either issued substantive amendments or new laws – in some cases, both. Other states have issued codifications for the first time, the most recent being the UAE at the end of 2005 and Qatar in 2006. In this study, these more recent instruments (issued over the last quarter century or so) and the literature that examines their substance, context, and implications are considered as part of a 'third phase' of Muslim family law reform in the Arab world.

The codes differ as to their detail and also as to how they are applied. In Jordan, Lebanon and Palestine, for example, the codes of Muslim personal status law are applied though a system of *shariʿa* courts separate from the 'civil court' (*nizami*) system. In Egypt, the system of *shariʿa* courts was abolished in the 1950s, with family law applied in the regular courts of the unified national legal system; in a recent (2004) major adjustment in the court system, family courts have been constituted to deal with all personal status issues, without this indicating a move towards a *shariʿa* court system. In terms of substance, many states continue to explain the provenance of particular provisions in their codifications through tracing them to the opinions of various past jurists and schools, combined with arguments made on the basis of changing socio-economic circumstances and the public interest. Scholars as well as political opponents are wont to criticise an approach that they consider to proceed by identifying the social or political objective and working backwards to find a justification, rather than seeking the construction of a coherent jurisprudence or taking responsibility for state choices in family law.

In the Western academy, commentary on the modern history of Muslim personal status law has developed from the observation of the late JND Anderson that family law is regarded by Muslims 'as partaking most closely of the very warp and woof of their religion',[6] to critiques and reassessments of the interests of colonial powers and the impact of their rule (and of resistance to their rule) on the attitude of different sectors of the subject populations to the nature and significance of *shari'a* rules and on the substantive content of codifications of Muslim family law subsequently issued by independent Arab states.[7] The discourses of reform, modernity and national unity employed by centralising and bureaucratising state authorities in their promulgation of family law codifications are scrutinised in recognition of the centrality of the state as represented in and reinforced through the codification process, and of the place of 'Islamic family law' as a symbol of religious and national identity. A range of contemporary literature starting in the late twentieth century seeks *inter alia* to evaluate the impact of such codifications on the position and options of women subject to their jurisdiction.

Some of this literature looks at the interactions of law and society, the practice of law in the courts and/or its varying significance in out-of-court negotiations and individual strategies of protection and advancement by women in different socio-economic sectors.[8] As lucidly analysed by Moors,[9] disciplinary shifts to legal anthropology, socio-legal studies and women's and gender studies, and the changing profile of researchers have variously expanded, challenged and nuanced academic understandings of 'Islamic family law' in its pre-codification applications and social practice, its 'translation' by colonial powers, and its current meanings and practices.[10] Recognition of the political contingency not only of institutions such as family and law but of scholarship have led to 'incentives to modesty' on the part of some researchers in Islamic family law.[11] The assumption that it is 'Islam' or 'Islamic law' that determines gender relations in specific contexts is critiqued; the meaning and nature of 'the family' are investigated;[12] the personalities and 'embedded positionings' of judges are considered.[13] Recognition of differences among women prompts both scholarly and activist (re-)assessments of the priorities and impacts of family law reform.[14] At the same time, on the level of public discourse, the texts of the laws promulgated by states are examined for the choices they make and the story of gender relations that they describe or prescribe, the constituencies whose voices are heard in these choices, the economic and political circumstances of their debate and promulgation, and the strategies, alliances and coalitions that develop around advocacy by different social actors, including broadly defined groups of feminists and Islamists.[15] At the end of the twentieth century, if family law (or personal status law) had become the 'preferential symbol of Muslim identity',[16] the rallying of different and opposing constituencies to the cause of proposed changes in statutory law on the subject was also analysed as a central element in civil society mobilisation and in the claiming and contestation of space in an 'emerging public sphere'.[17] These developments increasingly challenge governmental patterns of reliance on executive power or on other tactical strategies of avoidance to side-step or out-flank opposition to key legislative decisions on family law.

The focus of this study is on the most recent (third phase) legislation in each state, with indications of how the approaches and substance have either changed from earlier legislative interventions, or in the event of first-time legislation, how they can be compared with trends across the region. Reference is made to earlier, mostly English-language examinations of text and practice in different countries, where particular developments need to be set against earlier positions in the law. Every effort has been made to ensure the information is accurate up to the end of the year 2005, although in some cases information on practice and indeed of legislative amendment has not been easy to obtain.[18] The commentary and analysis focus on the legal texts, court practice where this information is available, the manner in which the state authorities present the texts, and public policy debates including the interventions of women's and human rights groups. There is consideration of interventions by Islamist legislators, but I do not investigate in any systematic manner the activism of Islamist or other political movements around family law issues; the focus is on interventions and assessments by 'women's rights' advocacy, broadly defined. [19]

Where this study makes reference to the *fiqh*-based origins of particular provisions, this is in the context of the arguments being made by different parties in the debate; otherwise, I do not investigate the jurisprudential provenance of different laws in the manner of earlier considerations of personal status law codifications in Arab states, such as those by JND Anderson.

It is also worth noting that I do not seek to assess whether or not particular approaches or provisions have a 'basis' in 'classical' Islamic *fiqh* (jurisprudence) or indeed in the foundational texts of the Qur'an and the *Sunna*.[20] These arguments are indeed made by legislatures and invoked by different advocates of change, and as such are discussed here in the specific context of contemporary policy debates. The premise of this study is that however much what is presented by contemporary states as '*shari'a*' (or as *shari'a*-based) differs in form and substance from previous articulations of '*shari'a*', the principle that Muslim family law is '*shari'a*-based' is still a notion explicitly deferred to by the state, and thus constitutes a form of basic 'legal postulate'.[21] This '*shar'i* postulate' is presented as informing the choices made by state legislatures in their national formulations of Muslim family law; it also informs the interpretation and application of statutory instruments by the judiciary. It has furthermore informed the different means and levels of engagement developed between the judiciary, the legislature and Arab women's movements seeking enhanced and expanded protection of women's rights within the family, whether through the content of legislation, or through access to justice and the conduct of the judiciary. It is at this level that these issues are engaged in this study.

The study begins with a consideration of various issues that recur in discussions and debates on the codification of Muslim personal status law in Arab states and on the application of codified law. These include the principle and processes of codification, the interaction of the judiciary with both the text and the legislature, and the wider interaction of women's rights activists and governments with relevant instruments of international human rights law. Different areas of Muslim personal status law are then considered thematically, with reference to the codified laws of the following member states of the Arab League: Algeria, Egypt, Jordan, Iraq, Kuwait, Libya, Mauritania, Morocco, Oman, Qatar, Sudan. Syria, Tunisia, UAE and Yemen. Occasional consideration is made of a draft Palestinian text of 2005. Member states of the Arab League not included in the preceding list are Djibouti and the Comoros Islands, due to my lack of access to and information on legislative sources; Lebanon, due to the absence of a 'national' codification of Muslim personal status law applying to all Muslim sects;[22] and Saudi Arabia and Bahrain. Certain developments in the last three countries are discussed in the course of this study, but Saudi Arabia has no codification of Muslim personal status law, and although I examine some aspects of the current debate over codification in Bahrain, I was not able to access any of the various draft laws to reference in the discussion. In addition, I was not able to access information on current family law practice in Somalia, but have provided occasional comparative reference to the 1975 code of the previous Socialist Somali government. At the end of the study I include translations of relevant provisions from the laws under consideration grouped in a number of specific subject areas: capacity and guardianship, polygyny, the marital relationship, stipulations, judicial *khulʿ* and comparable divorce provisions, and compensation for injurious or arbitrary divorce. The aim here is to give some substance to the comparative conclusions drawn in the body of the text on legislative patterns and developments in these areas.[23]

2 Codification of Muslim Personal Status Law in Arab States: principle and processes[1]

As the overview of recent legislation given in the following chapter indicates, the tendency towards national codification begun in earnest in the 1950s and continues today in Arab states as probably the major mechanism of state intervention in Muslim family matters. Where there is no codification, there is activism from women's groups advocating for the adoption of a code; where a code has been previously legislated, the text and application of the law are subjected to examination with a view to activism demanding – usually – expanded and more detailed intervention from the legislature through amendments, directives, guidelines and the establishment of particular fora for dispute processing in family law matters. On the other hand, as this chapter shows, resistance to codification takes place in specifically contingent political circumstances that may not immediately be related to the content *per se* of the law.

Note has already been made of the substantial and developing literature on and broadening disciplinary approaches to women and Muslim family law in the Arab world, in historical and contemporary perspectives. The valuable contributions of the work on historical sources have included illustrating the agency of women in accessing *shari'a*-based rights in legal dealings and *shari'a* courts in history, and equally illustrating the historical dealings of the judiciary with women petitioners and respondents. This scholarship has immediate contemporary significance. As Sonbol observes:

> By rediscovering these rights through court records, contemporary personal status laws can be questioned. Particularly important here is questioning the religious sanctity that the State gives to personal status laws on the books in Muslim countries today.[2]

Following on from this, another issue that is raised involves the choices made by Arab states in their post-colonial codifications of Muslim family law, with illustrations of the gendered nature of these choices and the proposition that since the codifications are based on 'state patriarchy', we have to examine the impacts of the particular choices (and reforms) on particular women, perhaps more closely than did scholars of earlier ages. In this as well as in other disciplines therefore, the necessary and universalised relationship of modernity, reform and the advancement of women may be unsettled. Finally, contrasts are made very ably by these and other scholars (such as Brinkley Messick[3]) between the 'closed' nature of the codes, as compared with the 'deliberately open' nature of the previous system of *fiqh* articulation and application, a system which largely left application of Muslim family law to the judge, mostly through the implementation of dominant rules from the judge's school, despite evidence of occasional central direction on particular issues at particular times.[4]

In regard to the latter point in particular, there has been some assumption that not only has the role of the *shar'i* judiciary in general, and the judge in particular, inevitably been altered through the process of codification, but that this role has been considerably constrained and that the codifications have almost terminally undermined the flexibility and ability of the judge to exercise discretion in seeking a just solution to individual cases. That is to say, the 'conscience' has more or less gone out of the application of the law as a result of its tighter central direction from the political (legislative) authority. On this point, it is important to draw attention to work that focuses on the court-based application of contemporary Muslim family law, seeking to understand the way in which the *qadi* conducts himself when deciding issues of justice in accordance with a codified law. Among this work is Nahda Shehada's *Justice without Drama*, an ethnographic study looking at precisely this issue in the Gaza City *shari'a* court.[5] She finds in a variety of cases that '[w]hen *qudah* find that strict adherence to the written code would lead to an unjust outcome, they strive to interpret the law in a way that brings it more in harmony with its objectives.'[6] Shehada's conclusions include that:

> even with the codification of Islamic family law, people, be they *qudah*, lawyers or litigants, are active social agents, working out their interests and values in the grey zone created by the interplay of codified law, uncodified norms and the multiple references of *qudah*.[7]

Shehada recognises that the Gaza and indeed Palestine context have their obvious particularities, but work going on elsewhere in the Arab world may well support these conclusions on the basis of observations in the courts. The proposition here is that the *qadi* will seek to protect the weak, the disempowered and the vulnerable, which means that within the gendered frameworks of law and society, he will often find himself in a protective role towards the female litigant, even though the instances and limits of this 'protection' are shaped by the *qadi*'s own social expectations, understandings, and professional education, as indeed they are under uncodified law.[8] The additional fact of a codified law may constrain the judge's choices of protective action in some cases, just as it may constrain strategies employed by women in the courts. Examples here might be the statutory limitation (normally one year) of the post-divorce *'idda* period during which a wife might claim maintenance from her husband, as well as the limitation of the period for which arrears of maintenance can be claimed. Another example comes in the general take-up, in codifications, of the position that a *talaq* accompanied in word or sign by a number or by any other expression of finality gives rise only to a single revocable *talaq*, rather than causing the immediate and irrevocable 'triple *talaq*' of traditional Sunni (but not Shi'i) law. The latter statutory provisions are officially explained as necessary to constrain the irresponsible, arbitrary and injurious use of *talaq* by the husband, invoking the debilitating insecurity suffered by women in their marriages as a result of the lack of such restriction in traditional Sunni law. Moors, on the other hand, notes that such reforms as '[a]bolishing conditional and triple divorce do not always work to women's benefit; in the past, women have made selective and strategic use of these in order to bring about a desired divorce'.[9]

On the other hand, codification – and its associated bureaucratic and procedural regimes – is clearly regarded as the form of state intervention most readily available for the political authorities in most Arab states to address the issue of women's rights within the family, and as the key to the implementation by the state of its commitments in regard to family law reform: rules on for example the minimum age of marriage, on consent, and on polygynous unions are executed and monitored through this process. In recent decades, women's rights activists have sought greater input into and participation in the formulation of these state interventions. This may be on specific issues, or more broadly in seeking the participation of women in

drafting committees, as well as monitoring the conduct of women legislators in debates on Muslim family law. However unreliable an ally the state
may be for women's rights activists, centralised law, carefully drafted and
properly implemented, remains the target of much women's rights advocacy
in the region.

Current debates: Bahrain and Iraq

One of the remaining Arab states yet to promulgate a codified family law is
Bahrain where, in 2003, a group of women advocating for a codified law and
reform of the *shari'a* court system ended up embroiled in cases at the civil
and criminal courts with members of the *shar'i* judiciary. Bahrain is a member of the Gulf Cooperation Council which in 1997 approved the 'Musqat document', a model codified Muslim personal status law which closely
influenced the codifications in Oman and the UAE. The Bahraini discussion
on a codified Muslim family law dates back over twenty years, and a Personal
Status Committee has been in existence for as long, so far without the promulgation of a code. In 2003, significant opposition to the codification of Muslim family law was led by members of the *shar'i* judiciary from both Sunni
and the majority Shi'i communities in Bahrain. As the debate heated up, it
became clear that this opposition focussed variously on the drafting and
promulgation processes, discussed further below, and on the principle and
the alternative forms of codification. On the principle, a judge in the Shi'i
court system told a local newspaper that:

> A unified law of personal status constitutes a risk that *shar'i* cases will not be
> given their full due by examining the considerations that vary from one case to
> another. The existence of a written law binds the *shar'i* judge, resulting in wrongs
> to men and women alike.[10]

The objection voiced here is the direct opposite of that made by those advocating for the adoption of a code. Ghada Jamshir, head of the Committee for
Women's Petition (established in 2003), describes her group's first goal as
'working for the promulgation of a personal status law to regulate the affairs of the Muslim family' and explains why:

The absence of such a law means that the *shar'i qadi* has the final say, he rules on God's command, what he says is obeyed and his order is binding. You find each *shar'i qadi* ruling according to his whim; you even find a number of [different] rulings on the same question, which has brought things to a very bad state of affairs in the *shari'a* courts. The demand for the promulgation of this law aims at eliminating many problems and at unifying rulings; it would reassure people of the conduct of litigation, and would guarantee women their rights rather than leaving them at the mercy of fate.[11]

These two arguments show the different values placed on, and the tension between, judicial discretion and legislative direction. The *qadi* stresses the need to leave matters in the hands of the judge in order to maintain the necessary flexibility in the approach to individual cases. The women's rights activist demands state intervention, in the form of a codified law, precisely to restrict the exercise of such discretion on the part of individual judges, to make the law 'known' and rulings more predictable. The *qadi* demands trust in the unknowable person of the individual judge; the woman's rights activist demands guarantees of justice from the amorphous and contingent entity that is 'the state'.

One of the key issues in the Bahraini debate that is not clear from this quote is the insistence by women activists on a single unified code that would apply to both Sunni and Shi'i Bahrainis. Many of the *shar'i* judges involved in the debate, however, if they conceded the validity of a codification process, wanted two separate codifications for the two separate communities. The Minister of Justice, quoted on the matter in a meeting in 2003, acknowledged that there were drafts of both forms in existence, and would not at that stage be drawn on the likely form that the government would ultimately propose.[12] In Lebanon, in contrast to other parts of the Arab Middle East, separate codified laws have long been the basis of family law regulation for different Muslim sects. Elsewhere in the Gulf, a slightly different approach has recently been taken in Oman, where the majority of the population is Ibadi, and in Qatar where the majority is Hanbali. In Oman, the 1997 law makes two specific exceptions to the application of the provisions of the code to Muslims. Where the *fiqh* school of the husband has 'stricter rules or particular procedures' regarding divorce, the *qadi* is to observe these conditions and procedures; and where the rules of the testator's school differ from the provisions of the code in regard to the inheritance of the daughter and grandfather, the judge is to apply the dominant opinion of the testator's school unless the heirs by consensus request the application of the provisions of the code.[13] In Qatar, the law provides that the Law of the Family will apply to 'all those subject to the Hanbali *madhhab*'. Along with non-Muslims, Muslims adhering to other schools of law may apply their own rules, or may opt for application of the state's codification.[14]

In Bahrain, the legal and institutional debate reflects both the size and the power of the Sunni minority in relation to the Shi'i majority. The separate expertises and institutional interests of the two sets of *shari'a* courts reflecting the communal make-up of the population is a key challenge to women advocating the promulgation of a unified code. In Iraq, an existing unified code is today under serious challenge from those who wish to re-institute communal jurisdiction. Writing in 1960, Norman Anderson compared the 1959 Iraqi Law of Personal Status with a pre-existing draft Code that had been approved by the relevant legislative committee the previous decade, but had never been promulgated by parliament due to 'the opposition it aroused in certain religious quarters – most of all, perhaps, among the leaders of the Ithna 'Ashari or 'Ja'afari' sect.' In this early draft code, just under half the articles provided rules that differed ('in whole or in part') for Sunnis and for Ja'afaris, including nearly all the rules on inheritance. Comparing the 1959 law promulgated by the new revolutionary regime to that previous draft, Anderson found that:

> It is far shorter, and therefore leaves much more to the discretion of the *qadi*; it is far more radical, and includes a number of quite daring innovations; and it eliminates all differences between Sunnis and Ja'afaris, even in regard to inheritance.

For his part, Anderson foresaw 'major problems posed by the brevity of this code', which was 'presumably intentionally silent' on a number of key issues. From a common law system himself, it appears that when it came to codification of Islamic family law, he found the lengthier and more detailed approaches of for example Syria more satisfactory than Iraq's 'economy in legislative precision and extravagant reliance on judicial discretion'.[15] Opposition to particular parts of the 1959 law continued, and when a new regime came to power in 1963, it repealed the controversial provisions on inheritance (which had applied Civil Code provisions to all intestate property) along with the stipulation that a polygynous marriage concluded without the consent of the court was invalid.

In 1990, Chibli Mallat reviewed the criticism on the part particularly of Shi'i scholars to Iraq's unified code of 1959 as 'a blueprint of a world debate to come'.[16] At the end of 2003, Iraq's then Governing Council, in the happenstance absence of a number of its female members, passed 'Resolution 137' in a move that portended the potential abrogation of the unified Iraqi Law of Personal Status.[17] Resolution 137 required the application of 'the provisions of Islamic *shari'a*' to all questions of Muslim personal status in accordance with the law schools of different sects. A range of women's groups mobilised against this move, supported by international interventions from a wide network of women's organisations who addressed themselves *inter alia* to the US occupying authorities in Iraq as the approval of the Coalition Provisional Authority's US governor was needed for 'Resolution 137' to be promulgated as law.[18] The resolution was suppressed, but in 2005 the debate was revived as the newly elected assembly engaged the process of constitution drafting, and the substance of Resolution 137 reappeared:

> Article 39: Iraqis are free in their adherence to their personal status according to their own religion, sect, belief, and choice, that will be organized by law.

The tragedies attending so many Iraqi lives today clearly impact the extent of attention to and concern about Muslim family law reform in Iraqi society, but nevertheless advocacy and debate continue, often with the support of trans-national solidarity networks. In a 2006 study focussing on article 39 of the Constitution, the organisation Women Leadership Institute Iraq finds this article to be a violation of Iraq's obligations under CEDAW.[19] At the time of writing, the future of the 1959 Iraqi Law of Personal Status (together with its numerous amendments) was unclear. Some women's groups and activists, in Iraq and elsewhere, insist that as it stands, the Iraqi code is still relatively radical in the Arab world, and that grave losses for women's rights would ensue on its repeal. Others call energetically for the institution of a national, unified, secular civil law.[20] The potential of the constitutional provision cited above is to allow different Muslim communities the 'choice' to regulate personal status issues separately from others. The fact that this is to be 'organized by law' means that different groups in Iraq, at the end of 2005, were engaged in considering legislative instruments that could fulfil the constitutional provision while protecting women's rights in the family to the greatest potential. In such a situation, procedure is key: for example, a requirement that individuals opt out of an existing national law is critically different from them having to opt in. A continuing national law may also make specific provision for sectarian differences on particular issues while maintaining a minimum of protection for women's rights in the family. It is not clear whether opponents of the unified code contemplate returning to the application of uncodified *fiqh* by Sunni and Shi'i *shar'i* judges in their respective courts, or whether they envisage continuing state control through legislative direction but in separate legislative instruments. However these debates turn out, it appears to be the first time that an Arab state stands to formally (and constitutionally) retreat from an established, nationally applicable statutory codification of Muslim family law. The fact that a range of women's rights activists oppose such a move is indicative, again, that many prefer the risks of 'state patriarchy' in the form of state intervention through a code to the risks of the state retreating from intervention in family law.

Legislation, judicial discretion and political process

More detailed consideration is given to the relationship between legislative direction and judicial discretion in the texts and workings of the codes in Chapter 4. However, in terms of the focus of the current chapter, it is important to recall that the practical application of the law not only affects the way in which the codification works but also influences its substantive content. Courtroom experiences clearly fed into the national codifications of family law in the region; in Iraq, for example, the 1959 law refers the judge explicitly to 'the rulings established by the judiciary and Islamic jurisprudence in Iraq' as well as 'in other Muslim countries where the laws approximate those of Iraq' in the event of there being no explicit text or a question of interpretation. The hierarchical structure of courts formalised in the twentieth century in different countries, and the increasing publication and dissemination of the rulings of higher courts, also stand to have an impact both on the application of the law and on the content of subsequent legislative instruments – whether this content comes to affirm or to overturn established judicial positions. In some cases the Explanatory Memoranda to laws refer to positions adopted or problems noted in the courts prior to promulgation of the codification. In this sense, it may be important to nuance Amira Sonbol's statement that:

> When modern States built new separate *Shari'ah* courts they did not apply precedents from pre-modern *Shari'ah* courts. Rather, modern States constructed legal codes compiled by committees and handed them to *qadis* educated in newly opened *qadi* schools...[21]

Sonbol's focus here is the nineteenth rather than the twentieth century, and on the rupture in form and substance that occurred between pre-modern application of Muslim family law and codification under new nation-states. In the twentieth century, Sonbol's arguments about 'state patriarchy' and the risk to women of codified law apart, the accumulated experience of the 'new style' application in the *shari'a* courts of different Arab states was clearly feeding into the substance of the law. In addition, members of the *shar'i* judiciary engage directly with issues of the balance between legislative direction and judicial discretion.

In the first codifications, the drafting committees were frequently headed by the Chief Islamic Justice (*Qadi al-Qudah*) and other senior members of the *shar'i* judiciary. It may be that the political authority mandated the drafting brief to senior members of the judiciary and establishment *'ulama'* (scholars) both in practical and strategic recognition of the particular *shar'i* expertise needed in this area of the law. Certainly, one of the changes in some more recent processes of codification – such as that in Morocco leading to the new law in 2004, and the temporary amendments in Jordan in 2001 – is the inclusion in drafting committees of those with expertise outside the *shar'i* system, including women: in Jordan this included the government-appointed Royal Commission for Human Rights along with the Office of the *Qadi al-Qudah*; in Morocco, different commentators describe the consultative committee appointed by the King as comprising 'scholars' (*'ulama'*), 'judges' and 'women.'[22] The processes of democratisation and increased participation have led women's movements in different Arab states to seek inclusion in such drafting processes, and while arguments are still made for the exclusivity of *shar'i* expertise, it is increasingly usual to find members of the *shar'i* judiciary and other *'ulama'* being joined in these appointed committees by those of other expertise, such as sociologists and psychologists. In Qatar, where the drafting committee was constituted of judges, the circulation of the resulting draft provided a forum for review and intervention *inter alia* by Qatari women, with the governmental National Committee for Women's Affairs submitting amendments for the consideration of the drafting committee.[23]

In the recent debates in Bahrain, *shar'i qadis* and *'ulama'* from both the Sunni and Ja'afari communities vigorously asserted their singular expertise to the exclusion of the legislative process. This point was made not only in support of the anti-codification position, but also by those who conceded the principle of codification but opposed the involvement of the legislature in the process. There were warnings that allowing the legislature, the National Council, to vote on drafts and promulgate a law would render *shar'i* rulings on personal status 'hostage to the Deputies', and that a parliamentary process could result in serious violations of the *shari'a*. One *shar'i* judge argued as follows to a local paper:

> There is no such thing as personal status law: it is an inseparable part of Islamic *fiqh*. These demands for a westernised law are demands supported by secularist and leftist movements which in various ways try to distance *shari'a* from life... I consider discussion of this by the members to be a crime. The members are not qualified from the point of view of culture, religion, *shari'a* or even law to discuss these matters, and this poses an unacceptable risk to the independence of the judiciary.[24]

An alternative drafting mechanism was proposed by a senior Ja'afari cleric in a meeting with members of the Women's Committee for Petition that was reported in the press as an attempt at bridge-building.[25] Ayatollah Shaykh Hussain al-Najati was quoted as follows:

> We are not against the principle of a law of personal status; it could be a very positive thing... What we are talking about is the mechanism of promulgating such a law through the parliament. We see certain risks – whether this happens through parliament or another institution, it is not a risk-free process... We of course believe that the personal status law must be in rigorous conformity with the Islamic *shari'a*: we are all Muslims, so naturally we all insist that the law must in all its provisions conform with the rulings of Islam. Now, assuming that the law were to be promulgated today by this current parliament and in conformity with the Islamic *shari'a*, scholars would still worry that in the future, even in coming terms, there may be those who will change provisions of the law in a manner

that does not in fact accord with the *shariʿa* [...] If we decide today that parliament has the authority to pass this law, then we can't take this authority away in the future... We are with the law, and I think that you too want the law itself, and are not so concerned about which institution passes it...

With this introduction, al-Najati proposed that the women's activists join his call for the Supreme Judicial Council to pass an internal regulation for the *shariʿa* courts: 'this will bind the judge and it will be like a law; what matters to us all is not the means but the result.' There is no report on the reaction of the Committee members to these proposals, although they do not appear to have changed their insistence on a unified family law to be passed through parliamentary legislative process. The significance of al-Najati's intervention lies not only in his concern to find common ground between the *ʿulama'* and women activists, but in his carefully phrased explanation of why he and others were so distrustful of the parliamentary process. In effect, this position would mean that Muslim family law would be permanently removed from direct state intervention through the legislature. During a time of increasing political participation and attention to democracy-building, this is presented as necessary in order to protect the law itself, and through it Bahraini society.

While countries without a codified family law see campaigns to achieve one, among the features of campaigns where codes are already in place are proposals for increasingly detailed legislation. In light of experiences of failed legislative projects as well as more successful ones, the argument here is that if women's rights in the family are to be protected by the submission of various acts (such as early marriage, polygynous marriage, divorce, etc.) to judicial scrutiny, then judicial discretion must be (increasingly) directed from the legislature in order to secure the intended impact of the desired legislative changes, and to avoid their being subverted by the exercise or abuse of judicial discretion. An example is how the new law in Morocco has changed the definition of injury as grounds for divorce. From the earlier and more standard phrasing of 'injury of any type that renders the marriage impossible for a woman such as she', which invites a relative social class-based assessment, the law has now moved to a definition of injury as 'any conduct or dishonourable or immoral behaviour from the husband that causes the wife material or mental injury making her unable to continue in the marital relationship.'[26] The law itself is extremely detailed, and illustrative of the more general point is the intention of the Moroccan legislators, as announced by the King, to invest substantially in training and equipping the family judges to apply the new law, in which their role is increased, including the production of a detailed manual or handbook for judges to assist in their application of the new law.[27] By contrast, the draft law prepared by the Palestinian *Qadi al-Qudah* and head of the *shari'a* court system proposes considerable and specific space for the judge's discretion in provisions that elsewhere are more centrally directed.

The attention that Amira Sonbol and other scholars have paid to the risks posed to women by the choices made by states in their codifications of Muslim family law, and their comparisons of pre-modern applications of *shari'a*, provide vital perspectives in the questioning, as Sonbol puts it, of the 'religious sanctity' that current states claim for their codifications. If Ayatollah al-Najati in Bahrain worries that there is no risk-free process in codifying Islamic family law, women's rights activists have had equal cause for concern in seeking to enhance rights protection through legislation on the family. The risk posed by the legislative process is not confined to that posed by the infusion of the laws with 'state patriarchy'. It may consist in the loss of established rights through a parliamentary vote, or the undermining of the principle of democratic participation through the by-passing or side-stepping of proper legislative processes by the executive in order to push through laws. Many women's rights activists are also committed social and political activists, and hold that the rights of women, as members of society, can only really be secured with the development of fully participatory social, political and economic structures. The less than democratic means pressed into service by various executives in the region to secure changes to Muslim family law that stand to benefit a large number of women thus pose particular dilemmas beyond the realm of the details of texts.

The 2001 Jordanian amendments discussed in this study are an example. The Jordanian amendments were passed as 'temporary legislation' in the absence of a sitting parliament and during a period of extensive use of the prerogatives of temporary legislation by the King and Cabinet.[28] When parliament reconvened, dozens of temporary laws were, as required by the Constitution, submitted to both houses for approval. While the majority of these laws were duly approved, problems arose with two laws closely affecting women's rights in the family: one the personal status law amendments discussed in this book, and the other a law amending the penal code on issues to do with 'crimes of honour'. While the appointed Senate approved the laws, the elected lower house twice rejected them through an unusual political alliance of Islamist and tribal deputies. Women's rights activists and other supporters of the amendments were put somewhat in the same position as those in Egypt when the then President Anwar Sadat issued key amendments to family law by presidential decree in 1979: that is, supportive of the aims of the amendments, but wishing for a properly democratic process and passage of the particular legislation.[29]

The anti-democratic nature of the executive's moves on personal status legislation has featured variously in a number of contexts; the top-down approach is perhaps most notably exemplified in the passage of the 1956 Tunisian Law of Personal Status, which was issued by decree of the Bey, the head of state, before his removal, sealed by Habib Bourghiba who was at that time Prime Minister, without parliamentary debate.[30] Algerian and Yemeni women objected to the manner in which drafts of Muslim family law were prepared and promulgated; in Algeria, Lazreg observes that 1984 'marked the year of the rupture between women and their government'.[31] A more recent example of the dilemma in which women activists may find themselves in this regard comes from Libya, where Hinz reports that a 1998 law passed by the General People's Congress removing the requirement of the first wife's consent to her husband's polygynous marriage was subsequently annulled by Muammar Qaddafi in what she terms a move of 'dubious legality'.[32] On the other hand, in Morocco the new family law (drafted by a Commission appointed and instructed by King Mohammad VI) was passed by parliament for the first time; previously, both the original law of 1957 and its subsequent amendments in 1993 had been promulgated by royal decree, without passing through parliament. Some observers feel that this was less of an achievement than it might at first seem, in terms of real democratic participation; others see it as an important precedent. In either case, the Moroccan example (discussed further in the following chapter) and those of other states mentioned here are illustrations of the entanglement of substance and process in codification and legislative reform of Muslim family law in Arab states.

3 Arab State Codifications and Women's Rights Advocacy in the Third Phase of Family Law Reform

Patterns of consultation, exchange and borrowings in the drafting of Muslim family laws in the region are well established and were remarked upon in the 'second phase' literature. This literature examined the texts and (in some cases) the application of the first national codes promulgated in the 1950s, which as noted drew in various provisions and jurisprudential arguments from Egyptian laws issued earlier in the century on particular aspects of Muslim family law, as well on the first codification, the Ottoman Law of Family Rights 1917. National codes increasingly also borrowed from each other, often explicitly, and continue to do so. Currently, two inter-governmental 'model texts' are also available, one drawn up by the League of Arab States (the Draft Unified Arab Law of Personal Status) and one by the Gulf Cooperation Council (the 'Musqat document' of 1996).[1] Appeal to a (very broad) shared jurisprudential heritage is bolstered by the idea of the standardization among states of approaches to particular areas of Muslim family law, including the assertion of state authority in imposing administrative and bureaucratic requirements in support of substantive elements of the statutory law. No two codes are the same, however, and official explanations of the laws assert the location of their particular formulations in the national context of the particular state; individuals and groups advocating for change also invoke specific political and social histories and circumstances in support of particular demands, as well as drawing on differences between the codes to support their challenges to any one governmentally endorsed position as uniquely representative of and required by 'the *shari'a*'.

For their part, those working on advocacy for change are in significantly different positions than in the first two phases of Muslim family law reform in the region. Besides the Islamist movements, women are likely to be found in government-appointed committees and commissions, and also in associations, organisations and groups that are independent from (and sometimes in opposition to) the governing authority. Compared to the earlier phases of Muslim family law reform when often 'reformism and women's rights were of a piece', or when women were part of revolutionary cadres in national liberation struggles, Val Moghadam's 1994 comment is pertinent in many of the countries of the region:

> Today, feminists and nationalists view each other with suspicion if not hostility, and nationalism is no longer assumed to be a progressive force for change – the panacea to problems of underdevelopment and social inequality, the path to a healthier and less dominated socio-economic order.[2]

The de-coupling of groups engaged in women's rights advocacy from governmental or party institutions can in some cases be linked directly to the processes of family law reform. Thus in Algeria, Lazreg notes that the setback represented by the debates around and eventual passage of the 1984 Family Law galvanized women more widely and an independent women's movement arose in opposition to an earlier 1981 draft.[3] In Egypt, Hatem reports the formation of formal and informal women's organizations with different approaches to family law following the passage of the 1985 law.[4]

International law and Muslim family law

Besides broad paradigmatic convergences in the construction of the codes, not least in their production in the geographical area of what Kandiyoti has called 'the clearest instance of classic patriarchy',[5] external fora also press for a degree of conformity. In 1976, Anderson noted that international law stood to challenge 'orthodox Muslim opinion [...] even though it has, at the present time, little or no relevance in practice'.[6] Since then, most members of the League of Arab States have become parties to the United Nations Convention on the Elimination of All Forms of Discrimination Against Women and all but one to the later Convention on the Rights of the Child. State reservations to the former, particularly to central undertakings with regard to womens' rights in the family, and their justifications thereof made on grounds of the normative precedence of their formulations of *'shari'a'* in this regard, have become the subject not only of scholarly examination but also of the reports, comments and questions posed by members of the oversight committee at the United Nations.[7] Among its provisions, the Convention – sometimes referred to as the Women's Convention – requires states parties to take appropriate measures to modify laws, customs and practices which constitute discrimination against women and to ensure equality of rights for women and men in a range of matters relating to marriage and the family. These areas are central to the ongoing international debates on cultural relativity versus the universality of rights and on articulations of 'women's rights in Islam'; the equality paradigm which underpins the women's human rights norms and discourse is held by critics to illustrate the 'Euro-centrism' of human rights norms.

The Women's Convention has drawn an unusual number of reservations from state parties around the world, but the particularly controversial nature of reservations entered by certain Arab states arises from their generality, purporting to subject commitments under the entire Convention to the principles or norms of 'the Islamic *shari'a*' or applying a reservation to the general undertaking to take legislative action to eliminate discrimination.[8] Substantive articles of the Convention to which reservations have been made by different Arab states include those providing for equality of women with men before the law, including in legal capacity and at all stages of court procedure, and in 'the law relating to the movement of persons and the freedom to choose their residence and domicile'; and requiring states to 'take all appropriate measures to eliminate discrimination against women in all matters relating to marriage and family relations'.[9]

In the 1980s, shortly after the Convention entered into force, objections were filed to certain reservations including the broad texts submitted by Egypt and Bangladesh. The Committee on the Elimination of All Forms of Discrimination Against Women (the UN committee responsible for monitoring implementation of the Convention) then proposed, in the context of its general concern at the number and type of reservations entered to the Convention, that the United Nations should 'promote or undertake studies on the status of women under Islamic laws and customs and in particular on the status and equality of women in the family... taking into consideration the principle of El Ijtihad in Islam'. Debates on these issues at the United Nations were heated; Connors reports allegations of 'cultural imperialism and religious intolerance' and warnings against 'using the Convention as a pretext for doctrinaire attacks on Islam', and the General Assembly subsequently agreed that no further action be taken on the CEDAW suggestion.[10] Objections have been filed to similar reservations entered by certain Arab states becoming parties to the Convention in more recent years, such as Saudi Arabia, and the Committee continues to seek information from states on progress towards the withdrawal of reservations. Some Arab states have reworded their reservations, and developments in law may be presented to the Committee in a manner that defers to the latter's dominant discourse and differs from domestic official exposition.[11] In their examinations of the reports submitted by state parties, the Committee may be informed by parallel reports from women's and human rights groups in the particular state. For their part, mainstream international human rights organisations based in the West have recently turned their attention to women's rights in the 'private sphere' of the family and its associated regulatory law and practice,[12] while some West-based international women's rights groups have opened local offices in the region.[13] Successive United Nations world conferences on women have mobilised and facilitated regional and international networking, and impacted both state policy and public discourse, in various and sometimes conflicting ways.

An additional international focus for many women's rights activists, in their approach to family law reform in the region, is the UN Convention on the Rights of the Child (CRC). Twenty-one of the 22 members of the Arab League have signed or ratified the CRC, the exception being Palestine which is as yet unable to accede to international instruments as a state. As is the case with CEDAW, there is a certain pattern to the interpretative declarations and reservations made by Arab states on signing or ratifying the CRC. Provisions of the Convention to which specific reference has been made include those regarding the right of the child to freedom of religion and the duties and rights of the parents or guardians in this respect (on the grounds that Islamic law does not permit a Muslim – child or adult – to leave the religion of Islam) and those referring to adoption, which in the institutional sense intended in the Convention is not recognised in Islamic law.[14] As is the case with CEDAW, some have made reservations in regard to the provision on a child's right to nationality, and certain states such as Saudi Arabia, Mauritania and Qatar have deposited general reservations to 'any provision incompatible with Islamic law'.[15] Advocacy work relying on the CRC includes work on violence in the home, early marriage, and education. In Morocco, commentators directly link the introduction of substantive provisions on the rights of child vis-à-vis his or her parents in the 2004 family law to the country's ratification of the CRC.[16]

Women's rights advocacy

State undertakings under international human rights law are a significant focus in advocacy addressing Muslim family law in the region, and here too major investments are made in regional and indeed international exchange, cooperation and strategising, particularly between different women's rights groups.[17] Discourses of equal citizenship rights and responsibilities, arguments on socio-economic change, the reality of women's lives, and the evocation of women's role in the national struggle also variously feature. Alongside these appeals to women's rights and state responsibilities are arguments insisting that proposed developments in family legislation, and in the position of women in general, are not antithetical to but rather in fulfilment of the principles of justice and egalitarianism underlying the *shari'a* and, concomitantly, that current law and practice denies women the dignity accorded them in the *shari'a* and denies the country the benefits of women's effective participation in development. Particular mechanisms from within the body of *fiqh* may be proposed for statutory implementation as offering jurisprudentially endorsed strategies for more effective protection, once given the authority of the state. Daoud describes this 'double movement' as simultaneously referring to international norms and to internal change within the normative framework of *fiqh*-based family law.[18] Demonstrations and mass petitions feature in campaigns, sometimes met in kind by opponents; in Morocco in 2000, the occasion of International Women's Day saw two opposing rallies for and against proposed changes to family law, one in Casablanca and one in Rabat.[19] In Bahrain, the series of petitions organised by the Committee of Women's Petition provoked a counter-petition which people were encouraged to sign against the principle of codification of Muslim family law.[20] In Algeria, activists working for the 2005 amendments produced a CD featuring 'women's angry voices' and making 'a fiery argument for women's rights using music and moving images'.[21] Paralleling such activism is what Moosa has called 'a fury of interpretive activity' around women's rights and the source texts of Islamic law.[22] Although some argue for a civil family law, whether as a replacement for the existing *shari'a* postulate or as an optional regime, the arguments for reform are mostly presented as lying within the existing normative framework, or at least as conforming to the underlying principles of Islam and not aimed at displacing 'Islam' as such from the public sphere.

Activists have turned their attention to procedure as well as substance, advocating for the establishment of integrated and specialised family courts or chambers (such as in Egypt and Morocco) and looking to court procedure as a way to either attenuate the effect of particular provisions of the law (such as the husband's power of unilateral divorce, or the requirements of 'obedience') or to underpin them (such as the prohibitions on underage or forced marriage, or the availability of interim maintenance orders).

In the region, the international networks of rights-based women's groups may afford them solidarity, support mechanisms, funds, profile, and a certain space, despite some tensions around a disproportionate Western influence over the priorities and strategies of the international women's rights movement. They are also however a focus for opponents of the 'women's rights' discourse. Opposition discourses display various features of the regional pattern of what Kandiyoti has called 'the privileged place of women and family in discourses about cultural authenticity'.[23] These include the conflation of 'cultural' or 'national' with a particular articulation of Islamic norms and religious principle. Invocations of biological determinism and appeals to what is presented as a monolithic and homogenous Arab-Muslim heritage may be accompanied by populist representations of class difference and the spectre of family breakdown, growing numbers of unmarried individuals, and general moral decline. The *fiqh*-based balance of 'equivalent' (rather than 'equal') rights in family law is presented as the ideal as well as the normative framework for the protection of women's rights, with problems attributed to a failure of conscience and an absence of correct, faith-based practice. Advocates of international women's rights may be accused of alienation, a lack of cultural authenticity, and seeking to undermine the unity and stability of the Muslim family and by extension Muslim society through the importation of Western ideas associated with moral laxity; in some cases charges of apostasy may be implied. References to 'international conferences on women' are not infrequent, and accusations that such activities are supported by 'foreign funding' evoke the same set of images. The rights discourse is directly targeted in light of empirically selective attitudes on the part of powerful Western states to the universality of the norms they promote. Opponents of the discourse of gender equality situate it, along with the discourses of 'Western feminism', within the larger context of colonial and neo-colonial agendas, cultural imperialism and hostility to Islam and the Arabs.

At the beginning of the twenty-first century, this narrative of polarization and resistance has resonance in the context of the use of vast Western military force against majority Muslim states and a declared interest on the part of the US administration, chief wielder of this force, in women's rights in the Middle East. For some observers, the current context directly invokes colonial experiences in the Arab world, when against the background of direct and prolonged subjugation of colonised territories and peoples, 'the treatment of "native women" by "native men" was singled out for attention and condemnation by missionary and colonial cadres, with religion forming a central divisor between colonials and colonised in struggles over gender relations'.[24] The particular contemporary (especially post-September 11th 2001) articulations and implications of this divisor as constructed by powerful Western states challenges the structuring of successful international alliances in support of change as well as the domestic positioning of advocates.

The privileging of women and the family in this political discourse means that Arab states' political interests may be served by the invocation of Islam over contested areas of law and policy, while 'Islamist' groups may attack the discourse of women's rights to undermine the credentials of existing regimes. In this context, Western scholarly literature on Muslim personal status law in the Arab world (and beyond) has expanded to include considerations of the dynamics and political implications of the debates around reform, and indeed to consider family law reform as an almost primarily political issue. Other recent publications are specifically aimed at supporting the research, activist and advocacy efforts of groups working internally in different Muslim countries and communities to change paradigms of authority and control within the family and society.[25] In the case of the international network Women Living Under Muslim Laws, for example, this is done by evaluating existing provisions by the degree to which they are 'option-giving' for the greatest number of women under their jurisdiction 'at the current historical moment'.[26] Website resources seek to serve similar purposes of information sharing and advocacy support.[27] In different countries in the region, research and law-focussed advocacy on the substantive provisions of the code is complemented by outreach and 'know your rights' activities, the provision of legal advice and assistance, and a focus on procedural issues such as integrated family courts, or particular documentary formats, such as the inclusion in the official marriage contract document of particular stipulations or agreements for the spouses to consider signing up to.[28] In Egypt, a women's legal aid organisation has produced a small book with reproductions of handwritten *shari'a* court records dating from the 16th – 18th centuries ce, in an effort to illustrate the way in which *shari'a*-based family law was applied prior to statutory legislation, and in particular how women accessed rights under the pre-modern system.[29] In some contexts, engaged feminist academics question the heavy investment of women's groups in the law and legal advocacy as a disinvestment in other areas of the public sphere critical to women's rights: criticisms of the 'professionalisation' of women's rights activism in project-based work rather than in broader social and political movements are part of the context of post-Oslo Palestine, mirroring broader areas of reflection on the roles of donor funding and civil society paradigms in the region.[30]

Recent legislative developments

In an age characterised *inter alia* by globalisation, new media and identity politics, Muslim family law in Arab states is thus a site of intense debate and contestation beyond national and regional borders and across disciplinary boundaries. Text-focused compilations and overviews can scarcely keep pace with events;[31] there is a lot to keep up with. Legislative developments in Arab states at the turn of the century have included the promulgation in Oman of its first codification of family law in 1997; Yemen's substantial amendments to its 1992 family law promulgated in 1998 and 1999; the adoption in 2000 in Egypt of a procedural law that also contained amendments to the law on divorce; and the Jordanian government's enactment, in the absence of parliament in 2001, of significant amendments to family law, and the refusal by the subsequently convened House of Deputies to endorse this 'temporary legislation' in 2003. The following year, 2004, opened with the parliamentary adoption of a new Moroccan code and the aftermath of the attempt by members of the Interim Governing Council in occupied Iraq to repeal Iraq's codified family law. In Algeria, President Bouteflika announced a draft of long-awaited amendments to the 1984 Algerian code, which were promulgated in February 2005. At the end of 2005, the UAE promulgated its first code of personal status; in Palestine a draft family law awaited debate by the next Legislative Council following elections initially scheduled for 2005 but subsequently postponed to 2006 and, eventually, won by Hamas. The summer of 2006 saw promulgation of the first Qatari family law. Beyond the substantive law, in Egypt the law establishing the new family courts envisaged under the 2000 legislation was promulgated in 2004, as was the law by which the Moroccan authorities re-organised the judicial system to create 'family matters sections' in every first instance court to apply the new family law.[32]

Besides being indicative of substantial ongoing legislative activity in the area of family law, these developments are illustrative of the different political contexts and legislative approaches in various states. The Omani codification is closely modelled on the Draft Law of Personal Status developed by the Gulf Cooperation Council; elsewhere in the Gulf, Kuwait has had a codified law since 1984, and discussions had been ongoing for several years in Qatar as well as in the UAE on drafts before the laws were promulgated. In Qatar, the draft was tested out in the courts in advance of promulgation; in Bahrain the codification debate in 2003 discussed in Chapter 2 included the trading of libel allegations in court battles between certain members of the *shar'i* judiciary and members of the Committee for Women's Petition. Yemen's 1992 law was produced following unification of the People's Democratic Republic of the Yemen and the Yemen Arab Republic, both of which had pre-existing codifications of law from the 1970s. The PDRY law (1974) was a radical piece of legislation aimed at transforming society in line with the government's social and economic policies, and many of its provisions were comparable only with the following year's socialist family law codification of Somalia; the 1976 YAR law was largely made up of rulings – both dominant and historically 'dissident' – from the Zaydi school.[33] The 1992 law of unified Yemen was drawn mostly from the YAR law, with certain changes drawing on the draft unified Arab law of personal status.[34] After the civil war of 1994 and constitutional amendments establishing *shari'a* as the sole source of legislation, the 1998 and 1999 amendments reintroduced a number of more traditionalist approaches.

Egypt has not yet promulgated a full code of family law, despite a number of drafts since the beginning of the twentieth century; the most recent substantive legislation on family law (of 1985) modified two key protections in the pre-existing 1979 law struck down by the Supreme Constitutional Court on the grounds that the manner of its promulgation (by presidential decree) had been unconstitutional. The procedural law of 2000 introduced divorce by judicial *khul'*, whereby a woman might petition the court for a divorce from her husband without his consent and without having to prove grounds, provided she return to him the dower she had received. This provision was extensively debated in Egypt, with much of the press opposed, and received considerable coverage internationally. In Jordan, the 1951 family law was replaced in 1976 by a new codification, which made certain relatively cautious changes to family law. The amendments issued in 2001 were less cautious, *inter alia* introducing a divorce procedure adapted from Egypt's controversial 2000 legislation, raising the minimum age of marriage and instituting certain regulations on polygyny hitherto absent from Jordanian law. As noted earlier, when elections produced a new House of Deputies, what the pro-government press referred to as an 'undeclared coalition of tribal and Islamist deputies' articulated vehement opposition to the temporary legislation issued by the government and after twice being rejected in the House, the family law amendment was sent to await a joint debate by lower and upper houses.

In Morocco, at the opening of 2004, after a lengthy build-up and significant polarisation in the public debate, the new family law was drafted under close guidance from the king but as already noted was debated and passed by the legislature for the first time. The new law widened women's rights and responsibilities in the family and, similar to the Egyptian legislation, received favourable coverage internationally, and contains internal references to Morocco's international commitments. Earlier recommendations made in the context of a National Development Plan had not been successfully passed through parliament, and some attribute the relatively smooth parliamentary (and, in the end, public) passage of the new 2004 law not only to the hands-on interventions of the King but to the relative absence from the public sphere, at that time, of dissident 'Islamist' mobilisation in the wake of the 2003 Casablanca bombings and widespread arrests.

In sum, the last quarter of a century has been witness to what might be identified as a third phase of Muslim family law reform in the Arab world.[35] This very broad description would take the first phase as consisting of Ottoman and Egyptian legislative interventions in the first half of the twentieth century and the second as the series of national codifications issued in the

1950s in countries in the Mashreq and North Africa. The third phase is distinguished by changed global, regional and national circumstances in Arab states, including but not limited to different forms of political and civil society mobilisation, modern communications and networking capabilities, and the increased levels of interventions from powerful third-party states. These circumstances impact the debates on the law, themselves more broadly based than was the case previously and involving a wider range of actors; they can also be seen to impact on the substance of the laws. In most of the region, women are more involved and at different levels than in previous phases of Muslim family law reform; they are also to be found organised in associations and movements independent of (and sometimes in opposition to) the ruling party or elite. And perhaps more than any other legislation, the promulgation of codifications of or amendments to Muslim family law demonstrate an intense political contingency reflecting national and international pressures and dynamics.

4 *Shar'i* Postulates, Statutory Law and the Judiciary

Generally, the codifications of family law explicitly invoke the '*shar'i* postulate' through directing the judge to a residual reference in the event of a specific subject not being covered in the text. This comes in a variety of formulations, which themselves may indicate either legislative (and political) history or aspiration. In Egypt, Syria and Jordan, the laws maintain reference to the dominant opinion of the Hanafi school, despite the inclusion of a number of provisions with non-Hanafi origins.[1] Legislated in the same decade as the Syrian and original Jordanian law, the Iraqi code of 1959 requires the application of the law itself to all questions dealt with 'in letter or spirit' (a phrasing taken up by Libya in 1984) and failing this, judgement is to be made 'according to those principles of the Islamic *shari'a* most appropriate to the provisions of the law', thus allowing for reference to both Sunni and Shi'i jurisprudence (the code containing elements of both); as noted above in Chapter 2, the court is then directed to case law and comparative jurisprudence.[2]

Elsewhere, general residual reference is made to the 'principles (or rules) of the Islamic *shari'a* most appropriate to' the provisions of the particular law (Oman, Libya) or, in Algeria, simply 'the rulings of the Islamic *shari'a*'.[3] Yemen's law of 1992 refers the court to 'the strongest proofs in the Islamic *shari'a*' without suggesting guidance in this by the provisions of the codified law, while Kuwait and Mauritania require reference to the prevalent Maliki opinion or in default in the Kuwaiti case to the 'general principles of the school'.[4] Until its new law, Morocco also maintained reference to the dominant Maliki position or to its 'prevailing practice'; in the new formulation, in a reprise of the King's discourse in the reform process, a general reference to the Maliki school is supplemented by '*ijtihad* that realises the values of Islam in justice and equality and good relations'.[5] The 2005 UAE law includes a detailed provision stressing that 'the provisions in this law are taken

from and to be interpreted according to Islamic jurisprudence and its principles', with interpretative recourse to the jurisprudential school to which
any particular provision is sourced, and in the event of there being no text,
ruling to be made in accordance with the prevailing opinion in the Sunni
schools in the following hierarchy: Maliki, Hanbali, Shafi'i and Hanafi.[6] Somalia's 1975 code directed the court to the dominant opinions of the Shafi'i
school followed by 'general principles of the Islamic *shari'a* and social justice'.[7] The Qatari law offers the first codification to have the dominant opinion of the Hanbali school as the residual source, 'unless the court decides to
apply a different opinion for reasons set out in its ruling'.[8]

Tunisia and the sharᶜi postulate

The absence of any such provision in the Tunisian Law of Personal Status of
1956 evoked comment at the time; given that the law ended the previously
separate Hanafi and Maliki jurisdictions, Anderson observed that 'the only
answer, presumably, is that the courts can draw from any school or from
the dicta of any jurist – at their discretion'.[9] More recently, Tunisian scholars focussing on women's rights and the law have argued against the assumption that *fiqh* should be the exclusive residual reference for interpretation
and application of the law by the courts, in a debate that provokes issues of
the attitude of the judiciary, the intentions of the legislator, and the authority of international norms. A particular focus of the debate has been the
marriage of Muslim women to non-Muslim men, considered invalid by a consensus of the traditional jurists, and explicitly prohibited in other state codifications of family law. Socially, Ltaief observes that '[m]ixed marriage of a
female Muslim to a male non-Muslim [...] is seen as an offence to the identity
and beliefs of the people'.[10]

In Tunisian law, no mention is made of the prohibition of this kind of
marriage in the section setting out impediments to marriage, which Anderson found 'noteworthy', while observing that an earlier general requirement
that parties to a marriage must be free of lawful impediments 'would no
doubt be called in aid by those who wished to prevent such a marriage'. His
feeling was that the Tunisian government felt it could not go further on this
issue at that time and 'was content to leave the solution of this problem to
the courts and the future'.[11] As he predicted, the courts interpreted the list-

ing of impediments to marriage not to be exhaustive; and although this issue was not addressed in amendments to the family law promulgated in 1964, a press statement made at the time by the Minister of Justice referred to the place of the 'sources of Islam and of *fiqh*' in the organization of marriage.[12] In what Chekir describes as a 'celebrated' case in 1966, a Cassation Court ruling (the 'Arret Hourya') pronounced the marriage of a Muslim woman to a non-Muslim man to be void:[13] it was 'incontestable that a Muslim woman who marries a non-Muslim commits an unpardonable crime, and that Islamic law holds such a marriage void and not recognised.'[14] In 1973 an administrative circular from the Minister of Justice explicitly prohibited the registration of such marriages.[15]

More recently, Ltaief sees new ground being broken in Tunisia by a 1999 District Court judgment invoking international law in rejecting arguments against the validity of such a marriage, although the judge in the case was careful to note that there was nothing in the particular case that 'proves that the husband is not a Muslim'. Ltaief may however be premature in her assessment that 'this precedent puts an end to speculation on various possible interpretations'.[16] Even were this decision followed by precedents from Tunisia's superior courts, it could still be over-ridden, ignored or, alternatively, endorsed in long-expected amendments to Tunisia's personal status law.

It is not only in Tunisia that this particular issue has become a subject of debate. Commentators in different countries note an increase in such marriages, due to a variety of factors that may include increased population mobility, migration and tourism.[17] Besides arguments based on equality norms and the principle of choice in marriage, it is pointed out that the recognition of such unions would consolidate the authority of national law and obviate the need for citizens of the country to travel abroad (if they are able) to conclude such marriages. The jurisprudential consensus on prohibition, however, continues to inform the legislatures. During the debate on a draft civil personal status code as an optional regulatory framework in Lebanon, al-Cheikh notes particular opposition (from both Sunni and Shi'i circles) to the draft's omission of reference to the religion of parties to the marriage, read as an implicit sanctioning of the marriage of Muslim women to non-Muslim men;[18] here, it would indeed seem unlikely that, were such a law to be passed, the civil courts empowered to apply it would interpret the lack of a specific permission for such a marriage in a deliberately secular text as entailing a prohibition. In Tunisia, if the recourse by judges to *fiqh* rules in interpreting the legislator's silence in the codified law was predictable for Anderson, it is contested on a number of grounds by those who seek full freedom for Muslim women in their choice of marriage partner. Chekir argues that the fact that, unlike most other constitutional documents in the region, the Tunisian Constitution does not identify the *shari'a* as a source of legislation implies the legislator's desire to establish 'the sovereignty of positive law and its primacy over religious sources'; that judges should be guided by the general principles of interpretation articulated in the civil law;[19] and that Tunisia's responsibilities under international law in regard to women's right to equality of choice in marriage should take priority over the provisions of the personal status code.[20]

Judicial interpretation and legislative direction

In other countries, as noted above, silence in the statute directs reference to a particular or the more general body of rules and principles of 'the Islamic *shari'a*'. Where the code's silence has left gaps in what traditional law provided, judges have sometimes used this to re-institute rules protective of women's rights and choices in particular circumstances. Thus, when the 1992 Yemeni law invalidated a guardian's marriage of his male or female wards before the age of fifteen (also the age of legal majority),[21] it also removed the reference that had previously existed in the YAR law of 1978 to the right of a female married as a minor to choose to have the marriage dissolved on reaching puberty.[22] Since the 1992 law provided no enforcement measures for the provision on the minimum age of marriage, Wurth notes that judges relied on the residual reference of 'the strongest proofs in the Islamic *shari'a*' to continue to allow the dissolution of marriages on the achievement of puberty.[23] The rules of traditional law thus supplemented the statute law when the state failed to follow through on its own legislation protecting young girls against coercion and early marriage.[24] In Egypt, some judges were awarding compensation to women divorced abusively by their husbands long before this right was enshrined in statutory legislation.[25]

Judicial interpretation is also of course relevant to the application of particular provisions of statutory law, and has sometimes frustrated the achievement of the intentions of the legislator. Chamari for example notes the problems encountered by women in accessing their right to compensation on injurious divorce under the original terms of the Tunisian law.[26] Judges applying the Jordanian rules on stipulations in marriage contracts, notably those where the wife seeks to secure for herself the option of divorce, for an extended period took a rather narrowly literal approach to the phrasing of these stipulations that denied legal effect to those not sufficiently expertly drafted.[27] In Morocco, Loukili and Zirari-Devif report that notaries fail to inform intending spouses of the possibility of inserting stipulations in their marriage contract (for example against polygyny) or of concluding separate agreements on the management of property acquired during marriage, on grounds that 'such deeds do not conform with Moroccan traditions and customs' or because 'there is no time to inform the persons concerned during the marriage celebrations.'[28] Widespread concern is voiced in the region as to whether judges empowered to permit the marriage of parties below the minimum age of marriage are ready to exercise a proper degree of scrutiny in order to protect underage females at risk of a forced marriage; a recent example comes again from Morocco where it is reported that minors are still being given permission to marry by judges after a 'visual assessment' rather than following the more in-depth procedures required under the terms of the 2004 law.[29] Antipathy towards particular legislative provisions can also go further; in Egypt, Chemais found a majority of judges whom she interviewed to be explicitly opposed to the controversial provision in the 1979 law establishing a husband's polygynous marriage without his wife's consent as in and of itself an act of injury on the grounds of which she might obtain a judicial divorce, and one judge claimed that he was deferring all such cases that reached him because of his refusal to implement this part of the law.[30]

The latter case illustrates the tensions that can arise between the political authorities of a state taking upon themselves the task of legislating on the family, and the judges charged with applying it, these latter, on occasion, not only under-applying or subverting intended reforms, but holding them illegitimate under the wider framework of 'traditional' *shariʿa*. This position is also voiced by political opponents of certain family law reforms. On the other hand, the state may consciously choose to leave certain matters to be decided by the courts rather than take a political risk through legislation, as in the examples given above. Like their counterparts elsewhere, judges are likely to rule in accordance with their own educational and professional training, social background and perspective on women's roles and rights within the family and in society in the light of a complex range of context-specific social and political engagements and constraints. On the one hand, this can lead to protective interpretations of the statute, such as when judges in Jordan established the principle that any unilateral *talaq* was to be considered arbitrary unless the opposite were proven, since it was undertaken without the consent of the wife, and therefore the wife would be entitled to seek compensation under the new rules established in the law of 1976.[31] This approach was clearly driven by the court's disapproval of *talaq*, even while upholding the validity of the husband's exercise thereof, an approach that accords with the *fiqh* position. On the other hand, Wurth has shown the different ways in which women from upper and lower social classes were treated in a Sana'a court in regard to the level of injury and distress in the marriage that would be regarded as cause for divorce.[32]

Another common practice is for the statutory law to instruct the appropriate Minister or *shar'i* official (notably the *Qadi al-Qudah*) to issue detailed directives to the courts for the implementation of the spirit of a particular provision, such as in the case of the 2001 Jordanian amendments raising the minimum age of capacity for marriage. The law instructed the *Qadi al-Qudah* to issue guidelines to cover the circumstances in which the *qadi* might permit marriage below the new set ages; the way in which the *Qadi al-Qudah* maintained a broad scope of judicial discretion for his judges, and the results of this on the application of the law, are discussed below (Chapter 6). In Palestine, in the absence of a statutory Palestinian law, successive heads of the *shar'i* judiciary in Gaza and the West Bank have issued a series of directives to the *shari'a* courts which have *inter alia* affected the substantive law as well as impacted on procedure.[33]

Another common feature of legislation, and one which illustrates again the interplay between legislative direction and judicial discretion, combines the desire of the state to direct with a particular reliance on the individual efforts of the judge. This is the incorporation, in different codifications around the region, and particularly with regard to divorce claims, of the requirement that the judge attempts to mediate between the spouses and to help them reconcile their differences, before proceeding with the claim. This traditional mediating role of the *qadi* may continue in all manner of claims off the official court record,[34] but its formalisation as a statutory requirement re-casts it as state-directed and arguably more bureaucratically 'functional'. Official explanations support the expansion of mediation efforts with a 'pro-family' discourse that emphasises the importance of maintaining established family ties and preventing any increase in the divorce rate or other manifestations perceived as indicating the weakening of 'the family' as the basic unit of society. In Egypt, the legislature significantly expanded the mandatory requirements in the provision on judicial *khul'* in the law of 2000 for reconciliation attempts by the judge before awarding such a divorce.[35] In her consideration of the Egyptian rules, Bernard-Maugiron observes another aspiration, that of regulation by the state authorities of 'private' disputes and conflict resolution, a reference to the jealousy with which the state is wont to assert 'the monopoly it exercises on the regulation of conflict' in the face of the established and continuing parallel (not 'alternative') intervention and mediation efforts of relatives, neighbours and others.[36] In Palestine, by comparison, Shehada reports the *Qadi al-Qudah* as situating his recent (2004) institutionalisation of a court-related family counselling department under his direct supervision in the context of the competing norms of 'customary law' mechanisms and his desire to 'minimize the influence of the tribes and tribal law'.[37] The official explanation on the other hand focuses on the rising rate of court cases and of divorce, and the need to protect the Palestinian family against the predations of the current circumstances; an official report on the Department of Family Guidance and Conciliation included among the results of its first three months' work a reduction in the divorce rate throughout Palestine, with one Gazan court reporting its divorce rate to have dropped from 15% to 4%.[38] Aspirations of reducing the number of court claims, resolving family disputes without adjudication and avoiding where possible the incidence of divorce may thus be accompanied by the assumption that the state, or the official legal system, is best placed to regulate conflict even beyond the court room.

In the Gulf, whence the Palestinian *Qadi al-Qudah's* initiative in this regard was drawn, the 2005 UAE law institutionalises this practice, requiring that parties be referred to the Committee of Family Guidance before their claim can be heard by the court; exceptions to this rule include cases of inheritance and wills, provisional and accelerated petitions including urgent provisional orders for maintenance and custody, and 'claims where reconciliation is not in issue' such as the establishment of marriage and divorce.[39] The Explanatory Memorandum says that this mandatory procedure is 'out of respect for the family, in preservation of its cohesion, and in protection of the secrets of the home'.[40] In Egypt, the 2004 Family Courts Law provides for Offices of the Resolution of Family Conflicts to be attached to each court under the Ministry of Justice, comprising experts from the fields of law, sociology and psychology, whose selection and methodologies of guidance and mediation are to be governed by directives from the Ministry. With certain exceptions, no claim is to be heard by the court until the parties to the dispute have applied to this office for mediation, which is to include 'making the parties aware of the consequences of persisting with the claim, giving advice and counseling in an attempt to resolve the dispute amicably in preservation of the family entity'.[41] The phrasing of the exceptions both in Egypt and in the UAE suggests that, for example, all claims by a woman for *khulᶜ* or for divorce on the grounds of injury will have to pass through the Office as well as, subsequently, to be the subject of mediation efforts by the judge. A serious criticism that is made of such statutory requirements in relation to mediation or reconciliation procedures, and particularly with regard to divorce, is the daunting prospect they are likely to pose to a woman seeking divorce from an abusive husband.[42] The state does not appear to statutorily countenance a decision by the *qadi* that a woman should not in fact have to submit to attempts to forge a reconciliation with a violent or otherwise abusive husband and thus to maintain the marriage. Particularly interesting and effective study might be made of how judges for their part deal with such situations.

Thus, the codifications of Muslim personal status law under consideration here are presented as '*shariᶜa*-based' whatever the court system where the laws are applied, and whatever the training of judges employed to interpret them. The relationship between the judiciary and the text remains dynamic; sometimes judges fill in the gaps left by legislation, at other times they display antagonism to certain of the legislative interventions, and at yet others their remedies to particular issues pre-date legislative attention and may inform the substance of subsequent legislation. In these roles of course, they can be compared to judges in other legal systems working with statutory instruments. For their part, legislatures in a number of states are asserting an increasingly directive authority in regard to the role and functions of the judiciary.

5 Registration Requirements

One of the areas where the bureaucratizing and centralising tendencies of state authorities come up against *sharʻi* postulates is the validity or otherwise of acts undertaken in accordance with traditional law but in violation of statutory rules. This was raised in the previous chapter, in regard to the validity in Tunisia of a Muslim woman's marriage to a non-Muslim man; more broadly it encompasses the basic acts of marriage and divorce. Official registration of these acts – that is, registration with some official of a central authority, rather than unofficial documentation – serves a number of purposes, including information on and a degree of control over the 'private' affairs of citizens,[1] but also the potential for ensuring that other laws issued by the central authority are being upheld. This refers to the enforcement, for example, of rules on the minimum age of marriage, consent of the parties, judicial oversight of the conditions related to polygyny, and a woman's rights on divorce.[2] Registration also serves protective purposes for parties to a marriage – particularly women – and court records in different countries show evidence of practices of registration at court among different sectors and at different times prior to the modern period, including under the notarization requirements issued at the end of the nineteenth century by the Ottomans as they sought to extend the reach of state law.[3] With codifications of family law by independent states came mandatory registration procedures, sometimes replacing those instituted by colonial-era powers.[4]

Nevertheless, the traditional jurisprudential consensus required no form of registration of marriage or divorce for these acts to be valid 'according to the *shariʻa*'. Holding a marriage or divorce invalid because registration procedures were not observed is, in this paradigm, asserting the laws of the state over those of the *shariʻa* in the regulation (and recognition) of 'private affairs' (including lawful sexual relations). Imposing administrative procedures as a state legal requirement may also challenge social perceptions of legitimacy, whether or not social practice would be found by the courts to be in accordance with *sharʻi* concepts of validity; but it is social practice that is the declared target of the reforms imposed by the law through the institution of administrative procedures.

On the other hand, the officially posed argument that registration procedures assist fulfilment of the *shar'i* requirement of publicity of the marriage finds broad social support in particular when concern arises (or is provoked) at the prospect of young people – particularly daughters – marrying 'secretly', that is without the knowledge of their family. Much of the public debate around what are called *'urfi* (customary, unregistered) marriages in Egypt and more recently in Palestine, discussed further below, has focussed on this; Zubaida remarks that in its current manifestation in Egypt this type of marriage is 'practised by university students and other young people, away from home and unknown to their families, getting over the expensive formalities and the parental involvement in proper marriage'.[5] While according to Zubaida this kind of marriage 'did not raise much interest in its old locations of secret second marriage', now it produces 'cries of indignation [that] echo in the press'. The adverse reactions to reports of such practices appear to mesh concern at the risks with discomfort at the loss of involvement and control, and the formalisation of registration procedures in which the family will be involved is presented as a matter of general support.

By comparison, the right of men to keep a marriage strategically 'secret', notably in concealing a polygynous marriage from his existing wife, is more likely to be defended, as discussed later in this study. In particular here, the strategic secrecy of *misyar* ('ambulant') marriages in Saudi Arabia is identified by 'Arabi as a key element in the development of the institution, and one which was subsequently addressed (with an insistence on publicity) by the Kingdom's Mufti.[6] The institution of *misyar* marriage involves the wife waiving her rights to maintenance, the provision of accommodation, and the husband's cohabitation with her. It is commonly understood as having developed over the last ten years and concentrated in the Gulf states, although an Iraqi-born scholar in the UAE states that this form of marriage spread in Iraq during the Iran-Iraq war to 'protect widows from committing sin'.[7] The link with registration procedures is seen in the UAE, where the Arab Women's Forum reported that the 2003 draft of the personal status codification originally made specific provision for the formal registration of *misyar* marriages for the first time, requiring 'limited publicity' or declaration of the marriage and noting that 'full publicity' was not essential for validity. The limited publicity stood to protect the roles of the wife's family, involving the knowledge of the guardian (who was to conclude the marriage) and family of the woman involved, but not requiring notification of anyone on the husband's side – meaning that the existing wife would not be made aware through formal procedures that her husband had contracted this type of marriage with another woman.[8] This proposal did not survive into the final text of the 2005 law, and the subsequent validation of the institution of *misyar* marriage by Saudi clerics provoked another round of public debate in the Gulf that is discussed further in Chapter 8.

More generally, different approaches have been taken to encourage registration and to deal with the issue of unregistered marriages, including those that also violate other provisions of state law such as the rules on minimum age. These may include the imposition of penal sanctions for non-compliance with the administrative regulations on marriage,[9] the waiving of fees for the required court procedures,[10] and the establishment of the official document of marriage as the standard form of proof to establish marriage, with various formulations allowing for establishment of a marriage by a ruling of court in the event that the statutory administrative procedures have not been complied with but the marriage fulfils the *shar'i* requirements of validity.[11]

Before considering different approaches to unregistered marriage, it is worth taking note of one further element in registration procedures that has been introduced by a number of states and is a feature of all three most recent codifications (UAE, Qatar, and the new Moroccan law). This is the requirement that couples intending to marry submit medical certificates as part of the documentation needed by the official charged with registering or notarising the marriage. The tests on which such medical certificates are based may cover both physical and mental diseases and disorders and be regulated by detailed directives under the authority of government health agencies.[12] In Morocco, a joint directive from the Ministers of Justice and of Health followed promptly on the introduction of the requirement of a medical check-up (with additional tests if it appears appropriate to the medical practitioner) in the new law;[13] in Palestine, an administrative directive of the *Qadi al-Qudah* issued in 2000 required all intending couples to undergo blood tests for thalassemia. In the UAE, the law requires attestation from the 'appropriate committee established by the Ministry of Health' that the parties are free of 'conditions on the basis of which this law allows a petition for judicial divorce' while the Explanatory Memorandum refers to genetic disorders, conditions preventing consummation, or those that stand to 'affect future generations'.[14] In Qatar, the 2006 law refers to a directive to be issued on this subject by the governmental health department, but already makes tests for inherited conditions mandatory. Thus, while some legislatures leave more to the discretion of the medical practitioner (such as in Morocco), others are stipulating particular checks which may focus on contagious diseases such as would subsequently establish grounds for judicial divorce, on sexually transmitted diseases, and on genetic disorders that may, for example, manifest in the event that both parties are carriers but not if only one is a carrier, and which may be particularly an issue in cases of cousin marriage. The texts require that the results of one party's tests are made known (for example by the official registering the marriage) to the other. The objective is thus to ensure that one party does not marry in ignorance of a particular health condition existing in the other. Less common are texts that address what should happen in the event that the test results are potentially problematic; Qatar's law however states explicitly that the official documenting the marriage 'is not permitted to refuse to document the contract because of the results of the medical test, in the event that the two parties desire to conclude it'.[15]

Unregistered and ᶜurfi marriage

In the efforts to render state registration of marriage not only mandatory but routine and exclusive of other social practice, a further step is taken when the state identifies the official marriage document as the only form of proof by which marriage may be established, whether in general (as in Tunisia[16]) or in particular circumstances. In Egypt as early as 1931, the courts were precluded from hearing any claim arising from a marriage that was not officially documented in the event that one of the parties denied the marriage.[17] Since a court can deal with claims arising from the marriage only when the marriage can be legally established, the effect is to deny access to judicial remedy sought by parties to a marriage that is not legally established, regardless of whether its constituent elements comply with the *shari* requirements of validity.

In Egypt, the impact of this approach on women involved in *ᶜurfi* marriages was widely debated in the context of the law of 2000. *ᶜUrfi* marriage is typically concluded with a customary document replacing the official marriage registration procedures. An ʿurfi marriage may technically fulfil the *shar‹i* requirements for a valid marriage, since these requirements did not involve state certification or involvement; nevertheless, one of the concerns expressed in this debate is that those involved in concluding such arrangements may not be properly aware of what the *shar‹i* requirements actually are and that the parties may therefore unwittingly be involved in an unlawful relationship. There is a range of motivations underlying this form of marriage, depending on the individuals involved, but the practice attracts strong disapproval from the authorities and public concern at the potential for exploitation and abuse of the rights particularly of young women in such arrangements, as well as objections to the possible avoidance of parental control. There are also political undertones to the debate, with certain Islamist elements declaring that ʿurfi marriage may be valid under the *shari‹a* if all it lacks is government certification.[18]

In its law of 2000, Egypt amended its long-standing position of excluding disputed ʿurfi marriages from judicial remedy to allow claims for judicial divorce or dissolution (depending on the case) to be heard where there was no official document and one party was denying the marriage.[19] Those objecting to the provision argued that it 'legitimised' ʿurfi marriage and risked encouraging the practice by providing a way out. Viewed by some observers as a concession by the official legal system to the unofficial practice, it is presented by supporters and by the authorities as providing a remedy for women affected by the injury of this situation, enabling them at least to divorce and marry again if they choose.[20]

Morocco has also seen hardship caused to women and children through the difficulties of proving unregistered marriages. Mir-Hosseini has described the procedure of legally regularising an unregistered (*fatiha*) marriage under the previous law as 'simple' in the event that both parties acknowledge it, but as standing 'very little chance of success' in the event of denial by the husband.[21] The 2004 law expands notarization requirements beyond those of previous texts, while allowing the court to hear claims for the establishment of marriage not documented at the time 'for overwhelming reasons' with particular consideration given to the circumstances of pregnancy or childbirth.[22] However, in an implicit reference to future discontinuation of this exception, the new law also specifies that such claims shall be heard 'for an interim period of not more than five years as of the entry into force of this law.' The Ministry of Justice's guide to the new law explains that the court will consider all forms of proof in considering claims to establish an unregistered marriage including hearing witnesses, considering the school certificates of children from the marriage, and circumstances such as parties celebrating the birth of children; it also mentions hearsay evidence and the knowledge of paternity of a child of the claimed marriage. These notes clearly refer both to marriages that are denied by one party and those that are acknowledged by both; all those wishing to establish their marriage are urged to apply to the court within the five-year interim period to regularise their situation, and the guide emphasises that 'the *lafif* certificate' (customarily used to establish an unregistered marriage) cannot take the place of the marriage contract.[23]

Other states continue to contemplate the establishment of marriage without the otherwise mandatory state-issued documentation. In post-independence Algeria the Supreme Court, before the promulgation of the 1984 law, relied on official registration as the standard proof of marriage, but allowed other marriages to be established (and so 'regularised') in accordance with *shar'i* requirements, a practice continued after the Code and which Dennerlein holds to be 'of utmost importance in cases in which women try to claim their rights as wives and mothers in court while their husbands deny the marriage by claiming that it was not officially registered'.[24] In Syria, the 1953 law allows a couple to establish a marriage concluded outside court only after they have complied with all the procedural measures required for a marriage in court, thus in effect precluding the courts from hearing claims to do with a marriage that has not been concluded in accordance with the statutory administrative regulations, completion of which needs the participation of both parties to the marriage.[25] However, these procedures are dispensed with in the event that the wife has given birth or is pregnant, in a permissive exception that conforms to practice and legislation elsewhere regarding, notably, underage marriage, as discussed further below. The two most recent codifications in the Gulf, in the UAE and Qatar, both stipulate that marriage shall be established by official document in accordance with legal registration procedures, but allow couples to establish a marriage by other forms of proof in circumstances that are in the discretion of the judge.[26]

Overview

States in the region have increasingly sought to regularise formal registration of marriage, with a view *inter alia* to tightening enforcement capabilities in regard to other key provisions of family law such as those on consent, minimum age of marriage and polygyny. Some are also using registration procedures to ensure that actual or potential medical conditions in one party are made known to the other before the conclusion of the contract. Differences remain as to the particular challenge of how to deal with unregistered marriages that may conform with the *sharʿi* requirements of validity although not with state administrative procedures. While those seeking stronger protection of women's rights in marriage are supportive of registration requirements and the consequent judicial scrutiny, concerns arise at the potential lack of judicial remedy for the parties involved, particularly for the wife, who is most likely to need recourse to the court to claim her rights and, assuming she is aware of the law's requirements, may not be in a position to insist upon their implementation. In their assessment of Muslim family laws across the world, the organisation Women Living Under Muslim Laws found that 'in most of our contexts [...] women have little control over the registration of their marriage' and the group therefore relates the 'option-giving potential' of registration requirements to the development context and the accessibility of the required processes.[27] In Morocco, women's groups commenting on the new law's grant of a five-year period of grace during which currently unregistered marriages may be regularised, while not against the principle, noted that it called for a major education and awareness campaign among the citizenry.[28] Making official procedure and registration the norm thus continues to be a goal, but not at the expense of the rights of women who, for whatever reason, are unwilling or unable to insist on this procedure.

6 Capacity and Consent

Issues of capacity for and consent to marriage have long attracted the attention of legislatures and activists in the region, and frequently continue to offer particular challenge to the assertion of a statutory norm over social practice and *fiqh* rulings, as well as to the assertion of an international norm over statutory law presented as representing a *shar'i* norm and a site of cultural distinction. Thus, the establishment of a minimum age of marriage by the legislator has been a feature of national legislation from the earliest promulgations, is supported by women's rights activists (who continue to seek an increase in the minimum age) and firmly in line with international norms and expectations. The Convention on the Rights of the Child does not itself identify a minimum age of marriage, and none of the Arab states raised this issue in their reservations and declarations. Nevertheless, the range of CRC protections apply up to the upper limit of eighteen and the lower limit of fifteen years of age, and under these terms, a number of the provisions in the codifications under review fall short of the protections set out in the Convention. This is most obviously the case where the marriage of minors (below puberty) is contemplated, but also where the law identifies actual puberty (rather than a set age) as the minimum.[1] In addition, in the region, practices of underage marriage in different sectors and areas often continue to challenge the statutory provisions setting minimum ages of marriage, the rights of those – especially females – married below the statutory minimum age, and socio-economic policies particularly outside the urban areas.[2]

Legislators have taken longer to address certain aspects of the rights and authorities of the guardian in a woman's marriage. While most statutory law excludes the guardian's coercive authority over his female ward in the matter of her marriage, many states continue to require the consent (or allow the objection) of the family guardian (or if not, the judge as a proxy guardian) to a woman's marriage either in general or in particular circumstances that do not apply to males. Objections to this on the grounds, *inter alia*, of women's equal citizenship, equal legal capacity and equal choice have had less effect than advocacy for a minimum age of marriage, despite a general tendency to increasingly restrict the scope of the guardian's authority recognised by the law. The issue of coercion remains a concern, despite increasingly specific prohibitions in the law.

Minimum age of marriage

There was, generally, less opposition on jurisprudential (or political) bases to the setting of minimum ages of marriage than to other aspects of the reform agenda; although the classical juristic consensus permits the marriage of minor wards by their guardians, the fact that consummation was not supposed to occur until puberty or later, depending upon the wife's physical maturity, along with the existence of isolated juristic support for the prohibition of marriages under puberty, supported legislative reforms on this subject in the twentieth century. Objections are voiced more often where there is a difference between the statutory minimum age of marriage and that of actual puberty of the party involved or the legal presumption of puberty (at fifteen lunar years according to the juristic consensus). Statutory legislation may also show the same concerns, allowing marriage below the specified minimum age to be permitted or regularised by the judge in case of a need or a benefit. Such need is likely to be recognised in the case of an out-of-court, unregistered marriage, especially where pregnancy or childbirth has resulted, and more broadly where there is or has been pre-marital sexual activity by an adolescent female, or where the guardian perceives that there is a risk of such activity.

Statutory legislation has taken two basic approaches. The first, adopted by Egypt in its early legislation on the family and continuing to date, took a procedural route, not allowing a notary to register a marriage of a male under eighteen or a female under sixteen, disallowing the courts from hearing claims arising from any marriage where the parties were not of that age when the claim was raised and, as noted previously, disallowing claims from any disputed marriage in the absence of the official marriage document.[3] The Egyptian legislation was (and is) unusual in the region for not substantively making the achievement of puberty (*bulugh*) a condition of capacity, unlike in other states where the legal formulation was presented as procedural.[4] Yemen is also an exception; while the 1992 law set fifteen as the minimum age of marriage for both males and females, a 1999 amendment removed the minimum age and validated the marriage of minors by the guardian, while not allowing consummation or requiring cohabitation until the wife is capable of intercourse 'even if she is over the age of fifteen' and requiring the establishment of an interest in the marriage of a minor male.[5] Equally exceptional in terms of statutory regulation of the contracting of minors in marriage is Sudan. The 1991 Sudanese code refers to the achievement of puberty without adding a minimum age in years when considering the guardian's role in marriage, but in a subsequent provision explicitly allows the guardian to contract a 'discriminating [minor]' in marriage in cases of an 'overriding interest' and with the permission of the judge. Here, it does set a specific age, providing that 'discrimination is achieved at the age of ten' and thus effectively making ten the minimum age at which a person can be contracted in marriage.[6] Like the 1992 Yemeni law before its 1998 amendment, the Sudanese law makes no reference to *khiyar al-bulugh*, the option of dissolution at puberty available to a minor contracted in marriage by the guardian, although the reference to dominant Hanafi opinions as the residual law presumably makes this available to those made aware of the rules.

In contrast to Egypt's primarily procedural approach, most states have followed the approach taken in the Ottoman Law of Family Rights of identifying set minimum ages at which marriage may be concluded (that is, rather than ages at which marriage may be registered). Frequently, there are two sets of ages of concern to the legislator (as there was in the OLFR),[7] the first being either actual puberty or a minimum age, and the second the age of full capacity for marriage, which may correspond to the age of legal majority in civil law.[8] In between these two ages (often different for males and females), particular requirements are made regarding the consent of the court and the guardian; here, the law may constrain the court from permitting the marriage until full capacity is reached in the event of the guardian refusing to consent, as well as constraining the guardian and the parties involved from concluding the marriage without the consent of the court, which is generally conditioned on the establishment of some interest or benefit to be realised through the marriage.[9] By way of example, Algeria set its ages of capacity for marriage at 21 for males and 18 for females in the 1984 law, allowing the court to permit a marriage before this 'if there is a reason of interest or in a case of necessity'; in the 2005 amendments the age of capacity was reduced and equalised, now at 19 for both males and females, with the same allowance made for underage marriages.[10]

Being of the age of full capacity for marriage does not necessarily remove a woman from the authority of her guardian in the matter of her marriage, as discussed further below. Penal sanctions may apply in the event of non-compliance with the age requirements, while a marriage concluded in defiance thereof may nevertheless be or become valid. Jordanian law for example provides for criminal penalties for non-compliance with registration requirements and for the marriage of an underage female, which is held irregular and liable to dissolution by the court. However, the courts are instructed not to hear claims for divorce on these grounds if in the interim the wife has given birth or is pregnant (which of course *inter alia* establishes puberty), or if at the time the claim is brought to court both husband and wife have reached the statutory minimum age of marriage.[11] Even without such explicit statutory direction, judges are likely to weigh such circumstances in recognising an out-of-court marriage, particularly where the union is acknowledged by both parties, or (in the case of pregnancy) to consider it an interest, benefit or necessity (as variously phrased) permitting a marriage below the age of capacity. In addition, the exceptional circumstances may include an argument that a sexually mature female under the statutory age of marriage is or will become engaged in pre-marital sexual activity unless the court gives consent for her marriage. The risk here may be posited as threatening not only the interests of the girl and her family, but society at large. In an analysis of the original 1972 Libyan law, Mayer describes the Explanatory Memorandum as clarifying that 'concern for the potential immorality of a minor female' would be a circumstance where the courts could grant permission for marriage below the statutory age, specifically cases of female orphans where it was necessary 'to prevent them from falling into that which will lead to their perdition and the corruption of society'.[12] This comment goes directly to the expected role of the father as guardian in controlling the sexual conduct of his daughter, whether before her marriage or through arranging it at an appropriate time.[13] In Morocco, the original code of 1957 specifically retained coercive authority over an adult woman in allowing the court to compel her to marry if there was an established fear that otherwise she would 'fall into corruption'.[14] Furthermore, in the case of non-consensual sex, judges may concur with the argument that the rape victim's social and family interest is best protected through her marriage, and permit an early marriage in such circumstances.[15]

Limiting the practice of early marriage, particularly of girls, has long been a concern of social reformers, the feminist movement and women's rights activists in the region as elsewhere, and is given weight in the international instruments and in its treatment as a developmental indicator.[16] Reformers focus on the physical and mental health risks of early marriage to very young women and girls and issues of their consent to the marriage, as well as the loss or at least substantial limitation of their opportunities for education and work outside family labour – a focus which for some indicated the class-based prioritisation of this issue in the early days of the discussions,[17] while finding more resonance now with the institution of compulsory terms of education. Reference is often made to the Convention on the Rights of the Child in advocacy that tends to argue for the setting of the age of legal majority as the minimum age for marriage, and to argue for the informed scrutiny of the court for any exceptions, depending upon the socio-economic context of the particular environment. As well as the attitude of judges and notaries, attention is focussed on the procedures required for the contract, including the production and availability of the various administrative certificates, and the availability and use of penal sanctions to support the requirement of consent as well as age.[18] Thus, while supporting the option for girls under eighteen to marry if they wish to do so, Women Living Under Muslim Laws notes that 'activists in systems with such provisions note that they can merely serve as loopholes for the continuation of early and forced marriage'.[19] In the process leading up to promulgation of Qatar's first family law, al-Thani notes that particular concern was raised at the draft law's proposal that marriage under the set ages could be concluded if both the parties to the marriage and the guardian agreed, and that it was the intervention of the National Commission for Women's Affairs that produced the inclusion in the final text of the need additionally for the court's permission.[20]

The Jordanian debate on raising the minimum age of capacity for marriage

As to objections to the tendency to increase the minimum statutory age of marriage, some features of the discourse were illustrated in the Jordanian debate on the changes legislated through government decision in temporary laws in 2001, setting the age of legal majority (eighteen by the solar calendar) as

the age of legal capacity, and reinstituting the need for the court to give special permission for a marriage from fifteen to seventeen.[21] In 1996, a draft of
suggested amendments to the JLPS prepared by the 'official' umbrella women's
organization, the Jordanian National Commission for Women, did not propose
a change in the age of capacity. However, among other groups the establishment of the Civil Code's age of legal majority (at eighteen for both sexes by the
solar calendar)[22] as the minimum age of capacity for marriage was identified
as a target for advocacy and campaigning. Justifications for this objective were
made on the evidence of social science research into the effects of early marriage on young women and with reference to international instruments such
as the Convention of the Rights of the Child.[23] Others suggested that while the
age of capacity should be raised to eighteen, the *qadi* should retain the discretion to assess the girl's circumstances in particular cases where her guardian
requests permission for her to be married below that age.[24] This type of formulation, which was in fact adopted in Temporary Law no.82/2001, constituted a partial return to the rules of the previous law, the Jordanian Law of
Family Rights 1951, when the judge's approval as well as that of the marriage
guardian was required for a marriage below the age of full capacity. Jordan acceded to the Convention on the Minimum Age of Marriage in 1992 without
reservation, holding the age of capacity under the JLPS 1976 (pre-amendment)
of 15 lunar years for females to be in accordance with the Convention on the
Rights of the Child.[25] In 1999, non-governmental organizations participating in
the submission of the NGO report on the implementation of the Convention
on the Rights of the Child in Jordan announced that they were:

> Intensifying their endeavours to increase the age of marriage, for both men and
> women, to eighteen, since they are convinced that the physical, mental and emo-
> tional development on which eligibility for marriage is largely based cannot be
> found in persons under eighteen years of age.[26]

The report then acknowledged 'fears that the incidence of offences against
the code of morality might rise in hot and remote areas if the age of marriage
were increased' and called for public awareness and education programmes
to be carried out by NGOs 'in an attempt to avert such fears'.

In Temporary Law no.82/2001, the age of capacity for marriage was increased to eighteen years by the solar calendar; the judge was empowered to
permit the marriage of males and females below this age provided they are

aged fifteen or above and that such a marriage realizes an 'interest' or a 'benefit' (*maslaha*) as to be defined subsequently by the *Qadi al-Qudah*.[27] A month later, the Chief Islamic Justice issued the necessary directive setting out the bases on which a judge might permit such a marriage, which included 'that the marriage prevents an existing cause of corruption[28] or avoids the loss of an established benefit'.[29] On the face of it, this clause maintained a potentially very broad scope of judicial discretion in the matter of underage marriage, and although the directive emphasised the need to ascertain the consent of the underage female and that her interest would be thereby served, concern remained that underage females might be pressurised into marriage in circumstances that could be explained to the judge as 'preventing corruption' or achieving a benefit.

When the contents of Temporary Law no.82/2001 were publicized in Jordan prior to publication in the *Official Gazette* and implementation by the courts, the print media gave substantial space to discussions on the rise in the age of capacity for marriage. In one feature, a sociologist and an educationalist (both men) supported the amendment on grounds *inter alia* of the negative impact of early marriage (particularly for females) on personal health and family relations, the opportunity for greater educational and productive capacities with a later age of marriage, and the idea that changing times and socio-economic circumstances fully justified this change in the law.[30] In the same piece, two male lecturers in *fiqh* objected on the grounds *inter alia* that marriage is a right of females and males after puberty, that one of the aims of the amendment was to reduce the birth rate ('especially in Arab states'), and that current social problems involved delays in marriage rather than early marriage, since there were some 400,000 single males and females in Jordan of all ages. One also warned against leaving such matters 'in the hands of committees concerned only with human rights and child rights' to the exclusion of adequate *fiqh* expertise. Elsewhere, another *shari'a* academic insisted that the incidence of early marriage was very low, that there was no need 'for this big media fuss' and that behind the pressures on 'Islamic states' to raise the age of marriage lay 'the tendencies of world conferences on women to facilitate the prohibited (*haram*) among adolescents; these are suspect calls for the corruption of Islamic society'.[31]

One *shar'i* judge justified the amendment with *fiqh* arguments (including constraining the permitted in order to realize a benefit) and in light of social, cultural and economic changes including the longer period of compulsory education.[32] Another was more circumspect, warning that 'Jordan isn't just Amman,' that outside the cities marriage tends to take place below the age of eighteen, that the measure might be 'shutting in front of them the door of the permitted (*halal*) and opening the door of the prohibited (*haram*)'; and that he expected the exception (of permitting marriage below eighteen) to become the rule.[33] Women's rights and social activists were more supportive, some stressing the risks of early marriage particularly to girls, others the need for *qadis* to be careful in their use of discretion to permit a marriage below eighteen.[34] These last two positions have turned out to be well founded. By early 2006, the human rights group Mizan had launched 'the country's first ever public campaign to raise awareness about the dangers of early marriage' having found that 'the exception clause in the current law was widely abused'.[35] Television and radio slots accompanied a poster campaign prominently featuring the text of the amended JLPS provision stipulating the age of eighteen as the minimum age of marriage, with no reference at all to the subsequent clause allowing for exceptions.

Guardianship in marriage

Apart from reinstituting court scrutiny over the guardian's actions in marrying a ward below the age of legal majority, the temporary Jordanian legislation of 2001 made no change to the existing provisions on guardianship (*wilaya*) in marriage. The authority in a woman's marriage of the male family guardian (father, son, grandfather, etc.) or, by default or in the case of the judge over-riding the veto of the family guardian, that of the court acting as a proxy guardian continues to be a focus in many countries of the region for those working on reform of family law. As noted above, Morocco repealed in 1993 the remaining reference in statutory law in the region to the legality, in particular circumstances, of a forced marriage, and increasingly the codes explicitly attend to the issue of consent, prohibit coercion and provide for remedies in the event that the wife is forced into marriage; Iraq's 1978 amendment to its 1959 law is one of the clearest and most detailed in this respect, detailing in three separate clauses the prohibition of forcing a person to marry and the criminal penalties to which those doing so are liable.[36] Algeria's 1984 law also explicitly forbids the *wali* (guardian) from forcing his ward into marriage or marrying the ward without the latter's consent, without referring to penalties.[37] Some codes also require special scrutiny of a marriage involving a young woman and a substantially older man.[38] Such provisions, initiated in Jordan in its 1951 law, may be officially justified in terms of ensuring spousal compatibility, but they are clearly provoked also by concerns over the joint issues of early and forced marriage; a 2006 Yemeni study on early marriage reported huge age gaps between the spouses, and the press noted that among the reasons behind early marriage is that 'parents are lured into marrying their daughters at a young age by rich men proposing to marry their daughters'.[39] In 2005 the Mufti of Saudi Arabia, where there is no national codification, declared that it was unlawful for fathers to force their daughters into an unwanted marriage.[40]

Nevertheless, despite the legislative consensus on the need for the woman's free consent to the contract, concerns remain over the implementation of the legal texts,[41] particularly with regard to young women and girls, and there is thus substantial overlap with the debate on minimum age of marriage and adequate procedural oversight. In 2005, the American Bar Association's Iraq Legal Development Project summarised its finding from fieldwork in this regard as follows:

> [A]lthough many respondents knew that forced marriage involved a penalty under the Code, no respondents knew of an instance where a woman received an annulment for a forced marriage. Several respondents also observed that the chances of a woman obtaining a separation under such circumstances are relatively small due to social morays; the expense of court costs; and cumbersome procedures. As one respondent stated, 'if the woman can reach a court and prove that she has been forced into marriage, she is protected by the law and she might be granted separation. But she will have lost a lot of time, money and energy'.[42]

Issues remain in the statutory law around the other aspect of guardianship in marriage: that is, whether a woman of full legal majority needs her guardian's consent to her marriage. Some laws continue to require that a woman's guardian concludes the contract on her behalf, rather than the woman doing it in person.[43] Where this is the case, clearly the woman's marriage is dependent upon the consent of the guardian required to conclude the contract. The original Moroccan text included this requirement; in 1993, after a sustained campaign by women's rights groups, this was amended to allow a woman to conclude her own contract of marriage in person in the event that her father was dead, while the 2004 law allows this option to any woman of legal majority.[44] The Ministry of Justice's *Practical Guide* to the new law emphasises that 'one of the most important things that women have gained from the new law is that guardianship is her right; [...] like the man, she exercises it according to her choice and her interests without being subjected to any supervision or consent'. The woman is entitled to conclude her own contract, continues the Guide, or to delegate this function; delegation requires the physical presence of the woman and the person she is delegating in the session during which the contract is made and signed. In explaining the law's continuing provision for a woman to delegate her father or other relative to conclude her marriage contract, the guide invokes some of the same societal and familial expectations that make the removal of guardianship from an adult woman contentious in some quarters: it is 'out of consideration for what is customarily done, and in preservation of traditions that are known in the cohesion of the family'. [45]

In Algeria, women's groups have likewise voiced particular objection to a provision similar to the previous Moroccan text in the 1984 Algerian law which, according to Dennerlein, followed previous rulings of the Supreme Court in 'formally reinstating' this requirement after French-era legislation removed it.[46] In the 2005 amendments to the 1984 law, the Algerian legislators finally allowed an adult woman to conclude her own marriage contract 'in the presence of the guardian, who is her father or a relative or any other person of her choice'.[47] The requirement of the guardian has thus not been removed; the amended text continues to require that the contract of marriage fulfils the set requirements including capacity of the parties and the guardian, although a later text adds 'when this is necessary'.[48]

Court practice will show whether Algeria's amended law has in fact removed the requirement of the family *wali* or allows the court to continue to invoke it, in line with the pattern of other codifications that – implicitly or explicitly – require the guardian's consent beyond the age of full legal majority, either in general,[49] or for a first marriage,[50] while allowing an adult woman to seek the over-riding of her guardian's veto by the court. If the court finds the guardian's objection misplaced, it is then entitled either to give its permission for the marriage, with the judge standing in as the guardian under his authority of 'general guardianship', or to order the guardian to give his permission and if he persists in refusing, ask a more distant guardian of the woman to marry her. In other words, an adult woman must have either the permission of her family guardian or the permission of the court standing in for guardian either due to absence or due to the court's assessment that his refusal to consent is misplaced. The 1998 amendments to the Yemen law changed from one position to the other in this regard; the 1992 law allowed the judge to undertake the marriage of a woman if her closest guardian refused the judge's order to do so, while as amended, the law requires the judge to order the next two guardians in line to undertake her marriage before being empowered to do it himself.[51]

In Kuwait, where the law continues to require a woman's guardian to conclude her contract of marriage for her, a 2004 amendment to the 1984 law exceptionally allows a previously married woman to ask the judge to conclude the contract of her re-marriage to her former husband, provided that the court contacts her guardian 'to hear his opinion'. In such circumstances of course the guardian has already given his consent once to the woman's marriage to the man in question.[52] Otherwise, the Explanatory Memorandum to the original article indicates that a 'meeting of views' of the woman and her guardian is required for the marriage of a female aged from actual puberty until the age of 25, a time it describes as 'a critical time for young women', indicating that their emotional make-up during this period cannot guarantee considered reflection of the long-term future; after the age of 25, the guardian is to conclude her marriage 'in view of tradition and in preservation of the status of the guardian' while in the event of his refusing her marriage, the *qadi* is entitled to intervene and marry her to a man of her choice if he considers it appropriate.

Unlike the Algerian amendments issued the same year, the 2005 UAE law follows the pattern of other Gulf states in requiring that a woman's marriage contract is carried out by her guardian, justifying this on the majority juristic view and in view of the 'potential hazards' of a woman undertaking her own marriage. However, the Explanatory Memorandum stresses that the wife's consent is necessary and that it is to ensure that this has been given that the new law requires the notary to have the wife sign the contract after its conclusion by her guardian.[53] The UAE is unequivocal on the need for the guardian, voiding contracts concluded without the woman's *wali* and ordering the separation of the spouses, although establishing the paternity of any children from such a marriage to the husband; the 'two contracting parties' to the marriage contract are 'the husband and the *wali*'.[54] An article in the *Khaleej Times* some years earlier had quoted scholars and judges in Dubai in-

sisting on the juristic basis for the requirement of the guardian, while setting their concern in a social context that clearly revolves around *'urfi* marriage. One of the sources referred to the public prosecution offices being
'packed' with cases of 'illegal' marriages concluded without the consent of
the guardian due to 'the ignorance of Muslim couples' and 'underlined the
common mistake among young couples who tend to challenge their parents'
will and get married without their approval':

> There are cases of young couples who conclude illegal contracts by just bringing
> two witnesses and write a contract on ordinary paper thinking that they have ful-
> filled the conditions of the legal contract. But when they come to the court to reg-
> ister this contract driven by the belief that the transaction is complete, or when
> the woman's guardian objects to this marriage and files a complaint, or even
> when they get caught in an apartment or hotel room living together with only the
> paper they signed as a proof, only to discover that this paper is worthless and
> cannot protect them from being prosecuted for having an illicit relationship...'
> [...] Islam has set this rule to protect women, who are known for being sentimen-
> tal, from falling for the wrong men and ruining their lives.[55]

This short extract from a locally published English language newspaper gives
some indication of the social practice targeted by the UAE law, which clearly
empowers the woman's male family guardian in the matter of her marriage.
It also indicates the common wisdom of the protective intention behind the
institution of guardianship, discussed further below, echoing the judgment
noted above by the Kuwait legislators that women are prone to being swayed
by emotional factors and in need of the rational guidance of their male relatives. At the same time, the fact that the laws allow a woman to take her
case to the judge allows for the possibility that the guardian cannot unex-
ceptionally be relied upon to decide solely in the woman's best interest; this
interest can, in such circumstances, be decided upon by the male judge.

The role of the guardian

The idea of the guardian's veto of a marriage being misplaced or unsub-
stantiated invokes *inter alia* the concept of the 'suitability' (*kafa'a*) of a particular marriage partner for the individual woman, whose guardian may

object if the husband is not the 'equal' of the woman on criteria that vary in the statutory law of different states. [56] These criteria generally restrict the potentially wide scope of objections that might be made, if the judge chooses to give preferential weight to the woman's choice. Where the physical presence of the guardian is not required for the validity of the contract (particularly in areas influenced by the Hanafi school), the law may allow him to object retrospectively to a woman's marriage if it was made without his consent, and to petition the court for the marriage to be dissolved in the event that court finds the woman has married a man who does not fulfil the stipulations of *kafa'a*.[57] Where the guardian is required to be present at or to conclude the contract, or where otherwise his consent is required before the contract (such as in the case of a marriage below legal majority), the concept may be employed by the court, along with consideration of the interest of the woman, to assess whether he is being arbitrary or abusive in his refusal to marry the woman to a particular man. It also provides the basis for either the woman or her guardian to seek judicial dissolution in the event that the groom misrepresented himself in order to secure the marriage. The quality of *kafa'a* is thus presented as 'a right of the woman and of the guardian' in an indication of the motive of 'protection' – of the woman in cases where she and her guardian have been deceived by the groom, or of her family (and their assessment of her best interest) against her choosing such a match on her own authority, whether or not she is deceived into making it.

Besides *fiqh*-based arguments in support of the institution of guardianship – which acknowledge that there are textual arguments to the contrary also – the justification for continuing authority tends to be made in terms of protection of women against predatory and dishonest suitors, through involving the greater experience of men, not least in the ways of other men. This protection argument may be voiced also in the context of increased social mixing in different milieus.[58] In its different manifestations and internal variations, it articulates what Kandiyoti has termed the classic 'patriarchal bargain' of 'protection in exchange for submissiveness and propriety', evidenced also in the textual rules on the marital relationship discussed below.[59] Contemporary commentators are sometimes at pains to underline that no inadequacy of reason on the woman's part is implied by subjecting her choice of partner to the guardian's approval.[60] Women's rights activists in the region disagree, with a variety of arguments including equal citizenship rights and responsibilities. At the same time, those proposing reforms may seek to integrate the social expectation of the family's role, an expectation highlighted for example in those debates around 'urfi marriage that focus on the prospect of young women marrying 'secretly' without the involvement or knowledge of their families, a scenario also clearly evoked in the UAE press report cited above. In Palestine, Khadr proposed a text making a limited space for the views of parents without conceding the principle of legal capacity of the individual or accommodating gender discrimination:

1. The approval of the wali is not a condition in the marriage of a sane woman who has reached her eighteenth year by the solar calendar;

2. Either or both parents may object to a contract of marriage, and the qadi shall rule on the objection, which decision may be appealed;

3. The objection shall be accepted only before the contract has been concluded or within one week of the parent's knowledge of it;

4. The judge may rule that the contract shall not be completed for a certain period, or may rule on dissolution;

5. The qadi shall not prevent a contract of marriage that the two parties insist on concluding two years after a decision [by the court] to uphold an objection [by the parents].[61]

In the debates in Palestine, as apparently was the case in Morocco regarding the new law, the requirement of the male family guardian was among the principles most vigorously defended by a range of religious, societal and political actors. A draft Palestinian law of 2005 explicitly requires the guardian's consent, in an approach that the Chief Islamic Justice has explained as primarily protective of women.

A final point to be made about the marriage guardian is the continuing assignation of this role to the father or other close male relative. In Mauritania, the law stipulates that where a woman has been appointed wasi by the father or is acting in the context of a contract of kafala[62] ('legal sponsorship'), and therefore otherwise exercises the full authorities of guardianship, she must appoint a man to undertake the function of marriage guardianship in her place.[63] In Tunisia, the law requires the consent of both 'the guardian and the mother' to the marriage of a person under the age of legal majority; thus even where the mother has been assigned all the functions of guardianship, she cannot act alone in this matter.[64] The 2004 Moroccan law requires the court to hear the views of both parents on an application for marriage below the age of legal majority, while suspending its consent on the agreement of the 'shar'i representative' of the minor. This representative is normally the guardian, who in turn is normally the father, unless he is absent or has lost capacity, when the law assigns this position to the mother. Here, the text of the law appears to contemplate the mother acting alone in this capacity in certain circumstances.[65] In this area, the 1975 Somali code was something of an exception, not only its own time, providing that the mother follows the father as marriage guardian for her children.[66]

Overview

Minimum ages of marriage are identified in the Muslim family laws of most Arab states; where they are lacking, procedural rules identify similar ages for the registration of marriage by a state official. The ages vary throughout the region; several set higher minimum ages of marriage for males than for females. A general pattern in women's rights advocacy is to seek the raising of the minimum age of capacity for marriage to the age of legal majority usually identified separately in the particular country's civil code, with the age of eighteen often the target. Differences remain as to whether advocacy should include the prospects of exceptions for marriage below these ages, and if so, how this might be managed. Beyond the law, efforts continue in seeking to raise awareness of the risks of early marriage, and in work on education and other areas of social policy; early or underage marriage remains a focus for many social activists in the region. Experiences in certain contexts have shown that judges may view the prospect of an early marriage with less trepidation than women's rights groups. As for guardianship, there is no statutory recognition of a guardian's coercive authority over his ward in the matter of her marriage, although even where laws specifically allow coercion as a ground for divorce, access to this remedy may be difficult. Most codes retain the need for an adult woman in at least some circumstances to have her guardian's permission for her marriage, or failing this that of the court in over-riding his objection. Here, the codifications of Muslim personal status law in Qatar (2006) and the UAE (2005) stand at opposite ends of the spectrum to the 2004 Moroccan law. The former, like other Gulf codifications, continue to explicitly require the guardian's consent (together with his conclusion of the marriage contract); the latter, like Tunisia before, no longer require any guardian's consent for the marriage of a woman who is above the age of full capacity for marriage. Public debates tend to uphold the view that the involvement of the family is, at the very least, desirable, particularly in the marriage of a female, and removal of this involvement from statutory legislation (through the removal of the need for the guardian's consent) remains contentious.

7 Polygyny

The institution of polygyny is in many ways one of the 'totems' of Islamic family law. Targetted by early reformists and modernists in the Arab world, including the early feminist movement, as anachronistic and almost the antithesis of 'modernity', it was also pointed up by colonial and imperial powers in the discourses of power and subjugation. These days it falls foul of the human rights norm of equality and non-discrimination and continues to be a target for women's rights activists in the region and beyond. At the same time, it is a prominent point of 'difference' between what are presented as the 'values of the West' and the text-based principles of Islamic family law. The classical law left the conclusion of a polygynous marriage formally unregulated by the courts,[1] while developing principles on the rights of co-wives vis-à-vis their husband. Developments in the classical rules are vulnerable to being attacked as encroachments by the legislature on the morality and structure of the Muslim family and hence society, and on the *shari'a* itself, at the behest of powerful Western players.

On the social side, statistics on the extent of polygynous marriages are hard to come by and equally hard to verify, although the highest rates in the region appear to be found in the Gulf states.[2] In her fascinating 'investigation of the phenomenon of polygyny in rural Egypt', Laila Shahd examines, through extensive fieldwork, the motivating factors behind polygynous marriage in the village setting, desegregating the data between different socio-economic classes. Her findings include a consideration of factors that are 'economic, cultural, social and sexual' and include for example infertility of the wife or her production of daughters but no sons ('among upper-class farmers', as compared to divorce in these circumstances among lower- and middle-class farmers); problems with in-laws, whether between the husband and his wife's family or the wife and her husband's family; and political alliances enabling advancement in powerful local political structures and elites.[3] Studies of this kind considerably expand the potential for activists and policy-makers to design legally and socially effective measures in their efforts to constrain or end polygyny.

Constraints on polygyny in contemporary legislation

Tunisia is still pointed to by women's rights activists as the example of what a determined legislator can do, for its prohibition of polygyny in the 1956 law:[4] Habib Bourghiba insisted that he was not contravening any 'notion of Islam', that many Muslims had long been demanding the prohibition of polygyny and that it had 'become inadmissible in the twentieth century and inconceivable to any right-minded person'.[5] The presentation of the prohibition within an Islamic jurisprudential framework in the accompanying explanations did not prevent significant opposition from senior members of the *shar'i* judiciary to this move and other provisions in the text, while Chekir observes that among its supporters were those who favoured a reformist approach to Islamic law and others whose support came more directly because of the strengthening of women's rights at the start of independence.[6] By way of contrast, nearly fifty years later, the UAE's 2005 law simply reiterates the 'classical' positions on the rights of co-wives, and in an expanded commentary takes on some of the arguments of the reformists, albeit not referring to them directly. The commentary examines the Quranic texts to conclude that since control over things of the heart is not within the human capability, 'a husband is not required to be equal to his wives in respect of his heart's affection' although 'the heart's inclination must remain between the created and his Creator, and no evident inclination towards one wife may arise therefrom'.[7] Commenting on the codification of the traditional rule that co-wives may not be made to live together unless they consent, the commentary notes to etymological derivation of the word for co-wife *(durra)* from the word for harm: 'the mere presence of a co-wife in the house provokes feelings of jealously and hatred, and hurts the wife's feelings.'[8]

In other Arab states, legislative approaches aimed at constraining and regulating polygyny have involved a combination of judicial scrutiny and bureaucratic procedure prior to the conclusion of a polygynous union, an approach which revolves around the institution of registration procedures and requires the court's consent – under specified conditions – to the conclusion of a polygynous marriage, with penalties prescribed for those marrying in violation of these regulations. On the other hand is the issue of remedy, the explicit acknowledgement in law that a woman may be injured by her husband taking another wife, and that she may have cause to seek dissolution of her marriage accordingly. Most states also allow a wife to retain a remedy or a deterrent against polygyny by the insertion of a stipulation in her marriage contract entitling her to seek divorce if the husband marries another wife, or providing for an increase in her dower should he do so. While specific features of these approaches appear in different codes, certain of them remain less established and more vulnerable to challenge. This is the case with regard to the notification and consent of the first wife, the assumption of injury arising from a polygynous marriage (as compared to the need for her to establish such injury), and the question of validity of polygynous marriages concluded in violation of the bureaucratic procedures required by the law. The combination and significant increase of bureaucratic procedures in Morocco's new law is described by its drafters and supporters as rendering polygyny 'almost impossible'. In an overview of his intent, the Moroccan king underlined the constraint of polygyny in accordance with the intentions and justice of Islam, and the 'distinctive wisdom of Islam' in allowing a man to marry another wife 'in a lawful manner by reason of urgent and pressing need, and with the consent of the judge, rather than resorting to unlawful *de facto* polygyny in the event of the total prohibition of polygyny'.[9]

Lawful benefit and financial capacity

The two elements on which the court's consent is most commonly conditioned in the codes are the husband's financial ability to provide for a new wife in addition to his existing wife and family,[10] and the existence of what is termed a 'lawful benefit' from the polygynous union.[11] These conditions, in various phrasings, are now common in state codifications in the Mashreq and North Africa, but were innovations in Syria in 1953 and in Iraq in 1959, after similar proposals to subject polygyny to the consent of the judge had failed to be adopted in Egyptian legislation. The first remains less controversial than the second; in Jordan's 'temporary' legislation of 2001, which introduced constraints on the conclusion of a polygynous marriage for the first time into Jordanian law, the government required the judge to ascertain the husband's ability to pay dower and maintenance, but did not introduce scrutiny of the motives for the marriage nor require the court to withhold consent should it fail to find a 'lawful benefit' established.[12] In Qatar, an initial draft which had omitted any regulation of polygyny was amended after public consultations and interventions to include a very restrained reference to financial circumstances.[13] Yemen included both elements in its law of 1992, in wording that, as Wurth observes, was taken from the Draft Arab Personal Status Law, although it omitted the latter's stipulation that polygynous marriage be conditioned on the consent of the court in accordance with these conditions, and therefore left the provision 'unenforceable'; in the 1998 revisions, the reference to a 'lawful benefit' was omitted.[14] Syria, on the other hand, added the condition of a 'lawful (shar‘i) justification' in its 1975 amendment, the explanatory note observing that the existing requirement for financial ability had been found inadequate.[15] Algeria's 2005 amendments require consent to be sought from the court in the present spouses' domicile.[16]

The terms of a 'lawful benefit' are not defined in the laws or indeed in their Explanatory Memoranda. However, the terms most generally recognised were set out explicitly in the 1974 law of the then PDRY, which allowed the court to give the required written permission for a polygamous union only in the event that it was established to the court's satisfaction (by medical report) either that the man's existing wife was infertile (and provided that the husband did not know this before marrying her) or that she had an incurable chronic or contagious illness. Mitchell reports an unpublished judicial circular similarly interpreting the reference to a 'justified motive' in the 1984 Algerian law.[17] Early in the twentieth century, Egyptian feminists had argued for polygyny to be permitted only in the event of the wife's infertility or her inability to engage in sexual relations due to chronic illness,[18] and it is these conditions that are most commonly cited by commentators justifying the continued validity of the institution of polygyny, as a preferable course to the husband divorcing his wife in order to remarry.[19]

These definitions of 'lawful benefit' thus focus on the circumstances of the existing marriage. Having been the first to legislate this condition in 1959, Iraq subsequently added a provision regarding the circumstances of the intended marriage: a couple of months into its war with Iran, Iraq excepted from the constraints imposed on polygynous marriage a union where the intended bride was a widow.[20] This amendment evokes a circumstance-specific argument made in defence of polygyny, the situation of society in times of war, with a 'surplus of women', with orphans and widows in need of protection and the community needing more children to compensate for the men lost in battle.[21] Away from legislation, the recent debate on 'ambulant marriage' in Saudi Arabia analysed by Arabi shows the rights discourse being used by commentators in relation to the second wife, with regard in particular to professional women who 'missed the opportunity to marry' because of taking up expanded educational and professional opportunities, as well as, on the other side of the debate, in relation to the first wife, whose rights are presented as implicated by the secrecy of such unions.[22]

A more general and permissive argument for polygyny presents as an 'unfortunate fact' the inability of many men to be satisfied with a single sexual partner, with the ensuing risk, were polygyny to be prohibited, of the proliferation of unlawful extra-marital unions (here a comparison is often made with legally monogamous societies of 'the West') which would be not only in violation of the *shari'a*, but would leave unprotected the rights of the female partner and ensuing offspring.[23] The 'biological' basis of this argument appears to be less readily acceptable in some contemporary official discourse; in the parliamentary debate in Morocco on the new family law in 2004, the press reported an Islamist deputy as arguing that 'there are men who, for physical reasons, cannot satisfy themselves with only one wife', and the religious affairs minister as responding that 'in that case, they should seek treatment'.[24]

Besides the elements of financial capacity and a 'lawful benefit', a third element that also features in a number of codes is that of 'equity' or 'just treatment'. This concept, along with the financial obligations to each wife, finds a basis in classical jurisprudence and is commonly included as a requirement of an ongoing marriage, that is, as a right of the wife to equal treatment with her co-wives, or as an obligation of the husband to treat his wives equally, including not obliging co-wives to share accommodation. This kind of formulation is the focus of the only provisions regulating polygyny in the Kuwaiti, Omani, UAE and Sudanese codifications, and in Jordanian law until the 2001 temporary legislation.[25] The Iraqi code, however, required the judge to evaluate prior to conclusion of the marriage whether there is a 'fear of injustice between the wives' and if so not to permit it; in the law of Morocco, where this element was first included in a codification, it is maintained without such instruction to the judge.[26]

Notification requirements and consent of the wife

Other conditions now commonly attached to the conclusion of polygynous marriages in states where the law subjects them to judicial control relate to notification procedures, the thrust of which is to seek to ensure that the intended bride is aware that the man is already married, and to inform the existing wife of her husband's intention to remarry or his remarriage after the fact. These regulations vary in detail and in timing. In its original law, Morocco required (in what Anderson at the time called 'a mild form of *ijtihad*') that a woman could not be contracted in a polygynous union until she had been informed that the man was already married; in 1993 it added the requirement that the existing wife was to be informed that her husband was intending to marry again.[27] In its new law, Morocco stipulates detailed procedures requiring the notification of the existing wife with a view to her attendance and participation in the court hearings on her husband's application for permission to conclude a polygynous union, while Egyptian law requires the notary registering the marriage to inform the existing wife after (rather than before) the conclusion of the contract; both also deal with the possibility of the husband frustrating these procedures.[28]

There continues to be some resistance in particular in relation to the notification of the existing wife, as shown during the Jordanian parliamentary debates on the 2001 'temporary' legislation which provided for her to be notified after her husband's conclusion of a polygynous contract: 'no judge,' one deputy was reported as saying, 'has the right to inform a wife of her husband's decision to remarry should the husband decide to keep it secret' – sometimes it was necessary to wait for 'the right time'.[29] In Yemen the 1998 amendments to the 1992 law retained the reference to informing the intended bride, but removed the reference to informing the existing wife that her husband was intending to take another wife.[30] In Qatar, objections were reportedly made by the Legal Committee of the Qatari legislature to the draft law's requirement that an existing wife (or wives) be notified of a husband's polygynous marriage after it is documented, declaring that it could find no *sharʿi* basis for this requirement, that it was not local practice, and that such a requirement 'could lead to problems'.[31] One way of viewing this resistance is as an acknowledgement of the substantial challenge that can be posed to a man's decision if the woman is empowered with knowledge of it; it may also express a resentment at the further reach of state law and bureaucracy into the 'private sphere' of the family, unsettling an existing power balance.

The issue of notification is connected to consent; the informed consent of a woman to enter a polygynous marriage, and the consent of the existing wife to a subsequent marriage by her husband, which was not a requirement in classical law, as well as her ability to challenge it. Amendments to the

1984 Libyan law require (in addition to existing pre-conditions) that either the first wife gives her written consent before the competent court or permission is given by the court following a successful action by the husband against her.[32] Algeria's 2005 amendments remove the 1984 permission for either wife to seek divorce if the polygynous union has been concluded without their consent and instead now require the court considering the husband's application to establish consent along with the other precedent conditions; the implication here is that the court can (or perhaps shall) withhold permission for the marriage if informed consent is not given. Similarly unusually, Morocco's 2004 law prohibits polygyny if there is a stipulation against it, thus acting on an expressed lack of consent to prevent the conclusion in law of a polygynous marriage; in effect this would oblige the husband to choose between remaining in his current marriage and concluding a new one, rather than obliging the wife to choose between leaving her current marriage or remaining in it with a co-wife.[33]

Divorce options and validity issues

Mostly, however, legislators have hesitated to condition the action of a man upon the decision of his wife, preferring to focus on the wife's options to leave her marriage in such circumstances. As noted above, most allow the insertion of stipulations to this effect in the marriage contract, and some specifically address a woman's lack of consent as grounds for divorce. The 1979 Egyptian law made a polygynous marriage without the existing wife's consent in and of itself grounds for her to seek divorce on the grounds of injury, *idrar*, and regardless of whether or not she had stipulated against polygyny in her own marriage contract.[34] The Explanatory Memorandum to the law adduced evidence for the legal presumption of injury from the social situation of modern-day Egypt.[35] This approach was attacked *inter alia* on the grounds that this was to say that something permitted by the *shari'a* was inherently injurious; on the ground, Chemais notes a 'high number of women' in polygynous marriages applying for divorce.[36] Vigorous public and parliamentary debates centred on this particular provision,[37] which was amended in the replacement legislation of 1985 with a formulation that allows the wife to sue for divorce if she can establish that she has been caused injury and allows for a relative assessment by the court: the mere fact of a polygynous marriage may be viewed as an injury in one class, for example, and not in another.[38] This brings it closer to the more general provision of divorce for injury or ongoing marital discord found in many of the codifications, where the attitude of the judge, rather than that of the affected woman, is critical in establishing whether and to what extent injury has been caused, and/or to whom the discord is to be attributed.

The original Moroccan law also invoked the concept of injury in addressing the remedies for women who had not inserted a stipulation in their marriage contracts. In the 2003 law, however, the focus is implicitly on the lack of consent; if the wife insists on a divorce during the hearing of the husband's petition for permission to conclude a polygynous marriage, the court is to rule for divorce upon the husband's deposit of a sum covering all her outstanding financial entitlements, with failure by the husband to make such deposit within a tight deadline (according to the law no more than seven days) is considered by the law a withdrawal of his petition for permission.[39]

Elsewhere, specific provision for divorce options in these circumstances is retained in the 2005 Algerian amendments in the event that the husband violates any of the rules regarding polygynous marriages or deceives either wife in this matter; in addition, the new law provides for a polygynous marriage conducted without the consent of the court to be dissolved before consummation, suggesting a finding of invalidity that is to be acted upon by the public authorities rather than depending, as in the case of a consummated marriage, on the decision of the wife to seek divorce.[40] Also succinct was Iraq's provision for divorce if the husband married a co-wife without the consent of the court.[41] This latter is related also to the question of validity: if a marriage concluded in violation of the statutory law is considered invalid, it will be dissolved by court, while if it is considered valid despite attracting criminal penalties, the wife will need to seek divorce. Syria, for example, noted in the Explanatory Memorandum to its 1953 law that although a polygynous marriage would be prohibited unless the legal conditions were met, it would still be regarded as valid in order *inter alia* to protect the rights of children from the marriage – although other states have held these rights protected even if the marriage itself is held invalid.[42] In the original text of the Iraqi law, a polygynous marriage concluded without the consent of the court was clearly invalid, which Anderson reported to have provoked considerable opposition, including from members of the *shar'i* judiciary; and it was this clause, together with the controversial provisions on succession, that was revoked when the new regime came to power in 1963.[43] The following year the Tunisian government took the opposite course. The original code of 1956, while prohibiting and imposing criminal penalties for polygyny, was silent on the issue of the validity of a polygynous marriage if it nevertheless occurred, and at the time Anderson again reported judges and jurists to be divided in their reaction to this, some arguing that the failure to stipulate invalidity implied validity, which would also be less of a direct challenge to the classical position; others held the opposite, to the effect that having prohibited a contract on the basis of public policy, the state could not then proceed to recognise it.[44] This latter argument, referring to civil law, is echoed today as noted earlier by those arguing against the invalidity of the marriage of a Muslim woman to a non-Muslim man. By 1960, Anderson was reporting that the Tunisian courts 'have now decided that a marriage in contravention of this prohibition is itself valid'; here, the government chose to follow up and in 1964 amended the law to include in the list of irregular marriages those concluded against the ban on polygyny.[45] More recently, Libya clarified that a polygynous marriage in violation of the law would be declared invalid,[46] while the 2004 Moroccan law did not pronounce on this issue explicitly, although keeping, as in the previous law, the constraints on polygyny at the end of the section dealing with temporary impediments to marriage. The Algerian amendments take a halfway position, providing for the dissolution of an unconsummated polygynous marriage concluded without the court's permission.

Iraq also took an opposite course to another legislator, this time the PDRY, on another polygyny-related issue. After legislating tight controls on polygyny in 1974, the government of the PDRY issued a further regulation constraining divorced men from remarrying during the *'idda* period of the wife divorced by revocable *talaq*. The preamble noted that during this time, the first marriage was still legally extant and the couple might agree upon revocation of the divorce, while the man's subsequent marriage would have avoided the constraints imposed on polygynous unions; it was a lesser prejudice to the man's rights to disallow his marriage during this period than would be caused to those of the woman.[47] Iraq's 1959 law had also not addressed this issue, but in 1982 a Revolutionary Command Council decision provided (also with retroactive effect) that if a man revoked a divorce while having in the interim concluded another marriage, this would not be considered polygyny under the terms of the family law provisions constraining marriage to more than one wife.[48]

Overview

In the recent decades there are thus differing tendencies among and some-times within different states in regard to the issue of judicial control in the regulation of polygyny as in other areas. In the Gulf, the first-time codes in Kuwait, Oman and the UAE refrained from instituting such control, and the Qatari law is cautious on this subject. Tunisia on the other hand consoli-dated its absolute prohibition of polygyny by specifically invalidating such marriages, while Iraq retreated to some extent from the particular controls it instituted in its 1959 code, first in the legislation issued when the previous regime was overthrown in 1963 and subsequently during the course of the 1980s, against the background of the war with Iran and increasing legit-imising reference to more classical Islamic norms by Saddam Hussein. Other countries have tended to move more steadily towards increased judicial con-trol, such as Morocco, Syria and Libya; Jordan's temporary legislation of 2001 instituted such control for the first time, but the law was rejected by the Lower House. Another sign of continuing resistance in some sectors to the introduction of judicial control in this area is reported from Libya, where in 1998, as noted in Chapter 2, the General People's Congress removed the re-quirement of the first wife's consent to her husband's polygynous marriage, although Muammar Qaddafi subsequently reversed this move by the Con-gress.[49] In Egypt, the debate on polygyny continues, with advocates of re-strictions still citing the views of the nineteenth-century jurist Muhammad 'Abduh but with successive legislative proposals – besides the provisions on divorce rights discussed above – shelved since the beginning of the twenti-eth century. In 2004, the debate revived when al-Azhar reportedly refused to approve a draft text prepared by Egypt's National Council for Women pro-viding for the imposition of fines and other 'harsh sanctions' on men mar-rying polygynously, without suggesting that the marriage would be invalid.[50]

Women's rights activists continue to seek either the absolute prohibition of polygyny, on the Tunisian model, or its significant constraint through ju-dicial control through the means instituted in some states as discussed above. In comments on the draft Moroccan law in 2003, one women's coali-tion proposed that the text be revised to constitute an absolute prohibition, while another suggested that the consent of the first wife be made a condi-tion.[51] In Palestine, a discussion among women on the reform of polygyny, at the inception of Palestinian Authority rule showed a difference between those participants who aspired to an absolute prohibition on polygyny, as in Tunisia, and others who sought reform and restriction of the institution.[52] In Algeria, a coalition of women's groups seeking reform of the 1984 family law argued for prohibition. Rights-based activist strategies towards polygyny may depend upon an assessment of feasible advocacy goals in the particular country, both in general and at different points in the legislative process. Furthermore, a commitment to the equality norm and to international human rights principles, and indeed on separation of religion and state, may prompt a position on abolition for some, while others argue for an incremental restrictive approach encouraging the social and economic decline of the institution. The summary of the discussion of the subject in Women Living Under Muslim Laws indicates some of the complexities in the debate, concluding that 'even while it may be strategically option-giving for women in particular circumstances, overall polygyny reflects gender inequalities in society and therefore ultimately cannot be considered option-giving'.[53]

8 The Marital Relationship

In the textual formulation of gender-specific rights and duties in the spousal relationship, the financial obligations of the husband (and the man in general) are set against his authority and control within the family. Besides the husband's obligation to pay dower to his wife, standard elements included in most of the codes are the husband's duty to provide maintenance and a 'lawful dwelling', the wife's duty to cohabit with her husband in such a dwelling and to move with him should he relocate or travel, provided the court finds no good reason for her to refuse; the wife's right to her separate property and to equitable treatment with co-wives; the husband's obligation to treat his wife well, or differently formulated to refrain from causing her physical or emotional injury; and the wife's duty of obedience in 'lawful matters'. It is worth noting that contemporary scholars point out that the detailed 'listing' of such rights and duties are very much a construction of the codes, and constitute a take on 'the family' informed by the modern patriarchal state (and in some cases its historical encounter with Western colonial powers) rather than a re-articulation of classical approaches.[1]

As discussed further below, the husband's financial obligations remain extremely significant, even when the enormous impact of socio-economic change undermines the functioning of the gendered roles as scripted in the laws.[2] When women choose or are obliged to enter the waged labour market, and to contribute financially to the household, the unaltered premises of the law in most countries mean that this contribution is not recognised as altering other elements of the equation. Nor, particularly in the absence of a joint conjugal property regime, is there recognition of women's unwaged labour in the family as contributing to the development of the material wealth of the conjugal unit after marriage. The provisions in the codes for compensation to be paid to a wife in the event of an injurious or arbitrary divorce by the husband are not phrased or applied in such a way as to redress this balance. While the separate property regime legally protects a woman's right to her own property, most laws still contemplate a husband having the right, depending on circumstance, to prohibit his wife from going out to work. Where women 'with means' are legally assigned certain financial responsibilities towards their husband or, more commonly, towards their children and parents, there is no impact on the rules of succession assigning a female half the portion of a male in most degrees of relationship to the deceased, customarily justified on the grounds that the woman 'is entitled to receive [her portion] without being required to undertake any obligations, unlike the man...'[3] The tenacity of the legal script of the marital relationship on these points and 'the reality of different women's lives' mean that activists do not necessarily call for the removal in law of the husband's responsibility for maintaining his wife and family.[4] Many argue that the law should not reduce the rights of women to maintenance and dower until it evens up inheritance, property during marriage, and the constraints on women going out to work. Abu-Odeh has suggested that the goal of women's substantive (as compared to formal) equality might require a position in statutory law where 'men maintain and women do not obey'.[5]

Dower

The institution of *mahr* (dower) is another area where positions differ. The dower remains in all the codes a central feature of the marriage contract; it is either an effect of the contract or a condition for its validity, meaning that if the bride purports to waive it in her contract, she will either be due an independently assessed 'proper dower', in the first case, or in the second risks having the marriage held invalid. Legislation on the dower focuses on when and what dower is due, including allowing the dower to be divided into that part payable at the conclusion of marriage ('prompt dower') and that part payment which is postponed until the termination of the marriage by death or divorce ('deferred dower'). The legislation also tends to focus on upholding the basic *fiqh* rule that the dower is the woman's sole property and may not be taken over by her husband, nor by her father or other relatives. The 1975 Syrian amendments showed that such matters were still the concern of legislators informed by the experience of the judiciary. A substantial proportion of the amendments addressed the dower, including the prioritisation of dower debts, the problem of the wife being coerced into reducing or waiving the dower, the practice of some families not transferring the dower payment to the bride, and social attitudes that prevented women seeking payment of their prompt dower after their marriage.[6] Some concern is shown at decreases in the value of dower, which particularly in situations of political and economic crises can render the deferred dower of little effect in providing some protection to a divorced or widowed woman. A 1999 decree in Iraq provides that in the event of divorce, the deferred dower stands at its gold value at the date of the marriage contract.[7]

Besides these concerns, attention among legislators and other officials, including the religious establishment, has frequently focussed on what is perceived at different times as unacceptable inflation in dowers and in associated costs including the wedding and furnishing the marital home. Concerns have been voiced over the dower and other costs being so high that young men are unable to get married, leaving young women marrying older husbands and the youth of society in general more vulnerable to the temptations of extra-marital sexual activity. In poorer countries there may be concern that nationals are unable to match the dowers that can be paid by richer suitors from overseas; and, as evidenced in the report from Yemen cited earlier, there is a concern that penurious fathers or other male guardians may marry off young female wards against their interests for a substantial dower from a considerably older and richer man. Alongside these social and national concerns are set the religious and symbolic intentions of the dower and the exhortations particularly on the bride's family to reduce their financial demands on the groom in the best Islamic tradition. Thus, the 2005 UAE codification invokes existing legislation setting a maximum limit on the dower, with the Explanatory Memorandum referring to 'social problems and corruption caused by inflated dowers that prevent the youth from getting married' as well as to the *shar'i* arguments.[8] Elsewhere also occasional legislative attempts have been made to set upper limits on the dower, in some cases by precluding the courts from hearing claims in excess of the set amount and in some providing for the confiscation and redistribution to charitable causes or national development projects of the amounts paid in excess.[9] Enforcement proved difficult against established custom even where the issue of dower and associated marriage costs continues to be perceived by the authorities as a social challenge, for example in Yemen.[10] In Tunisia the 1993 amendments removed a requirement that the dower be 'not trifling' in a move that Sharif reflects 'abrogated the focus on the financial value of the dower which might invoke the idea of 'women's inferiority' which used to prevail'.[11] Morocco's 2003 law insists that 'the *shar'i* basis of the dower is its emotional and symbolic value, not its material value' and that 'what is lawfully (*shar'an*) required is keeping the dower low'.[12]

Activists have joined their voices to demands for dower to be reduced particularly in critical periods of national history. Badran notes Egyptian feminists campaigning to lower the dower in the 1930s against the background of economic crisis.[13] In Algeria, Lazreg records attempts by the nationalist FLN to limit the maximum level of dower during the war of liberation against the French; nevertheless, despite feminists holding it as 'an antiquated custom that objectifies women', she notes its persistence as a major feature of marriage.[14] In Palestine during the first uprising, the deteriorating economic situation and the exigencies of the national struggle added to religious exhortations to reduce dower levels, and women's groups were reported to be seeking to 'decrease or eliminate' the dower as a 'burdensome custom'.[15]

Thus, beyond the social challenges variously posed by dower, some object to the dower in principle, as a transactional exchange that cannot but represent, even symbolically, the 'monetary value of the wife',[16] her 'inferior position' in the contract, as evoked by Sharif, or consideration for the husband's right of sexual access. Across the region and elsewhere, there continues to be disagreement as to whether the institution of dower 'should be viewed as a useful financial resource for married women or should be viewed as the equivalent of selling a wife's sexual services and a purchasing of her "obedience"'; there is no disagreement that religious principle stands against excessive dowers.[17] Within the existing framework of marital relations in different countries, studies have shown how women from different classes use the institution of dower – including associated requirements such as furnishing the marital home, with the furnishings being registered in the name of the bride – within informal strategies for the protection of their rights, including protection against divorce by their husband, or in support of their own demand for divorce.[18] Moors has noted that setting upper limits on dower might have a positive impact on the marriage choices of elite and employed women but a negative impact on the situation of women with no other sources of economic security.[19] In Palestine, looking at the increasing registration of a 'token' prompt dower and accompanying patterns of gift-giving, she concludes that in real terms women may have a decreasing access to and control over property through dower than previously, rendering women more economically dependent upon their husbands in a societal structure increasingly emphasising the conjugal tie over kinship relations.[20] In general, the variable patterns and changing social significances of dower observed by different scholars make little impact on the legislative texts governing this institution; on the other hand, these patterns and informal strategies may either underwrite or constrain the overall script of marital relations of which those texts form a part.

Maintenance and obedience

Beyond the dower, the husband's primary financial obligation towards his wife is that of maintenance. This obligation effectively lapses only when the wife is formally held to be 'disobedient', and it is this construction of relations that Moors refers to as the 'gender contract'.[21] In some codes the spouses' respective rights and duties are set out in the form of 'lists'. By way of exception, under the socialist visions in South Yemen (1974) and Somalia (1975), the spouses had equal financial responsibilities, according to his or her means, although the Somali law still specified that the wife was to submit to her husband's authority unless there was a legal reason not to.[22] Apart from these, the codes under consideration here maintain the husband's primary duty of maintenance, even where the wife is required, in certain circumstances, to share or assume financial responsibility for the family. The volume of maintenance claims submitted by women to the courts, for themselves and/or their children, testifies to the continuing significance of this obligation, both as part of women's protective strategies and as an economic reality in family life, constituting a primary reason for women's recourse to the courts.[23] The effective implementation of maintenance rulings for wives and children where husbands are able but unwilling to meet their obligations in this regard is a major preoccupation for poor women, although their voices were not the first to be heard in the efforts to reform family law in the region. Demands for state intervention may propose the state advancing payments to the claimants and then seeking to recover them from the man (for example through deductions from his salary if he is a public employee). Iraq's Revolutionary Command Council established a 'temporary maintenance fund' of this type from the general budget in 1980. Egypt's 2000 legislation instituted a system based on payments from the Nasser Social Bank, but serious problems arose in the early years of its implementation, and it was not until late 2004

that further legislation provided the resources needed to advance maintenance payments. In Palestine, a law establishing a 'maintenance fund' that
had been the target of advocacy efforts by women's groups was approved before the legislature turned its attention to the substantive text of family law.[24]

The textual construction of the 'gender contract' around the duties of
maintenance and obedience remains the rule; in the codes under consideration here, only those now in force in Tunisia, Libya, Algeria and Morocco
make no mention of the wife's duty of obedience to her husband – in the
last two cases as a result of the legislation of 2005 and 2004, respectively. The
original text of the Tunisian law required the wife to obey her husband and
to 'heed him as head of the family' and to undertake her marital duties 'in
accordance with custom and usage', while recognising that 'the wife partic-
ipates in maintaining the family if she has means'. This was amended in 1993
to make most of the previously spouse-specific duties mutual under what
Sharif terms the 'new concept of cooperation';[25] thus, both spouses are to
treat each other well, both are to undertake their marital duties in accordance with custom and usage, and they are to cooperate in looking after the
children; the husband is to 'maintain the wife and children in his capacity
as head of the family' while the wife 'shall participate' in maintenance if she
has means, the language indicating an obligation.[26] Women's rights activists
welcomed the removal of the reference to ta'a (obedience) but were more
critical of the remaining reference to custom and usage, considering it to
evoke outdated social patterns and practice. There is also criticism of the
identification of the husband as 'head of the family' which, as Dargouth-Medimegh had previously observed, may be 'faithful to Muslim tradition' but was
also 'common to all Western legislation before the sixties'.[27] Chekir finds
this reference to qualify the wife's 'cooperation' in managing family affairs
as in the nature of helping her husband, rather than a 'recognition of real
power sharing'.[28] She finds the wife's participation in maintenance to have
passed from a possibility to a duty in the new text, but one that can be called
upon when there is need, rather than paralleling or replacing the husband's
obligations in this regard; she holds that 'this corresponds with the women's
evolving status in the family'.[29] Jurisprudence under the previous law had
similarly held that the husband was under an obligation to maintain his wife
even if she was a salaried worker, nor did the fact that the wife contributed
to the household expenses mean that he was exempt; only his poverty ex-
cused him in this regard.[30]

The Tunisian courts, in applying the original provision, had taken the same position as statutory text in Libya. Libya's 1984 law requires a wife with means to maintain her husband and their children at times when her husband is needy. It makes no mention of obedience in its listing of the wife's and husband's rights, and declares the retrospective abrogation of all rulings of *ta'a* ('as if they did not happen'). On the other hand, it is considerably more explicit regarding other expectations, not leaving these to 'custom and usage' as in Tunisia. Thus, the wife's 'management and organisation of the affairs of the marital home' is specified as a right of the husband, as is her 'concern for his repose and his emotional and mental stability'.[31] There is no textual suggestion of reciprocity in the event that the wife is obliged to maintain the family. The Libyan law also disallows a woman with means from seeking divorce from an impoverished husband on grounds of his failure to maintain her, requiring her instead to maintain him and their children.[32]

The changes in the 'script' of spousal relations introduced by such provisions thus entail potential legal claims on a wife's capital or income that in the older script was protected as her independent property.[33] Nevertheless, both the Tunisian and the Libyan laws maintain the principle of the wife's sole entitlement to her personal property, over which the husband has no right of disposal,[34] and thus preserve the traditional separate property regime with regard to goods and wealth acquired before and during the marriage. Under the traditional law, the standard rules on the division of household goods on divorce was that, in the event of dispute and the absence of proof, 'those things usually used by men' will be assigned to the husband and those by women to the wife. Otherwise, property such as the marital home, real estate and business ventures, which are more likely to be registered in the husband's name than the wife's, are likely to be treated as his legal property, and the separate property regime excludes claims by the wife. In Tunisia in the late 1990s, the government turned its attention to this; Sherif recalls the authorities in 1996 'taking measures to sensitise spouses when concluding their marriage contracts to the possibility of agreeing to follow a joint regime in regard to property acquired after marriage' in an attempt to 'ease the negative effects' of the separate property regime otherwise applying to such property.[35] In 1998, a law was promulgated providing the option for spouses to adopt a joint property regime for such goods.[36] The 2004 Moroccan law sets out the principle of separate spousal property, while also allowing the couple to agree on other terms for the management and investment of property acquired during the marriage in a document separate from the marriage contract; the Algerian amendments of 2005 followed suit. The Moroccan provision goes further, however, requiring the notaries to inform the spouses of this option at the time of their marriage, and providing that in the event that no such agreement is made, the new law requires the judge to apply 'general rules of evidence with regard to the work of each spouse, the efforts they have put in and the burdens they have carried in order to develop the property of the family'.[37] This provision could be understood as providing space for the courts to recognise the contribution to family wealth made by women's waged and unwaged labour, a development that, depending upon implementation, could address some of the criticisms made of this aspect of the previous text as compared to the socio-economic reality of women's labour.[38] The guide to the new law issued by the Ministry of Justice firmly distinguishes between the new provision and a joint property regime, and notes that if no agreement is made, each spouse will be able to make claims as to his/her contribution to property acquired after marriage 'in light of what the claimant has done and his/her efforts and burdens that have contributed to the development of this property and the expansion of its investment; the meaning here is not an equal division...' Disappointingly, the guide gives no direction to the courts in terms of what might be taken into consideration in terms of 'work, effort and burden'; this 'is naturally left to the court which has to assess the extent of the effort, its nature and impact on what property has been acquired during the marriage'.[39] How the new network of family law chambers apply this new provision will determine whether the space provided by the legislature is used by the judiciary to provide more equitable settlements to women through an expanded recognition of their contribution to the material wealth of the family. In the meantime, however, as already noted, commentators report that notaries are not consistently fulfilling their duties to inform intending couples of the possibility of drawing up a separate document to manage property acquired during the marriage.[40]

A further common approach in the new laws of both Algeria and Morocco is the replacing of the pre-existing 'lists' of gender-specific rights and duties pertaining to wife and husband with a single provision on 'mutual rights and duties of the spouses' which include jointly managing the affairs of house and children and, in uncommon reference, sharing decisions on family planning (Morocco) and the 'spacing of births' (Algeria).[41] At the same time, the laws leave the wife's maintenance an obligation on the husband.

Rather than employing the term 'disobedience', the Moroccan law allows for the lapse of the wife's right to maintenance where she refuses to comply with a court ruling requiring her to return to the marital home.[42] These circumstances are the same as those in which the previous law allowed for a wife's right to maintenance to lapse; the difference in the new text is the absence of the term 'disobedience', the different construction of spousal rights and duties (as mutual and shared, apart from that of maintenance) and the textual elucidation of conduct by the husband constituting 'injury' of the wife already mentioned above, all of which are clearly expected by the legislators to have an impact on the circumstances in which a court would rule for the wife to return home.

In the codes that still invoke the wife's duty to obey her husband 'in lawful matters', while this duty is not usually expanded, more specific attention is given to describing a situation of 'disobedience' (*nushuz*) which would entail the lapse of the wife's right to maintenance. This aspect is first and foremost concerned with the wife's physical presence in the marital home, and the specific circumstances in which she may leave it without the consent of her husband. These rules often include rules from *fiqh* regarding the wife's right to visit her parents and other close relatives, or to attend to her own business affairs, or for emergencies or in matters recognised 'by custom or the law'. They also usually deal with the wife leaving the marital home in order to go out to work. Here the formulations tend to combine all or some of the following elements: the nature of the work (that it be 'lawful' or 'permitted'); the husband's consent, or a definite prohibition articulated by his prior request that she stop going out to work; the motivation for his prohibiting her work (that is, whether he is being arbitrary or malicious); and whether her going out to work affects the 'interests of the family'.[43] In some cases developments in these rules were preceded by court rulings recognising the increasing need and legitimacy of women going out to work, such as in Egypt, while in others such as Jordan a fairly 'closed' text has been interpreted by the courts with attention to the above elements in light of changing socio-economic circumstances.[44] Iraq amended its law in 1980 to release the wife from the duty of obedience *inter alia* if the marital home prepared by the husband 'is far from the wife's place of work such as to make it impossible to reconcile her domestic and employment commitments'.[45]

The codes thus give legal regard to 'disobedience' in situations where the wife refuses to go to or has departed the marital home 'without *shar'i* reason' or refuses without good reason to travel with her husband, and has refused to respond to a court ruling for her return on the basis of a claim for *ta'a* submitted by the husband.[46] The court may decline to make such a ruling in various circumstances specified in the law, such as – variously – if any part of the prompt dower remains unpaid or under the control of the husband, if he has taken over his wife's property or injured her person and therefore cannot be trusted with her, or if the marital home does not fulfil the various requirements of a '*shar'i* dwelling'. If the husband succeeds in obtaining a court ruling for his wife to return or come to the marital home, the immediate legal effect is to cut a previous maintenance order or to establish the husband's defence to a future claim if the circumstances persist; it may also however impact the wife's rights, notably for compensation, should the husband subsequently divorce her. In Iraq, as discussed further below, a wife is entitled to a divorce two years after a ruling of *nushuz* is made against her. Beyond this, the texts on 'disobedience' have tended to be softened in the later years of the twentieth century through an explicit or implicit abrogation of coercive implementation of a *ta'a* ruling – that is, meaning that a wife cannot be forced back to the marital home against her will, for example by the intervention of the police, in processes which had drawn protests since the early twentieth century.[47] Proposals in Yemen in 2001 to re-introduce forcible implementation of *ta'a* rulings were dropped by the government after non-governmental organisations mounted an intensive campaign that Wurth describes as setting arguments invoking general principles of *shari'a* and customary practice against the proposed statutory amendment.[48]

The 2005 UAE law stands in contrast to the recent legislation in Algeria and Morocco through introducing lists of rights and duties: one relating to those shared by the spouses (including lawful sexual relations, cohabitation, mutual respect and bringing up children from the marriage), one to the rights of the wife and one to the rights of the husband. The Qatari law follows suit. The wife's rights include maintenance, and the husband's include his wife's obedience and her stewardship of the marital home and its contents. The Explanatory Memorandum to the UAE law adduces a detailed jurisprudential justification of this provision focussing on the *qiwama* (in this context, authority) of the man in the family, arguing that the man is 'more able to allow reason to rule and to control his emotions' and observing that 'all laws – civil or religious – put men a degree over women'.[49] This traditionalist perspective nevertheless shows some interesting attention to contemporary concerns. Firstly, the rights of the wife include that she will not be prevented from continuing her education. Secondly, as is the case in various other codes, the law specifically rules out the forcible implementation of rulings for obedience, on the grounds that such action would violate the woman's dignity, and that coercion cannot be a basis for marital life.[50] Thirdly, when regulating the wife's right to go out to work without being held 'disobedient', the law instructs the marriage notary to 'inquire about' the insertion of a stipulation into the marriage contract on this matter – although it does subject even the implementation of such a stipulation to the 'interest of the family'.

Special stipulations in the marriage contract

This instruction to the marriage registrar can be seen as an attempt both to raise awareness of the lawfulness and potential utility of such a stipulation, and to procedurally facilitate its uptake, the initiative being taken by the official. The widely codified option of inserting special stipulations in the contract of marriage which seek to vary its contractual effects has been presented as another way of rescripting the spousal relationship. Such provisions allow stipulations that address areas of permission rather than requirement: that is, a stipulation that no dower would be payable would not be regarded, since dower is a requirement of the contract, but a wife may stipulate that her husband will not marry polygynously, since he is not required to have more than one wife. The official justifications for such provisions, starting with the OLFR 1917, are based on Hanbali *fiqh*, which gave value to such stipulations in the sense that violation of their contents constitutes grounds for a judicial divorce. In Saudi Arabia, where Hanbali *fiqh* is the official regulatory framework, Wynn has noted the use of stipulations among the urban middle class.

Elsewhere, the dominant *fiqh* did not give legal value to such stipulations, in the sense that while the husband was free for example not to marry polygynously having undertaken not to, his existing wife could not seek dissolution on the grounds of breach of stipulation should he renege on his agreement. Abu-Odeh considers Hanafi *fiqh* in this regard to be particularly close to a narrative of status rather than contract,[51] with the effects of the contract flowing from the established and spouse-specific framework of rights and duties, rather than open to enforceable agreement between the parties. Hanafi *fiqh* did allow the conditional delegation of *talaq*, which would allow the wife to exit her marriage on the occurrence of certain events. Although in the Hanbali-based rules 'enforcement' still depends ultimately on the wife's ability to seek divorce, the emphasis is more on the mutual agreement of the spouses at the time of the marriage to certain parameters of their relationship which thus attach to the marriage contract. The non-Hanbali countries that have issued codifications of family law have included provisions of varying length and detail on stipulations, with those of Yemen in 1992 and Algeria in 1984 being the most textually restrictive. Dennerlein observes that the restriction of stipulations in the Algerian code means that 'the contractual character of marriage loses importance'; Algeria's 2005 amendments add to the pre-existing text two examples of 'clauses that the spouses might consider beneficial, notably concerning polygyny and the wife's work'. Somewhat similarly, examples given in the short Mauritanian text on this subject comprise stipulations against polygyny and against the husband absenting himself for more than a given period, and stipulations protecting the wife's right to complete her studies or go out to work. By contrast, the new Moroccan law gives substantially more attention to stipulations than was previously the case, and the 2005 UAE law also has a very detailed provision on the subject.[52]

Certainly, the approaches taken to the option of stipulations in the last decades of the twentieth century focussed on the idea of negotiation and clarification of such parameters, with the prospect of legal remedy. Scholars have observed that prior to codification, this was already a practice among certain socio-economic classes, at different times and in different places, whether carried out in the marriage contract itself or in other parallel documents agreed to by the spouses.[53] The 'authenticity' of this approach within *fiqh* and historical practice has been stressed by women's rights activists seeking the institutionalisation of such practice beyond the text of the law.[54] Egyptian activists invested years in an effort to have certain stipulations included in the standard marriage contract document, a campaign that after a number of years had the cooperation of the Ministry of Justice. The Egyptian campaign aimed at shifting the burden of initiative in the pre-marital negotiations from the party wishing to insert stipulations altering the terms of the established framework (usually the wife) to the party wishing to retain the more traditional parameters under the existing law (usually the husband), by obliging the latter to take the initiative of refusal (by having the pre-worded conditions struck out, for example) and relieving the former of the often socially awkward burden of proposal.[55] Such campaigns also seek to make more women aware of the possibility of using such stipulations, through 'know-your rights' activities, and to counteract prevailing social attitudes disapproving of such initiatives except in certain circumstances. On the other hand, activists have criticised states for leaving the greater legal protection of important women's rights to the initiative of the individual woman (and her family), rather than themselves shouldering the burden of modifying the substantive law.[56] In Bahrain, one of the proposals made by Ayatollah Shaykh Hussein al-Najati to the women activists seeking a codified law was that they might start work on a 'marriage contract document' in the form of a pamphlet containing nearly fifty special stipulations that spouses could agree to govern their relationship, 'such as is done in some Islamic countries'.[57] Al-Najati might have had both Iran and Egypt in mind in relation to this project. In Egypt, the new marriage contract document includes a list of stipulations as an annex or booklet attached to the contract, rather than in the body of the text; there are anecdotal tales of the husband-to-be removing the attachment before his wife-to-be sees it.

Within the framework of spousal relations, special stipulations may seek to clarify or modify the parameters of the wife's duty of obedience, or to expand the obligations on the husband. Subjects of stipulations that have been documented in different countries and from different times (including pre-codification) include the agreement that the husband will not marry polygynously, that the wife's children from a previous marriage will live with the new couple, and that the marital home will be in a certain town or village. In regard to the latter, a number of codes, when articulating the wife's duty to move to live with her husband in the place where he chooses, add a caveat releasing her from this duty should there be a stipulation to the contrary in the contract. Other more recent focuses include that the wife will be entitled to go out to work and/or to pursue her studies and, increasingly, that the marital home will be independent from that of the husband's family; the choice of stipulations may be differentiated according to class and sector (urban/rural).[58] Activists have also focussed on the use of stipulations for the division of property acquired during marriage, an issue which as noted above is addressed in the 2004 Moroccan law through the option of separate regulations being offered to the parties to the contract.

In general, while the bride's family may argue for the insertion of stipulations in circumstances where they perceive their daughter to be particularly vulnerable, unless 'normalised' within certain socio-economic groups, the insertion of stipulations may be perceived as awkward and potentially disruptive, including by members of the judiciary. The delegation to the wife by the husband of his general power of divorce appears to evoke particular antagonism; Wynn notes that in Saudi Arabia such a stipulation is 'uncommon and is considered somewhat shameful'.[59] Such a stipulation, which in theory gives the wife the same power as the husband in unilaterally ending the marriage, is a recognised principle in *fiqh*, but is perceived as more troubling to the overall narrative of the spousal relationship than when her power of divorce is circumscribed to a particular eventuality and cause, such as the husband taking another wife. The possibility of such general delegation, despite the obstacles to the realisation thereof, was relied on by the Moroccan authorities in presenting *talaq* as 'the dissolution of the bond of marriage exercised by the husband and the wife [...] If *talaq* is in the hand of the man, then it is in the hand of the wife, by *tamlik*'.[60] The difference of course is that while the husband possesses the power of *talaq* from the existing text of the spousal relationship, the wife 'is possessed' (*tamlik*) of the same power only through the action of her husband. Writing in 1993, Mir-Hosseini noted 'a pronounced reluctance to insert conditions in the marriage contract, which would enable women to use the option of divorce', adding that 'some [notaries] told me that they would never agree to contract a marriage with such a stipulation, as it sets a shaky foundation for the union'. [61]

Misyar *marriage*

While various women's rights activists have advocated the inclusion of stipulations as a mechanism through which particular rights can be protected for the wife, or the general power balance addressed, the institution of *misyar* marriage rests on mutually agreed binding conditions that are regarded by such activists as compromising the rights of the wife and more broadly the institution of marriage. Arabi observes that the legitimacy accorded to contracts of 'ambulant (*misyar*) marriage' is based on the principle of consent to these contractual terms, which significantly alter the assumptions traditionally arising from the contract.[62] Specifically, as noted earlier, the wife waives her rights to maintenance, accommodation and cohabitation, and generally accepts a condition requiring lack of 'publicity' to the marriage. The husband 'visits' his wife by day or night, without setting up home with her.

In the UAE, despite reports noted earlier to the effect that the draft law proposed to give statutory recognition to *misyar* marriage, the text of the law as promulgated appears to rule out recognition of such arrangements: stipulations by the husband that he will not pay maintenance are included among the examples provided in the Explanatory Memorandum of stipulations that are void because they conflict with the requirements of the contract.[63] This does not mean that *misyar* marriage as such would be regarded as unlawful in the UAE; it might mean that women undertaking such marriages would not be held to their agreement to waive maintenance, for example, should they take a case to court. Nevertheless, the explicit lack of male commitment under the *misyar* contract might mean a woman contracted in such a marriage would be unlikely to pursue her rights at court, being either personally persuaded of the benefits of the arrangement, or expecting divorce if she sought to challenge the mutually agreed conditions and bind the husband to responsibilities he explicitly sought to avoid.

Women's rights have been vocal in their objection to the institution, in a public debate that was renewed when, in April 2006, the Saudi Arabian *Fiqh* Assembly ruled on the legitimacy of *misyar* marriage along with so-called 'friend marriage', the latter aimed specifically at Muslim men and women studying in the West and enabling them to establish a lawful relationship that, similar to *misyar* marriage, would give rise to no obligations on the husband to cohabit or provide accommodation or maintenance to the wife.[64] Commenting on the lawfulness of *misyar* marriage, one scholar noted that 'the only difference [from a normal marriage] is that the woman abandons voluntarily her right to housing and support money. There is nothing wrong in relinquishing one's own rights'.[65] This emphasis on the consensual nature of the arrangement is echoed by other supporters of *misyar* marriage, along with an insistence on the opportunities it offers to women 'unable to enjoy' a standard form of marriage – divorcées, widows, and 'spinsters' beyond the 'normal' age of marriage (having spent their 'marriageable' years in study or work) are those normally referred to. In his consideration of Saudi Arabian public debates on the institution in the 1990s, 'Arabi shows how the arguments both for and against *misyar* marriage were couched in terms of rights: in the case of supporters, the rights of these groups of women to enjoy the companionship of a husband, perhaps have children and so on. 'Arabi also notes that the dower paid in such marriages is substantially lower than that in a standard marriage, which adds a further financial incentive for men beyond the absence of housing and maintenance costs; a Reuters report on the institution in 2006 was entitled: 'Saudis turn to '*misyar*' marriage to beat inflation.'[66]

In the case of opponents of *misyar* marriage, 'Arabi notes an emphasis on the rights of the existing wife to at least be informed of her husband's polygynous union. Women activists also question the degree to which such arrangements can be regarded as truly 'consensual'. In January 2006, a Saudi newspaper published a set of unhappy testimonies from women who had agreed (knowingly or retrospectively) to *misyar* marriages, alongside interviews with two professional 'matchmakers' or marriage-arrangers (one man, one woman), both of whom confirmed that secrecy remains a prime condition. According to one:

> Men look for *misyar* much more than women, especially older, rich men...The basic requirement for a man looking for a *misyar* marriage is that he doesn't want his wife or family to know anything about this... Most don't want to bear the costs of expenses of a family, they don't want to be constrained by it, and most men also lie and say that their wives are sick and cannot perform their *shar'i* duties...[67]

Women commenting on the Fiqh Assembly's ruling argued that rather than being 'primarily of benefit to women', *misyar* marriage 'relieves men of responsibility for their wives' and 'destroys the fundamentals of a family'.[68] Together with a stress on contemporary views of the role of the husband and father in a stable family, the interventions indicate disapproval of what some clearly perceive as the 'strings-free' licensing of sexual indulgence by men, and continuing concern at what some present as the 'betrayal' of the existing wife inherent in the secrecy underpinning *misyar* marriage. Thus, one denounces the 'exploitation of women of advanced years or who happen to be divorced or widowed' and asks her audience: 'Tell me, what need is there for *misyar* marriage when we have polygyny in Islam?'[69] Another declares that 'the aim of this marriage is first and foremost sexual, at least for the man' and that '*misyar* is a marriage [...] of cowardly men who are scared of their wives so they secretly undertake a *misyar* marriage!'[70] A third addresses interventions she had received to the effect that *misyar* marriage was primarily of benefit to women, specifically 'those women who do not have the opportunity for lawful [sexual] pleasure', contrasting these assertions with text messages being sent to mobile phones 'announcing the availability of young women willing to undertake *misyar* marriage with the slogan "we guarantee you complete secrecy!"'[71]

Besides the text messages, the determinedly 'modern' nature of such arrangements are illustrated by reports of 'special *misyar* websites' where postings facilitate the meeting and matching of would-be partners.[72] The *misyar* marriage appears to represent a rescripting of the conjugal relationship in which men drop most of their responsibilities and women most of their rights. This leaves a reduced dower, lawful sexual relations and companionship without cohabitation, and the legitimacy of any children from the union, should the husband 'allow' them (in practice rather than in the contract) in the *misyar* marriage. While some women no doubt happily engage in such arrangements, this does not indicate an equal relationship either between the particular couples or more broadly in terms of the availability of *misyar* marriage. The public debates described above acknowledge the prevailing power balance between the sexes that structures the general prospects for remarriage of divorcées and widows, and for marriage of women beyond a certain age.[73] The consensual nature of the stipulations that characterize *misyar* marriage does not in fact mean that such marriages are equally 'chosen' by men and women.

Overview

The texts of Arab laws in this area reflect the assumption that here, as elsewhere in the world, it is mostly men who will have access to capital and cash income, and rights and responsibilities are accordingly divided on a gendered basis. Most of the codes do not contemplate a change in the scheme of statutory rights and duties should this assumption be challenged in practice, and the question of how statutory law does or does not conform to the social practice of marriage is one that is increasingly attracting the interest of researchers as well as of activists. The codes do not legislate for the routine accounting of a wife's contribution to the family wealth through her waged or unwaged labour, although this may be taken into account in their assessment of the amount of financial compensation – usually subject to a maximum limit – she may be due after an arbitrary divorce as discussed in the next Chapter. The 2004 Moroccan law appears to provide space for such accounting, including of the burdens of women's unwaged labour in the family, but it is the courts that will determine to what extent this becomes court practice. Women have been assigned increasing financial responsibilities in some laws, but this does not challenge the continuing presumption that the husband/father is the 'head of the family' and exercises authority over his wife and children; although rulings for 'obedience' made against the wife can no longer be forcibly implemented by the police or other executive authorities, they remain part of family law in most states, the exceptions being in North Africa, where more egalitarian laws and amendments have characterized the third phase of reform. At the same time, women's rights advocacy often recognizes that many women remain critically dependent on male income, and may focus immediate efforts on securing more effective mechanisms of support in this regard, through interim maintenance orders and/or the establishment of state-funded sources to cover awards. To a certain extent, advocacy around protective stipulations in marriage contracts, whether by individual initiative or by means of state facilitation and endorsement, along with recent developments in Morocco, Algeria and Tunisia in regard to the management of property acquired during marriage, and also the elaboration of *misyar* marriage in certain states, can all be traced to an emphasis on the advantages of a (limited) 'freedom of contract' approach to the Muslim marriage contract.

9 Divorce

Most of the codifications maintain a variety of divorce procedures based on traditional *fiqh*, consisting of divorce by *talaq*, the unilateral divorce or, as often translated in English, 'repudiation' of the wife by the husband; by *khul'*,[1] a divorce by mutual consent, where a *talaq* is pronounced by the husband as part of a mutually agreed arrangement which may involve a renunciation of the wife's remaining rights and possibly a further financial consideration in exchange for the divorce;[2] by judicial divorce (usually termed *tatliq* or *tafriq*) which may be sought on a number of specific grounds primarily but not only by the wife; and by judicial dissolution (*faskh*) which terminates a marriage that is or has become invalid.[3]

From the earliest statutory interventions in Muslim family law in the region, legislatures have addressed themselves to divorce law in a general pattern of constraining a husband's facility of *talaq* and widening the grounds on which a wife can seek judicial divorce and her rights on divorce. So far, Tunisian law is alone among those under consideration here in providing for statutorily equal access to divorce for men and women. In addition, while the divorce procedures of judicial divorce and dissolution occur in court and after litigation, under the traditional rules the procedures of *talaq* and *khul'* are non-litigious and may occur extra-judicially without the intervention of the court. In seeking to make divorce a judicial procedure, legislatures face similar challenges in regard to the validity of out-of-court divorce as they do in regard to unregistered marriage.

Statutory approaches to unilateral talaq *and judicial divorce*

The earliest statutory initiatives on family law in the region, under the Ottomans and in Egypt, addressed themselves to reforming divorce law in two main approaches which have been adopted and in some cases developed in subsequent codifications. The first approach aimed at constraining the impact of the man's pronouncement of unilateral *talaq* in certain physical and psychological circumstances, which mostly go to undermining the presumption of intention on the part of the husband. In such circumstances, the statutory laws provide that either no divorce takes effect, or a single revocable divorce[4] is effected in place of what dominant Sunni *fiqh* (with some differences among the schools) would have ruled a three-fold and irrevocable *talaq*.[5] The formal target of such legislation is not the husband's power of *talaq* itself, but the arbitrary and unreflective use of this power by men who may themselves not intend their action or realise the legal consequences of their use of a particular formula of divorce.

Thus, various laws around the region now provide that no divorce occurs if a man pronounces the *talaq* when intoxicated, under duress, overwhelmed or incoherent with rage; if he uses indirect or metaphorical expressions of *talaq* that were not in fact intended to cause a *talaq* to occur; and if he uses an oath or another form of suspended or conditional *talaq* that was actually intended to have someone do or not do something (rather than being intended to cause a divorce).[6] Further to the last approach, some have simply required that *talaq* be immediately effective, thus disallowing a suspended or conditional *talaq*. In addition, there has been a general take-up of the position that a *talaq* accompanied in word or sign by a number or by any other expression of finality gives rise only to a single revocable *talaq*, rather than causing the immediate and irrevocable 'triple *talaq*' of traditional Sunni (but not Shi'i) law. The latter statutory provisions are officially explained as necessary to constrain the irresponsible, arbitrary and injurious use of *talaq* by the husband, which is 'classically' described by various Western scholars as 'the unfettered power to repudiate his wife at will'.[7] These justifications have resonance with the protestations by rights activists in India at the failure of the All India Muslim Personal Law Board to address and restrict the 'triple *talaq*' in its 2005 text, invoking the debilitating insecurity suffered by women in their marriages as a result of the lack of such restriction. In a similar vein, Munira Fakhro attributes the high rate of divorce in certain Gulf states in the early 1990s to a lack of statutory regulation of the power of *talaq*.[8] On the other hand, as noted earlier in this study, such reforms may also work to constrain the strategic use of classical rules by women seeking a divorce.[9]

Other efforts to constrain the husband's facility of *talaq* – notably by increasing the financial burden on him, and attempting to reduce the occurrence of out-of-court *talaq*, which opens the way for greater judicial scrutiny of and intervention in the processes of *talaq* – began in the second phase of Muslim family law reform in the region, and are discussed further below. Also discussed below is the most recent approach to *talaq*, that of 'balancing' the husband's power of *talaq* with the introduction of 'judicial *khul‘*' at the unilateral demand of the wife, which belongs firmly to the third phase, and has arguably been the most controversial.

The second approach to divorce law established early in the twentieth century, particularly in countries officially dominated by Hanafi *fiqh,* was the expansion of the grounds on which the wife could seek judicial divorce, through adopting rules from other schools. Broadly speaking, this last approach involves the specification of circumstances that are considered to cause harm or injury under the existing description of the husband's obligations.[10] Current codifications thus allow the wife's divorce petition on the specific grounds of the husband's failure to pay maintenance,[11] his disappearance or his unjustified absence or effective (and sexual) desertion of his wife for a specified period, and his being sentenced to a custodial term of more than a specified period. Other grounds, which may also extend to the husband, include the violation of a stipulation in the marriage contract, and having or later developing a chronic mental or physical illness or condition that would (or could) cause harm were the marriage to continue, or preventing consummation or sexual relations. The UAE law is rare in referring explicitly to 'AIDS and similar illnesses' (the Explanatory Memorandum refers also to herpes) requiring that the judge divorce a couple where such a condition is established in one spouse and there is a fear that it will be passed to the other, or to offspring.[12] The wording here implies that the judge is not to attempt to reconcile the couple or otherwise seek continuation of the marriage, but is obliged to rule for the divorce if so petitioned.

A wife's right to seek divorce in the event of her husband marrying polygynously has been discussed above; otherwise, marital infidelity is referred to as grounds for divorce explicitly in the law of Iraq (including 'any act of homosexuality committed by the husband'), in the UAE (applicable to both spouses) and implicitly in Algeria, while practice establishes it elsewhere as a component of 'injury'.[13] Yemeni law allows a wife to petition for divorce if the husband is addicted to alcohol or narcotics, while Iraq amended its law to specify these as well as gambling in the marital home as establishing injury to either spouse.[14] Iraq is also unusual in specifying that a wife has the right to divorce if her husband is or becomes infertile and she has no living child by him.[15] A variation on this has been taken up in the 2005 UAE code, allowing a wife or husband aged under forty and without her or his own children to seek dissolution in the event that the other spouse, in a marriage that has lasted more than five years, has been medically established to be infertile and has already undergone possible treatment for the condition.[16] Other amendments to Iraqi divorce law were promulgated by decisions of the Revolutionary Command Council during the war with Iran, allowing a woman to seek divorce if her husband deserts to the enemy, flees his military service or is convicted of treason.[17]

As noted above, various of these more specific grounds, although not articulated in statutory law elsewhere, may be considered by the courts to establish 'harm' on the grounds of which the wife and often also the husband are entitled to seek divorce. If the wife is unable to establish her husband's harm of her, or if otherwise either spouse establishes ongoing problems ('discord' or more generally incompatibility) in the marriage, the codes provide for an arbitration process involving, where possible, two arbitrators appointed from each of the spouses' families, empowered to attempt to reconcile the spouses and otherwise to assess proportions of blame to be attributed to each spouse, with financial consequences upon the court ruling for divorce. Where the wife is held largely or wholly blameless for the marital discord (or 'incompatibility'), she will keep all or most of her rights to dower and maintenance during the ʿidda period, which she stands to lose if found wholly or largely to blame. In Iraq, 1980 amendments additionally entitled a woman to a judicial divorce two years after a court has made a ruling of nushuz against her, making her forfeit the deferred dower or half of the full dower if she has already received it.[18] In effect, this recognises incompatibility by the wife's refusal to return to the marital home over the set period, without her needing to establish this further, and on forfeiture of a lesser sum than required by the new Egyptian rules on judicial khulʿ disussed below; it does however require prior action by the husband in petitioning for a ruling of nushuz. Sudanese law has a somewhat similar procedure where a wife has been ruled disobedient, although the divorce is guaranteed only where the husband acknowledges his wife's claim; where he denies it, the court will proceed to the appointment of arbitrators, rather than causing the divorce to occur on her unilateral insistence.[19]

Jordanian law on the other hand does not empower the court to rule for a divorce on the wife's establishment of her husband's injury of her, but rather requires evidence of this injury in order for the court to proceed with the appointment of arbiters in a claim for divorce on the grounds of 'discord and strife' (*niza' wa shiqaq*). This position has been criticised in both Jordan and Palestine as clearly disadvantageous to the wife; in the initial stages of the claim, it may be difficult to establish injury occurring in the 'private space' shared by the spouses, while should this be achieved, even if the wife has for example suffered serious physical injury, the text requires the court to attempt reconciliation and should these attempts fail, then to turn the matter over to arbiters who must likewise attempt reconciliation before recommending a divorce with the apportioning of blame.[20] A similar position in the Kuwaiti code was amended in 2004 to allow the court to rule for judicial divorce if injury is established by either spouse, without the need to proceed to the appointment of arbiters.[21]

Criticisms of statutory provisions allowing the court to make relative assessments of 'injury' depending on social group have already been noted; Chemais observes that '[t]he determination of the level of harm "normally" endured by individuals of a particular social group is particularly problematic in a socially mobile society, as Egypt is, where one's current situation and one's aspirations are not necessarily the same'.[22] Even without such statutory provisions, the attitudes of the judiciary towards domestic violence and other forms of abuse, and problems in proving the husband's abuse of his wife, short of hospital reports or assault convictions in the criminal courts, may obstruct a wife's access to divorce on these grounds. Social attitudes to divorce and to domestic violence may further complicate the viable remedies available to a woman wishing to leave her marriage on these grounds.[23] A considerable amount of campaigning work – much of it internationally supported – has been focussed in recent years on the various manifestations of violence against women, and the connection with the practice of divorce law is clear; as Hajjar notes, when women go to court to seek divorce on the grounds of violence, 'saving the marriage often is prioritized over saving or protecting women from violence'.[24] Other criticisms that are raised are procedural, often focussing on the length of time it can take for a claim for judicial divorce to be processed, with the result at the end being uncertain. Women seeking divorce may submit their petition on the grounds most likely to achieve the aim of dissolution, and these may change accordingly to place, time and court practice. In other cases, women seek to persuade their husbands to agree to a divorce, negotiating away some if not all of their remaining rights in exchange for the divorce, without the intervention of the court.

Judicial khulᶜ *in Egypt*

In Egypt, powerful support for a third approach to divorce law reform was provided in the abundance of stories about women – particularly poor women – being forced into giving up their financial rights in exchange for a divorce from their husbands, after investing considerable time and money in the courts petitioning for a judicial divorce, because of the inability (or failure) of the judicial system to bring them prompt and equitable resolution of their application.[25] In 2000, the Egyptian legislature responded to lobbying by women's rights activists by introducing the option of a judicial *khulᶜ*. This option was presented as building on the traditional divorce procedure of *khulᶜ*, which as noted above involves the spouses agreeing upon a divorce settlement effected by the husband pronouncing a single but immediately final *talaq* (that is, not subject to his subsequent revocation) in return for a consideration by the wife. Often presented as wife-initiated divorce, this procedure is still dependent upon the husband's consent, but could occur out of court, often with the intervention and mediation of the respective families or other non-judicial third parties. In Palestine, research in the records of the *shariᶜa* courts from the 1960s to the 1990s showed the most common form of divorce to be a *talaq* by the husband in exchange for a general renunciation (*ibra' ᶜamm*) of her remaining financial rights by the wife.[26] This form of divorce (*mubara'a*) differs from *khulᶜ* in being based on a renunciation of outstanding rights, rather than a return of rights already received by the wife, notably the prompt dower. Nevertheless, where the codes cover the procedure of consensual divorce they tend to render the default 'exchange' in a *khulᶜ* settlement to be the lapse of the wife's outstanding rights, rather than a further payment by her to the husband. In his examination of Egyptian *shariᶜa* court records in the first half of the twentieth century, Shaham similarly found that most such divorce settlements involved a renunciation of outstanding rights, rather than an additional payment by the wife.[27] Needless to say, the court records in this regard establish the legally enforceable results of negotiations between the spouses, rather than the actual settlements, which may include arrangements involving payments either by the wife or by the husband.

Broadly speaking, the two most significant steps taken in the Egyptian legislation on judicial *khulᶜ* were, firstly, to statutorily empower the wife to insist unilaterally on a divorce from the court, without establishing fault on his part and without her husband's consent; and secondly to establish the consideration for this right as the payment of a sum to the husband – that is, the return of any dower she has in fact already received – in addition to her renunciation of outstanding rights. The terms of Law no.1/2000 thus provide that, where a woman's husband refuses to consent to a divorce by mutual agreement, she may ask the court to rule for the divorce instead, incorporating in her petition certain formal statements as to the impossibility of the marriage continuing, and returning the dower that she has received as well as waiving remaining financial rights.[28] The new procedure was expected to reduce the burden of litigation both on the courts and on female petitioners. It was presented, as discussed below, as both addressing the difficulties of access to judicial divorce by women, and as providing 'equal access' to divorce for women, balancing the unilateral power of *talaq* held by the husband.

The provision was hotly debated in public, press and parliament, and the law as a whole was dubbed 'the law of *khul*^c' as a result of the attention to and controversy over this one provision. Those in support of the law emphasised its provenance from within the Islamic tradition, the urgent (and social) need to speed up court procedures to reduce women's suffering. Official discourse made textual arguments in support of the provision, and placed the provision as a whole within the jurisprudential framework of removing injury. Despite the major contribution made by elements of the Egyptian women's movement, Tadrus found domestic official discourse keen to avoid association with those calling for equality of the sexes; the dominant voices speaking in support invoked the concepts of the stability and security of the family, rather than those of women's rights or indeed the violation of their rights. Similarly she found little use made of the discourses of citizenship or constitutional rights.[29]

Those who were opposed to the provision similarly argued from the *fiqh* texts and sources, to the effect that removing the need for the husband's consent to a *khul*^c was a direct violation of the rules of the *shari'a*. It was argued that all the Sunni schools had required the husband's agreement to a *khul*^c divorce; that giving the court the power to over-ride his refusal to agree effectively removed the husband's 'authority' (*qiwama*)[30] over his wife. In an analysis of the treatment of the *khul*^c provision in the press, Tadrus identifies a range of other arguments made by critics, including that this was an attempt to 'make the Egyptian family a carbon copy of the Western family';

that it did not address the real problems in society, which were economic rather than related to personal status law; that women were governed by their emotions and were liable to make rash decisions on divorce; that the law would destroy the Egyptian family, lead to huge increases in the number of divorce cases and 'compound the problem of spinsterhood'. She further notes references to 'external forces imposing the bill', links drawn with the programmes of international conferences such as the International Conference on Population and Development in Cairo and the Beijing Fourth World Conference on Women, and the idea of the law as 'the fruit of the alliance between Western women's movements and the Egyptian women's movement'.[31] Legal challenges to the provision made promptly by opponents of the law were dismissed in a lengthy argument by the Supreme Constitutional Court at the end of 2002. [32]

The idea of 'women divorcing at will' provoked (and/or was used to provoke) substantial opposition to the new law: that women could divorce their husbands without having to prove grounds, indeed with no 'fault' on the part of the husband, and against his will. There are clear points of resonance here with the antipathy noted in different countries of the region to the insertion of a stipulation in the marriage contract empowering the wife with the husband's power of *talaq* over herself. On the broader popular level, Nadia Sonneveld finds the following in an examination of Egyptian cartoons addressing the issue of *khul'*:

> They depicted women with moustaches, women flirting with other men, men in shackles and men pushing prams, all conveying the same message: once women were given the right to unilateral divorce, they would misuse it. As a result, Egyptian family life would fall apart. What is particularly interesting is that many, if not all, cartoons depicted women as westernized Egyptian women who did not wear the veil, but instead wore tight garments and walked on high heels.[33]

Sonneveld's descriptions suggest that such vehicles also seek to depict the end of the husband's *qiwama* over his wife, linking this with the transfer of the very qualities of maleness away from men and to women. As elsewhere, claims of 'equality' are shown as meaning the diminution of males. A 2003 cartoon with some resonance to these descriptions appeared in the Jordanian press as the parliament discussed the introduction of rules on judicial *khul'* there.[34]

The idea of equal access to divorce for women under the rules of judicial *khul‘* does however need examining within the broader framework of the script of marital and socio-ecocomic relations. Just as under the rules on *talaq* a man can unilaterally divorce his wife for no reason on her part and against her will, paying her deferred dower and financial compensation as required by Egyptian law, so the deal presented by the *khul‘* provision – at its most basic – requires the wife to pay 'compensation' to her husband in the event of her exercising this option. It is in this sense that the Egyptian National Council for Women later that year, responding to questions from CEDAW, presented judicial *khul‘* as 'women's equal right to divorce for incompatibility without need to prove damage':[35]

> An important step has been taken to promote equality between women and men in the area of Family Law which will pave the way to make Egypt's withdrawal of its reservation to Article 16 possible. Law no. 1 of 2000, effective as of 1 March 2000, gave women the equal right of divorce through "*Khul‘*," or repudiation, which is the indigenous Islamic formulation of women's equal right to divorce for incompatibility without need to prove damage. The law also enhanced justice, including social and economic rights of women, and put an end to the suffering of over one million women each year involved in divorce cases. Such cases used to last from five to seven years on average and sometimes end with denial of divorce.[36]

While the provision is regarded as a substantial gain by many elements in the women's movement, critics sympathetic with the aims of the law remain nevertheless concerned that poor women have considerably less equal access to divorce under this rule compared with both men and women with more financial means, particularly given the requirement not only to waive remaining rights (as noted above, a common out-of-court divorce practice) but to pay back the cash sum of the received prompt dower; and there has also been criticism of the early stages of implementation of the new rules.[37] For her part, Sonneveld asserts that the majority of women seeking divorce by judicial *khul‘* are 'Egyptian women from the lower middle classes' who may have been deserted by their husbands, are unable to obtain from them any contribution to the family income, or other such circumstances. Research of implementation of the provision over a longer period would be needed to make a more precise evaluation of the various aspects of this provision. Nevertheless, in the meantime, the Egyptian law has attracted considerable regional and indeed international significance. The international angle is shown not only in presentations of the law abroad as equalising women's access to divorce, but by the attention paid to it by the international media and human rights organisations.[38] Within its regional and jurisprudential framework, El-Alami calls it 'nothing short of revolutionary' and Arabi finds evidence that it 'marks a radical discontinuity with extant Islamic family law'.[39] It has also been copied by a number of other Arab states, most closely in Jordan, where many elements in the public debate can be directly compared with those in Egypt.

Judicial khul[c] in Jordan

In 1997, Jordan's initial report to the CEDAW noted that '[i]n the articles relating to marriage, repudiation, alimony and divorce, the Personal Status Act gives men and women equal rights'.[40] In regard to divorce, it noted that 'the wife has the right to handle her own divorce, provided that was specifically provided for in the marriage contract'[41] – referring to the delegation of the husband's unilateral right of talaq – and goes on to detail the grounds on which a wife can seek judicial divorce. This possibility does not of course constitute 'equal rights' or access to divorce. In 2001, however, Temporary Law 82/2001 included a provision on judicial khul[c] closely modeled on the Egyptian provision of the previous year.[42]

In the context of the parliamentary debates on the 2001 amendments in 2003, interventions were made both for and against the khul[c] provision. A detailed examination in support of the provision had been prepared by a member of the Shari'a Appeal Court,[43] including a rigorous examination of the fiqh sources backed up by the broader argument that a woman whose husband refuses to agree to a khul[c] may not resort to underhand stratagems such as gossiping, threats or deception in order to force him to agree, and so has the right to resort to the judge. If the reason is from his side, the principle of removing injury is invoked;[44] if from her side, the principle is 'justice between human beings and their equal entitlements in human freedoms'. A khul[c] procedure avoids the need to reveal the intimacies of marital problems in court, summon witnesses and go through lengthy procedures. The paper also brought regional precedents from a 1976 Abu Dhabi case, from Yemeni law, from a first draft of Kuwaiti law and an interview with a senior Kuwaiti palace official. The Egyptian provision of 2000 is cited at the end, as is a feature about *al-khulʿ* on al-Jazeera satellite television in the *Li'l-nisa' faqat* ('for women only') slot.[45]

An example of an opposing intervention came in a memorandum prepared in advance of the lower house's debate by an Islamist Deputy and published in a local newspaper in a feature entitled 'the battle of al-*khulʿ*'.[46] The memorandum focused primarily on the need for the husband's consent, and thus began by arguing for the need for consent in light of the textual sources in the Qur'an and the Sunna, and judicial and legislative practice 'until the start of the 21st century' when countries such as Egypt and Jordan allowed the judge to grant a *khulʿ* without such consent. It then notes the hundreds of cases in the Jordanian courts in less than two years, compared to perhaps three from the time of the Prophet to the Caliph ʿUthman, underlining the need to limit the phenomenon. A complaint is made that those who work in the *shariʿa* court system are not properly consulted about amendments to personal status law, and points to problems encountered in practice; it notes that if the wife had received a large prompt dower, only rich women would benefit from the provision,[47] while if was a token dower (one gold dinar for example) and the woman was required to return only that dower to her husband, this would be doing a great wrong to the husband (as 'in reality nobody marries for a dinar'). The author asserts that 'many believe' that the amendments came not in response to actual local needs but to 'an agenda [set by] foreign Western thoughts, on recommendations from conferences or conspiracies aimed at destroying the integrity of the family on the pretext of liberating women' with a specific reference to the Beijing conference. He criticizes the equality paradigm as against the law of the family in Islam, insisting that *qiwama* and *talaq* are the right of the husband while maintenance is the right of the wife; giving the right of *khulʿ* to a wife whose husband is fulfilling all his duties towards her is 'taking the wife's side over the husband's'. He also underlines the need to narrow the doors of divorce rather than open new ones, and observes that women are 'mostly very emotional and quick-tempered' while men are ('mostly') more capable of being ruled by their heads and their reason, 'which is why Islam gives men the right of *talaq* for the sake of family cohesion'.[48] A final point that has resonance elsewhere is that as currently applied, the *khulʿ* provision 'usurps the right of the *qadi*' by obliging the latter to simply respond to the wife's petition. The author's conclusion is to propose alternatives, including the simplification of establishing existing grounds for divorce on the wife's petition, such as *niza' wa shiqaq* ('discord and strife') and setting a time limit of three months to such cases.

The next day, the same paper published extracts from a roundtable it had convened on *al-khul'*, bringing together a female and a male Deputy, a *shar'i qadi*, and a specialized *shar'i* lawyer.[49] All articulated support of the provision except for the male Deputy, who had voted against the amendments in the House. The feature, covering one side of broadsheet print, gives an overview of the dynamics at work in the somewhat emblematic debate over *khul'* in Jordan – and indeed in wider debates over amendments to Muslim personal status law in the country and perhaps, with variations, in the region. From a reading of the published extracts, the male Deputy appears to be promoting a populist traditionalist position dismissive of the practical experience of the lawyer, the 'humanitarian' interventions of the female deputy, and the legal opinion of the *shar'i qadi*, seeking to invoke solidarity with the poor, the religious, the 'authentic' citizens, and indeed with the established *shari'a* court system. His final appeal is to legislative standing of the elected House of Deputies. The *qadi* is part of the *shar'i* establishment, which supports the government-led amendment, and can be read as defending his own expertise against the challenge to the provision voiced by the Deputy, as well as more generally against 'alternative expertises'. The female Deputy defends the provision as being in accordance with the *shari'a* and of benefit to women, particularly poor women, as well as to the well-being of children, and denies the existence of 'American pressure' in the matter ('nobody would accept such a thing'). The *shar'i* lawyer argues from his court experience that women seek divorce only as a last resort, and emphasises indigenous Arab inspiration of the *khul'* provision. There is supportive reference to expert regional discussions but no mention (in the published extracts) of international norms apart from hostile (or denying) references to 'international conferences' dominated by 'American interests' and more generally to 'Western pressure'. And all participants invoke the healthy, stable family as a primary focus, whether arguing for or against the amendment.

In the public debate in Jordan, the interventions of women's rights activists focused *inter alia* on the validity of the procedure under *shari'a* and the likelihood that it would be used as a very last resort and remedy by despairing wives needing a dignified and expeditious exit from a marriage.[50] Some

activists were concerned at delays in the proceedings in practice, which undermined the aim of a speedy remedy, at difference in application of the provision by different judges, and at difficulties faced by women who could not
return their dower; some held that the *khulʿ* law was an inadequate remedy
in any case to the larger picture of family law in Jordan.[51] The picture is thus
mixed, and as in Egypt, research into the uptake of the provision would be
needed to assess the competing predictions and claims. On the other hand,
unlike in Egypt, the manner in which the *khulʿ* amendment was passed into
law by the executive may yet affect its application, as the lower house twice
refused to approve the temporary law in which it was included.

Other approaches to judicial khul^c

Other Arab states have also introduced the possibility of judicial *khulʿ*, although
not as clearly modelled on the Egyptian provision as that in Jordan. The 2005
Algerian amendments explicitly introduce the phrase 'without the husband's
consent' into an existing provision allowing the wife to divorce by *khulʿ* and
previously giving the court a role only in the event that the spouses disagreed
on the amount to be paid or forfeited by the wife.[52] In the UAE, it was reported
that lawyers in the UAE working around the draft law had lobbied for the inclusion of a provision for judicial *khulʿ*, and there appeared to be some confu-
sion over the result.[53] In the end, the 2005 text establishes the mutual consent
of the spouses to *khulʿ* as the norm, with the Explanatory Memorandum noting explicitly that 'this law has not taken up what certain Arab personal status codes have done – such as Egypt and Jordan – in considering *khulʿ* an
individual act from the wife'. Nevertheless, in a final clause in the same article, the law does in fact allow the court to rule for *khulʿ* for an appropriate exchange in the event that the husband is being obstinate or arbitrary in his
refusal and where there is 'fear that they [husband and wife] will not live in the
limits of God'. Here, the UAE Explanatory Memorandum stresses that this provision applies where there is a fear regarding the conduct of both spouses 'if
the relationship continues despite there being no desire on the part of either
spouses for it to continue'.[54] The 2005 draft Palestinian personal status law, as
already noted, includes a provision for judicial *khulʿ* giving the judge a particularly substantive role in assessing the need for such a divorce, while the 2006
Qatari law stays somewhat closer to the Egyptian model.[55]

Elsewhere, the Moroccan legislators declined to adopt this approach in the 2004 law, despite advocacy from some women's groups for the inclusion of judicial *khul*.[56] Loukili and Zirari-Devif consider that the Moroccan law takes a route potentially better for women than that provided by judicial *khul* through introducing divorce for *shiqaq*, whereby either or both spouses may petition the court for a divorce on the grounds of irreconcilable differences making continued married life impossible. The court is to appoint arbitrators who must attempt to effect reconciliation; the court is to rule for a divorce if reconciliation efforts fail, establishing the responsibility of each spouse for the marital breakdown and assessing financial rights accordingly. Although this procedure is available elsewhere, the Morrocan law adds a requirement that all such petitions be ruled upon definitively within six months from the submission of the claim. Loukili and Zirari-Devif hold that this in effect gives the wife 'an equivalent right to dissolution of marriage to the right of repudiation recognised for the husband' and cite government statistics showing that more than half of all divorce rulings in the year 2006 were issued by way of the *shiqaq* procedure: 'women didn't wait long to make use of this new judicial possibility of divorce.'[57] Assuming the courts are held to the deadline of six months, and (as these commentators imply) allow a wife to insist unilaterally on her aversion to the marriage continuing, then unlike in judicial *khul* the wife has the prospect of being awarded at least some proportion of her financial rights while securing a judicial divorce within a reasonable period.

In Mauritania, the 2001 law provides an explicit remedy for women who can establish that they agreed to a *khul* divorce only in order to get out of an injurious situation.[58] Wurth notes that the Yemeni rules on dissolution for 'hatred' or aversion (*karahiya*) 'resemble a *khul* administered judicially against the wish of the husband' as in the later Egyptian law.[59] In addition, the Sudanese procedure of judicial divorce for *fidiya* (ransom or redemption) open to women ruled disobedient by the court requires the wife to state explicitly in her submission that she is 'unable to give her husband his marital rights and has been injured by remaining in his *'isma*''.[60] A few texts already allowed a procedure similar to judical *khul* in a marriage before consummation, including the Draft Unified Arab Law, in provisions that in essence allow a wife to withdraw unilaterally from the contract before cohabitation has commenced.[61] The UAE 2005 law took this up with the Explanatory Memorandum explicitly noting that the judge could rule for a *khul* in an unconsummated marriage against the consent of the husband 'in order to prevent the further spread of the injury'.[62]

Libya's legislation has shown a somewhat contrary trend in regard to judicial *khulᶜ*. The 1972 law included a text on judicial *khulᶜ* that was at the time unprecedented in the Arab laws, in a provision that Mayer called 'an unexpected development'. Nevertheless, she held that in practice it would be likely to make little difference to the wife's access to divorce; she further noted the resemblance of the Libyan provision to the practice of judicial *khulᶜ* established by the Pakistani courts since the 1960s.[63] The provision was changed in the 1984 text to limit its application to where the husband retracts ('through obstinacy') an offer of a *khulᶜ* settlement, although in such circumstances the court is entitled to allow deferral of the wife's payment of the consideration if she is unable to meet it immediately.[64]

Otherwise, legislators have focussed on issues such as protecting the wife from being coerced into giving up her rights in a *khulᶜ* or consensual divorce settlement,[65] and in disallowing recognition of a waiver by the woman of her right of custody over her children as consideration or 'exchange' for a divorce. Libya is again an exception here, reversing the position in its 1972 law to allow the right of custody to be waived in a *khulᶜ* divorce.[66] In most cases, the codifications allow the wife to take on the child's maintenance herself as well as to waive her right to a fee for custody as part of the compensation for *khulᶜ*; in the event that she becomes unable to live up to her commitments, the father is obliged to provide for the child's needs with the amount becoming a debt against the custodian.

As noted above, the regular, non-litigious form of *khulᶜ* and other related arrangements for divorce rely on the principle of mutual consent of the spouses. The attraction of the idea of judicial *khulᶜ* for those seeking to increase women's access to divorce lies not only in the anticipated brevity and non-intrusiveness of the procedure, but in the prospect of women being able to insist unilaterally on a divorce where they cannot establish judicial grounds under the available law and legal system. This may be presented as the closest parallel to the husband's power of unilateral *talaq*. At the same time, the requirement by the Egyptian provision that the court undertake efforts to reconcile the spouses before granting the wife's petition for a judicial *khulᶜ* applies to this procedure an approach also increasingly being taken by laws around the region to any application for divorce, requiring the intervention of the court in unilateral and consensual divorce procedures as well as in those requiring litigation.[67] The expansion of such mandatory mediation procedures, which have been introduced in countries from North Africa to the Gulf, has been discussed above in Chapter Four.

Divorce as a judicial process

The different ways in which the region has seen the expansion of the formal role of the court in divorce procedures can be grouped as a fourth approach to divorce law reform. The motivations include persuading the husband to desist from his intention to unilaterally divorce his wife, or encouraging the couple agreed upon divorce to settle their difference through the assistance of mandatory court or other, formally established third-party mediation that requires the presence of both spouses;[68] they also include securing established and sometimes additional rights for a woman divorced unilaterally by her husband, and in some cases allowing the awarding of damages to whichever spouse is injured by a divorce. The primary focus of this approach has been the institution of *talaq*, with an increasing insistence on the need not only for registration but for court procedures in order to establish the divorce.

In moving towards establishing the court as the proper location for divorce, states have taken different approaches. At issue, ultimately, is the question of the validity of an extra-judicial divorce; and just as in the case of marriage, traditional law did not require court process or registration to render a *talaq* valid. Most states have not taken the radical step of completely denying validity to an out-of-court *talaq*, although they have taken different steps to establish formal registration procedures and to normalise in-court divorce. The current laws in Jordan and Yemen, for example, require registration of the *talaq* at court, with criminal sanctions applicable in the event of an out-of-court *talaq* not being registered within the set deadline.[69] Jordan's legislators in 1951 had excluded the courts from hearing claims by the husband (but not the wife) to establish an out-of-court *talaq* in the absence of such registration.[70] This procedural approach stood to oblige the husband to register his *talaq* if he wished it to have any legal effect, while allowing the wife to prove the occurrence of a divorce if the husband was refusing against her wishes to register it. The legislators subsequently retreated from this position, without giving any explanation for the omission of this provision in the 1976 law, although objections to the effective denial of validity of an unregistered *talaq* indicate the jurisprudential grounds on which opposition may be based. Taking a slightly different tack in the absence of further statu-tory legislation on the subject, administrative circulars have instituted bu-reaucratic procedures at court designed to delay (and therefore discourage) the husband's registration of the third of three *talaqs*.[71]

The statutory laws in other states have made firmer attempts to make di-vorce a judicial process. In Iraq, the 1959 law required a husband to petition the court if he wished to divorce his wife by *talaq*, but allowed him to regis-ter it with the court during the *'idda* period if he was unable to comply with the standard procedure; while marriage contracts were to be held valid until formally cancelled by the court as a result of a divorce, it has been noted that subsequent court practice did not hold that a *talaq* not so registered was inherently invalid.[72] The laws of Libya and Algeria both provide that divorce may only be 'established' by a court ruling,[73] and Dennerlein notes as 'rather exceptional' a 1989 decision by the Algerian Supreme Court recognising the validity of an out-of-court *talaq* on witness testimony.[74] Nevertheless, the lan-guage of these codes, while firmly institutionalising court procedure in di-vorce, do not adopt the unequivocal position of the Tunisian law which in 1956 held that 'divorce occurs only in court', thus denying not only recog-nition but also the validity of out-of-court divorce.[75]

Egypt's legislators have taken a strictly procedural approach to this issue, and were also obliged to retreat at one point. Coming later than its early and widely emulated substantive constraints on *talaq*, a provision in Law No.44 of 1979 required husbands to document their *talaq* with the appropriate no-tary and provided that the consequences of the divorce as far as the wife was concerned would take effect only from the date she was made aware of its oc-currence – that is, rather than from the date it occurred, a controversial po-sition for some.[76] The 1985 law that replaced the 1979 legislation constrained this suspension of the financial effects of divorce ('in terms of inheritance and other financial rights') to circumstances in which the husband deliber-ately conceals it from his wife.[77] The official explanation was the need to 'prevent injury [of the wife] without constraining the husband's right of *talaq*'.[78] This was supplemented in the 2000 law by a provision to the effect that in the event of a *talaq* being denied, the court will find it established only by the formal notarisation and documentation process confirming the occurrence of the *talaq* in or out of court.[79] Critics of this provision voiced concern at the apparent denial of legal validity to a contested *talaq* other-wise perfectly valid under the *shari'a*. Others argued in support on the grounds that it would further protect women's rights and oblige the husband to document his *talaq* and have the wife notified accordingly. Fawzy reports particular support among a sample of lawyers and members of the judiciary familiar with what he describes as the 'predicaments' of the complexities of existing procedure.[80] In a draft explanatory memorandum to the first draft of the law presented to the People's Assembly, the government argued that this provision effectively brought legal recognition of *talaq* into line with legal recognition of marriage – which, in the event of denial and as discussed above, has long had to be established by official document in order for any claims related to that marriage to be considered by the court.[81] In an explicit recognition of the normative pluralism involved in this approach, the draft memorandum noted that while such a *talaq* would not count in law (*qanunan*), 'this does not take away from the fact that the *talaq* occurs in religion (*diyanatan*)'.[82]

The new Moroccan law takes a decisive step in introducing the requirement of judicial oversight in its definition of divorce.[83] The official guide to the law makes no mention of out-of-court *talaq*, and explains the role of the judiciary as being:

> to protect the marriage bond from frivolous or arbitrary exercise of *talaq*, guarantee the rights of the divorcée and the children, and strengthen the mechanisms of mediation and reconciliation.[84]

Besides this, the law substantially increases the bureaucratic procedures to be followed in the event that a husband – or a wife to whom the power of *talaq* has been delegated – has to follow in seeking the court's permission for the notarisation of the *talaq* to occur. The approach is the same as that taken to the constraint of polygyny, with substantial bureaucratic and financial requirements relied upon to support the conciliation attempts undertaken by the court before the court will allow the divorce to be notarised. Also similar is the position that if the husband does not deposit the sums specified by the court (including the wife's deferred dower, *mut'a* and maintenance) within thirty days, his application to have his *talaq* notarised by the court is considered to be withdrawn.[85] These procedures were anticipated in the 1993 amendments, which Buskens observes seemed to have had the unintended result of an increasing number of men 'who abandon their families and disappear, instead of "properly" repudiating their wives'.[86]

By comparison to developments in North Africa, the two most recent laws in the Gulf make fewer inroads on traditional divorce law. The UAE codification states that '*talaq* occurs by declaration from the husband and is documented by the judge'. The 2006 Qatari law has the same wording, although adding a requirement for the *qadi* to attempt reconciliation prior to hearing the husband's divorce pronouncement. Both laws then provide that a *talaq* pronounced out of court can be established by means of acknowledgement or proof. In regard to this clause, the Explanatory Memorandum to the UAE law states as follows:

> The conditions governing *talaq* and its occurrence do not require that it occur before the judge or before two just witnesses[87] (unless it is by deputisation) because divorce is an expression of the husband's will. Accordingly, and given that *talaq* is one of the matters related to the right of God Almighty, if the husband causes *talaq* to occur outside the court and then he takes the matter to the judge and establishes that it has occurred in a manner that fulfils the [*shar⁽i*] conditions, then the judge rules for its occurrence as of the date it happened. This is because not granting its occurrence leads to the continuation of an unlawful marital life in which illegitimate children proliferate in society, which must be protected therefrom.[88]

The focus on the lawful parentage of children at the end of this explanatory passage is repeated when the UAE Explanatory Memorandum deals with paternity and modern reproductive technologies, as discussed in the following chapter. As a whole, the passage implicitly rejects the approaches taken in other Arab states to the matter of out-of-court *talaq*, whether in terms of conditioning validity or recognition of a *talaq* or the implementation of its effects on a judicial or registration process. Bolstering the statute with such arguments, in an official explanation of the law, complicates the prospects for successful advocacy for change.

Compensation

A fifth approach to the reform of divorce law, aimed this time at deterring certain divorce practices and expanding the rights of the wife on divorce, can be identified in the legislative establishment of a wife's right to compensation. Different forms of this requirement, first introduced in statutory legislation in Syria in 1953,[89] have been adopted in all the codifications under discussion here, and it has thus become a standard feature of statutory law in the region. This is despite the reservations of certain jurists, who object *inter alia* to the effective penalising of the husband for exercising a right lawfully recognised to be his, and to obliging the husband to reveal his reasons and thus potentially to air in public things that should remain confidential out of respect for the marital relationship enjoined by the Qur'an.[90] In official justifications made within the *fiqh* framework, the provisions are presented as a broadening of the 'gift of consolation' (*mut'a*) variously required or recommended for divorced wives in different circumstances according to the schools of law.[91] The purposes are explained as deterring the husband from arbitrarily exercising his power of *talaq*, compensating the wife for the injury she has sustained, and increasing the financial obligations on the husband towards his divorcée beyond the dower and maintenance for the *'idda* period; some also refer to the principle of compensation for the abuse of a right. A common approach is to award the compensation by way of monthly maintenance instalments after the end of the marriage. Although this can be seen as a separate approach to divorce law reform, it is dependent on the increasing court involvement in and judicial scrutiny of divorce, since it involves an assessment by the court of the husband's reasons or motives for his exercise of *talaq*, along with the impact upon the wife.

Differences among the various statutory texts on this subject include whether there are maximum or minimum limits to the amount of compensation that may be awarded, and how it is to be paid; whether the provision applies only to cases of unilateral *talaq* by the husband, or also applies to injury established in other divorce procedures; whether the text empowers the court to rule for compensation when ruling for the divorce, or requires the wife to initiate a separate claim; whether the text focuses on the husband's abuse of his right, the wife's material position, or indeed the husband's financial circumstances, and/or specifically requires the court to take into consideration the length of the marriage.[92]

These distinctions, and judicial interpretations of the respective provisions, have a substantial effect on the actual and potential impact of compensation awards. In Syria and Jordan, the courts have established a legal presumption of arbitrariness in unilateral *talaq* and therefore placed the burden of proof on the ex-husband to establish that he had a legitimate (or *shar'i*) reason for his divorce.[93] Still, the wife has to claim separately for this award. Research in the records of the *shari'a* courts of the West Bank applying the 1976 Jordanian law shows that although claims for compensation for arbitrary *talaq* are rarely successfully defended by the ex-husband, it is also rare to see the maximum amount of compensation being awarded.[94] The judge will exercise his discretion in awarding a reduced amount if, although the ex-husband is unable to prove a *shar'i* defence, or is unwilling to have it recorded, the judge is nevertheless convinced that the man was not totally and absolutely to blame for his action. Conduct by the wife which would commonly be considered unreasonable, while not amounting to 'reasonable cause' as such in *shar'i* terms, will serve to reduce the amount of compensation awarded, and the maximum is awarded only where the judge is convinced that the wife was totally wronged and entirely blameless in the affair.[95]

In Syria, the court's discretion is limited not only by the maximum limit of three years' maintenance but by the material impact (of poverty and neediness) on the wife of the arbitrary *talaq*.[96] Appellate decisions have thus held that 'the fact that the divorcée has someone to provide for her prevents a ruling for compensation for arbitrary *talaq*'.[97] On the other hand, once the award of a fixed amount is made, it does not necessarily lapse by a change in circumstance: 'The remarriage of the divorcée does not prevent her entitlement to the compensation for arbitrariness in *talaq*'[98] and nor does the divorcée's entitlement to a substantial deferred dower from her ex-husband mean that she is not entitled to claim compensation.[99]

In Egypt, once it is established that the woman has not been at fault in the divorce, the court is bound to award a minimum of two years' maintenance, which avoids the prospect of a token or symbolic award, but is unconstrained by a maximum limit; it is also instructed to take into account the length of the marriage when assessing the award. It thus allows a wider degree of discretion to the judge, and heightens the potential impact of the principle of compensation. Al-Kashbur cites an Egyptian case where a man took over his wife's inheritance from her deceased parents and then divorced her and married a young woman working as a clerk in his office; the court took a particularly dim view of the arbitrariness involved in his exercise of *talaq* in this case and awarded the woman compensation by way of maintenance until she died.[100] Similarly, el-'Alami notes a case where a woman had been divorced for no reasonable cause after 33 years of marriage and had been awarded the minimum compensation of two years maintenance by the first instance court. On appeal, the award was increased fivefold by the judges of the higher court in view of their assessment of the extent of arbitrariness in the husband's conduct.[101]

In addition, although the Egyptian text is not explicit on this subject, the higher courts have upheld the principle articulated by the Mufti of the Republic to the effect that the compensation would be payable in the event of "any divorce effected without a wife's consent, whether by court decision or by an act of the husband... She is to be denied a *mut'a* compensation only if she is guilty of an offence".[102] El-'Alami reports an appeal decision setting aside a ruling by a first instance court which had rejected a claim for compensation made by a woman divorced from her husband by the court on the grounds of injury. The Appeal Court argued that 'it is an established principle' that in cases in which it is possible for a ruling to be given for judicial divorce, the judge is in effect acting in place of the husband in effecting the *talaq*: 'Where a wife seeks judicial divorce on the grounds of injury, this injury is deemed to be a factor forcing her to seek divorce in order to avert the harm, and the divorce is therefore considered to be against her will.'[103] Kuwaiti and Sudanese law also recognise this principle, with certain exceptions, as do the 2005 Algerian amendments, and the 2006 Qatari law.[104]

Tunisia's broad rules of compensation arise logically from its radical reformulation of divorce law dating from 1956.[105] The Tunisian statute gives women the same right as men to petition the court for divorce without having to establish any grounds. The other procedures for divorce are a petition by one spouse on the grounds of injury by the other, and divorce by mutual agreement.[106] Commentators observe that the original law included the principle of compensation to either spouse in order to limit exercise of the option of the first 'no grounds' type of divorce;[107] in circumstances where divorce was effected on the unilateral insistence of one of the spouses, the court would determine what compensation the wife should be granted for the damage she has sustained, or what compensation she should pay her ex-husband.[108] Chamari points out that this formal equality in matters of compensation for the financial consequences of divorce was applied in a context of economic and juridical non-equality of the spouses, women nearly always feeling the financial repercussions more than men; this fact combined with a general antipathy towards the provision by members of the judiciary and together they 'translated into the non-effectiveness of the principle of equality in practice and the diversion of the law from the goal towards which it was aimed'.[109] Chamari therefore welcomes the introduction in 1981 of an amendment which 'breaks, in favour of divorced women, the strictly egalitarian rule of the original article'.[110] The amendment entitles both men and women to compensation for the emotional and material damages inflicted on them by a divorce 'without grounds' or a divorce at their petition for injury, but specifically provides that women may opt to have the material part of the damages paid not as a lump sum but as an ongoing monthly stipend, which continues 'until the woman dies or her social circumstances change by way of by a new marriage or by her attaining something that enables her to do without the compensation'. In early implementation of the provision, lower level courts again refused to award the monthly stipend; Chamari notes that such decisions were overturned on appeal, but that not all women had the means to proceed to appeal.[111] Appellate decisions have held that 'material compensation is awarded in the form of a life stipend to she who has no income and no regular work, and as a lump sum to other women', and that regular (for example salaried) work and a 'respectable income compared to that of her divorcer' allow review of the stipend reparation for material injury.[112]

The statutory rules on compensation, depending on how they are formulated and applied, have clearly added a further dynamic to the judicial and social practice of divorce in the region. This dynamic depends also on the overall approach of the law to divorce. In Jordan, where statutory judicial oversight of unilateral *talaq* is minimal, an official note accompanying an earlier proposal to raise the maximum level of compensation justified its failure to propose even higher limits on the grounds that this might encourage husbands to refrain from *talaq* 'for quite the wrong reasons' and to coerce their wives into agreeing to give up their rights (including compensation) in exchange for a divorce.[113] On the other hand, in Algeria, Mitchell notes a substantial proportion of judicial divorce petitions submitted by husbands in the early years of the application of the 1984 code, which she attributes to the compensation rules applying to instances of unilateral *talaq*. She observes that 'the notion of fault in these cases plays a large part in Algerian court decisions'; although in her case material the fault was mostly held to lie with the husband, she finds that the compensation awarded the wife did not amount to a substantial sum.[114]

Post-divorce rights to the marital home

The adequacy or otherwise of compensation payments is linked to another major issue in post-divorce arrangements: that of the divorced wife's accommodation and more specifically rights to the marital home. As has been seen, the statutory laws retain the presumption that the wife will move to live with her husband, who is assigned the obligation of providing the marital home. Deeds of ownership and rent contracts are likely to be in the name of the husband. The separate property regime protects the wife's home if it happens to be her own property, but otherwise means she acquires no rights in it, but proposals that the wife be assigned certain rights (albeit temporary) to the home itself have met with significant resistance from legislatures. Iraq is unusual in having amended its law to allow a woman to stay rent-free in the home owned by her ex-husband for a period of three years following the divorce, provided she does not herself own somewhere to live and that the divorce was not by reason of her *nushuz* or marital infidelity or by her agreement.[115]

Elsewhere, attention by the legislatures has been confined to the situation of the divorcée with custody of children from the marriage. The traditional rules require the former husband to pay a wage to his divorcée with custody, and to pay for his children's maintenance; such provision does not however necessarily amount to an obligation to provide an independent dwelling. In Jordan for example, where the statutory law has not specifically addressed this matter, the courts have held the father obliged to provide accommodation only in the event that the wife does not have any.[116] In Algeria, a draft text on this subject in the 1984 law was weakened during the parliamentary debate to apply similarly only where the wife had no guardian willing to take her in with her children and to exclude any claim on the marital home itself where it was the only one in the husband's possession; in an indication of the way things are moving on this subject, the 2005 amendments remove this text and in the event of divorce require the father of the wards to provide either decent accommodation or rent for such for the female custodian, while the wife has the right to remain in the conjugal home until such time as he has implemented the judicial ruling made in regard to her accommodation.[117]

The Egyptian debates on this subject have similarly shown the sensitivity of this subject as a target for legislative intervention. Egypt's 1979 legislation gave the mother the right to remain in the marital home (including one owned by the husband) following divorce for the duration of custody. According to Najjar, this was among the provisions of the 1979 law that provoked the most controversy, producing 'the most abrasive exchange between the proponents and opponents of the law, for the simple reason that Egypt has been suffering from a "suffocating housing shortage," as the Egyptian newspapers described it'.[118] The replacement law in 1985 maintained its recognition of the right of a wife and children to an independent dwelling during the period of custody, but excluded the marital home owned by the husband.[119] The codifications in the Gulf states have not addressed this matter explicitly, although the debates in Bahrain indicate that it is a matter of concern for women's rights activists.[120]

Overview

Earlier scholars have noted that it was the problems caused by the difficulty of access to judicial divorce for women under the Ottoman-preferred Hanafi school that first prompted legislative intervention in family law by the late Ottoman authorities; in 1915, decrees widening grounds for divorce petitions by women were issued in advance of the 1917 promulgation of the OLFR. The other main target for reform in the early laws was the institution of *talaq*, and although various constraints have been placed on a man's legal facility of *talaq* in different laws, the structural imbalance created by the husband's unilateral power to end the marriage remains of concern to many. One approach to this, starting in Syria in the 1950s and now widespread, has been the introduction of provision for financial compensation for a wife divorced in injurious circumstances and thus seeking to increase the cost for a husband minded to abuse his power of *talaq*; the circumstances in which such compensation may be awarded, and the limits on the award, vary according to the particular law, and the judiciary generally retains significant discretion. A more recent approach has been the introduction of judicial *khulʿ*, which may sometimes be presented as providing the wife with a counterbalancing unilateral divorce procedure; as noted above, the way these provisions work to the advantage of women in different socio-economic circumstances is a matter of debate among activists both in support of and opposing such developments in divorce law. The take-up of the Egyptian model of this procedure has not been unanimous in the laws issued since the

2000 Egyptian law; arguments against the procedure include the assertion that giving women such authority over themselves in the matter of divorce is unwise in light of women's 'emotional' nature, while others object to what they perceive as the erosion of male authority in the marriage occasioned by the recognition of a unilateral divorce option for women. Making divorce a wholly judicial procedure remains an aim for many women's rights activists in the region, with considerable success in this area in states in North Africa but little in the Gulf states. Complex challenges also remain in relation to the issues of a divorcée's and a mother's accommodation rights, particularly in regard to the marital home.

10 Parents and Children

Family laws in the region mostly maintain the overall approach of the *fiqh* texts in which, as Meriwether puts it, 'at least in law and theory, children "belonged" to the father's family'.[1] Broadly, the laws divide the functions of parenting into those of the custodian and the guardian, and identify the former with the mother or other close female relative and the latter with the father or other male guardian. In this description of the relationship, the custodian has duties of physical care and upbringing of minor children, while the guardian has duties and authorities in regard to their financial affairs (including management of any property), their education, their travel and other areas where the ward meets the 'public' world outside the home, as well as being financially responsible for them. The distinct duties of mother (custodian) and father (guardian) reflect gendered assumptions of 'ideal-type' social and familial roles in the care and upbringing of children. To what extent practice matched the 'ideal' is unclear. Fathers were entitled to appoint the person of their choice as *wasi* (legal guardian) to undertake the functions of guardianship, including management of financial affairs, in the event of the father's death, rather than this passing to the next male agnate in the recognised order of guardianship authority. Margaret Meriwether found that in records from late 18th and early 19th century Aleppo, 'women were appointed as *wasi* more often than men' – most often, the mother being appointed in his will by the father, but also close female relatives.[2]

Current laws tend to point out that while the marriage is extant and the spouses cohabiting, the care and upbringing (and custody) of children is the shared responsibility of both parents, although the authorities of guardianship are not alluded to as shared in similar fashion. When the spouses are living separately or the marriage has ended by death or divorce, the custodian is assumed to have physical charge of the ward. Unless the marriage is extant, the custodian is entitled to a fee from the guardian in addition to the guardian's financial support of the ward.[3] While the ward lives with the custodian, the latter may be prevented from moving to live elsewhere within the same country, if this would constitute an obstacle to the guardian discharging his duties, or travelling abroad with the ward without the guardian's permission. The guardian may also have recourse to court if he wishes to travel temporarily with the ward in the latter's interest and the custodian objects.

Period of custody

The different schools of law identified either set ages (two, seven, nine, eleven) or stages of life (puberty, marriage) as marking the end of a woman's custody over her children, while the guardianship of the father might continue in certain aspects. In particular, as has already been discussed, the guardian is likely to maintain an authority in the marriage of his female children or wards; there may also be a continued authority in financial and property matters exercised by the guardian beyond the end of the period of custody. When the period of custody is over, the guardian is entitled to seek the physical removal of the ward to his household, assuming that the ward has not married and moved away from the custodian; the ward may by then be of an age to choose with whom to live, according to the views of some of the schools. The *fiqh* rules did not allow the removal of a child from his or her mother's custody in the event that the child 'would not accept anyone other than her'. In the presentation of the traditional rules, the right of the child to the best (most appropriate) custodian is an underlying theme; the 'right' of the parent is either a duty or a right shared with the ward. The mother's (or woman's) custody is estimated to be terminated when the ward can 'dispense with the care of women' – that is to say, the physical care and nurturing function expected of the custodian. The transfer to the physical household of the guardian is presented as related to particular (gendered) needs of a male or female child at different stages of their life. Thus, according to different schools, the end of a woman's custody over the boy child may be contemplated when he is at an age to need to 'learn the ways of men', while the girl child may need to be in her guardian's physical protection, rather than that of her mother, when she comes of an age to be married or to be the target of predatory male interest.

Earlier overviews of developments in Arab personal status laws noted general tendencies to extend the period of custody normally assigned to a woman over her children following divorce beyond the age limits contemplated in the majority of the *fiqh* rules. In addition, they noted statutory references to the concept of the 'interest of the child' on which the judge may modify this and other related parts of the law, including primary allocation of custody rights. These patterns have continued in the more recent laws and also in amendments to the older laws such as those in Syria (where the 2003 amendments followed a focussed advocacy campaign), Jordan, Iraq, Tunisia and Morocco.[4] The 2004 Moroccan law subjects almost every substantive rule on custody to the child's interest. In the draft UAE codification approved by cabinet in 2005, a provision ending the mother's custody over girls at thirteen and boys at eleven provoked public condemnation by lawyers who had consulted on previous drafts and held these ages to be a curtailment of existing custody rights.[5] The text of the law as passed maintained this position, while allowing the court to extend a woman's custody until the male ward reaches puberty and the female marries. It also provides that the woman's custody continues indefinitely if the ward is mentally or physically disabled, presumably on the assumption that this ward will remain in need of the functions of care normatively assigned to the mother.[6] Both of these clauses are subject to the best interest of the child.[7] Addressing the selection of the ages thirteen and eleven from beyond the rules of any one particular school of *fiqh*, the Explanatory Memorandum observes as follows:

> We can't avoid the fact that it is not beneficial to rely on the opinion of the child, as the child does not well evaluate how things may develop [...] And it is not just to assume that the father is extremely stern and a dominating force, and the mother is always the pinnacle of complete caring and superior solicitude. It is not up to the legislators to work out which of the schools best befits the love of mothers, or the love of fathers. Rather, they have to look at which most responds to the interests of proper social upbringing and education of the child. Thus the law holds in this regard that the age for males shall be reaching eleven years, and the female thirteen. After this stage, the boy goes to his father to learn the bases of masculinity and men's counsel. The girl goes to her father in view of the circumstances of society that make it difficult for women to control girls.[8]

A different example, from Palestine, shows the *shariʿa* courts extending the period of a mother's custody in advance of the promulgation of a Palestinian law of personal status, to the disgruntlement of at least parts of their constituency.[9] Towards the end of 2005, the press reported the Legal Committee of the Palestinian Legislative Council criticising recent action of the *shari'a* courts in 'raising the age of custody to fifteen' in advance of any legislative change. Institutional sensitivities were evident in comments reported from the Committee, to the effect that the *shari'a* courts should not act on a draft text, and should await decisions from the Legislative Council to unify Muslim family law in the West Bank and Gaza Strip. However, there was also evidence in the report of objections springing from cultural practice and expectations, rather than institutional caution: the report noted that the Committee had examined this matter as a result of the complaints it had received to the effect that:

> raising the age of custody to fifteen will lead to many problems, especially as it gives the girl the right to live in the house of her maternal uncles, away from her father and her paternal uncles, who are closer to her in lineage (*nasab*), for fifteen years; and she may marry directly afterwards, so her father will have no role in her upbringing. [10]

Such comment illustrates a number of the assumptions that may have supported the more traditional *fiqh* rules, including the primacy of lineage through the father and the prospect of marriage for the female ward at a relatively young age. It also illustrates the internal connection and inter-reliance of different areas of family law currently targeted for reform: here, for example, efforts to increase the age of marriage, particularly marriage by girls under the age of eighteen, with the extension of the period of women's custody over minor children. Another connection raised implicitly in the comment is the possibility that women in unsatisfactory or abusive marriages may feel freer to seek a divorce if they know that even after divorce they stand to keep custody of their minor children until the latter reach adulthood, or at least an age at which they are entitled to choose with which parent to live. On the other hand, in a reflection of socio-economic circumstances in the Arab states, contemporary statutory texts and court practice in different countries have held that a woman who goes out to work will not be held to have forfeited her right to custody, provided that she provides proper supervision and child care in her absence.[11] Increasingly, the texts make reference to professional institutions for the care of children for whom no family custodian is available, and (for example in the new Moroccan law) to the involvement of social services in assisting the court in its assessment of various needs of the ward.[12]

Paralleling the general developments in the period of women's custody, there has been a tendency in some laws to legislate for an overlap in the guardian/custodian roles. They may for example require the mother to financially provide for her children where the father is unable to and she has means, rather than leaving this responsibility (at least in the theory of the law) with the extended agnatic family through the order of male guardians, notably the paternal grandfather.[13] While on one level this could be seen as reinforcing practice in the law, on another level it is not matched in the text by the transfer of the authorities of guardianship from the indigent father to the providing mother. In some cases, more recent developments have also included the assignment of significant administrative and institutional functions of guardianship to the mother in circumstances where the father is dead, absent or otherwise unable to properly discharge his duties.[14] The 1984 Algerian law passed full guardianship to the mother where the father of minor children died; in 2005, more unusually, the amendments provided that in the event of a divorce, guardianship is to be conferred upon the parent to whom custody has been assigned by the court.[15] In theory, this means that if a woman is assigned custody of her minor children after a divorce, she will be empowered to take all decisions and act in all their affairs on their behalf, rather than their father (her ex-husband).

Allocation of custody

Regarding the allocation of custody, in the traditional *fiqh* rules, the jurists took the approach of listing a hierarchy of relatives entitled, successively, to custody of a minor child. Certain requirements have to be met by any theoretically entitled relative, such as freedom from any dangerous contagious disease, failing which the right to custody passes to the next entitled relative. Generally, the *fiqh* rules establish the mother as the first in the hierarchy, followed by her mother and then by the father's mother. Although the order changes according to school, female relatives are prioritised over male, and mostly those on the mother's side over those on the father's. The assumption is that the closer the relative, the better the prospects for the ward's care and upbringing. In the event that a male becomes entitled to custody, most con-

137

temporary laws require that he has with him 'a woman' who can undertake the physical functions of custody; this also reflects the assumption that women are best placed to look after children, even if it is a man who holds the legal duty and entitlement. Morocco's 2004 law breaks from this pattern.[16]

Some of the Muslim personal status laws in Arab states have introduced modifications to this approach – although mostly not, as yet, to the gendered assumption of the functions of custody as normatively assigned to women. Many of the texts make explicit reference to the 'interest of the child' being considered in such allocation in normatively assigning custody to a succession of relatives. The Qatari law is unusual in setting out what qualities the *qadi* is to consider in making such an assessment of the interest of the child. These include the custodian's affection for the child and ability to raise him or her, the provision of a sound environment in which the child can be brought up and 'protected from delinquency', the ability to provide the best education and medical care, and the ability to prepare the child in terms of morals and customs for the time that he or she is ready to 'leave the custody of women'.[17]

More specifically, some laws, including most recently the 2005 Algerian amendments and the UAE law, have established the father as following the mother in the presumptive order of entitled custodians, before the maternal grandmother and other female relatives.[18] Apart from this, the UAE law reflects the more traditional approach, with a list of some seventeen individuals or categories of relatives successively entitled to claim custody of a minor child; the Qatari law has eighteen. For its part, Tunisia has dropped any explicit statutory presumption of the mother's precedence as the 'natural custodian of her children', and its law requires the judge to observe the interest of the child in assigning custody after divorce to 'either spouse or to another person'. Nevertheless, Tunisia maintains the traditional requirement noted above that where a man is assigned custody, there must be a woman to perform the actual tasks involved.[19] Under such rules, fathers stand to acquire custody rights in circumstances beyond those contemplated in the traditional rules while, in most cases, maintaining the primary authorities of guardianship. Mothers, on the other hand, acquire particular functions of guardianship only in exceptional cases.[20]

As for the mother, the general rule that she loses her right to custody if she remarries a man not a close (*mahram*) relative of the ward[21] continues to be included in statutory texts, which may or may not be nuanced by a specific or general caveat in regard to the court being allowed to rule otherwise in the interest of the child.[22] This and other circumstances in which a mother may be ruled to have forfeited her right of custody may be further softened by a provision that when such circumstances arise if the person entitled to claim custody from the mother stays silent after knowing of them for a year, this person's right to claim custody itself lapses.[23] Nevertheless, the specific issue of remarriage remains a target for advocacy in different countries, *inter alia* on the grounds of discrimination (the father not being subject to such restrictions) and on the choice it imposes on women, whose ability to remarry may be constrained by the threat of losing custody of their children, as well as on the grounds of the rights and best interest of the child.

Iraq is something of an exception in this regard; in 1986, against the background of continuing casualties in the war with Iran, a law was passed allowing a widow to remarry without losing her custody rights over her minor children, provided *inter alia* that the court is convinced there would be no injury caused to the child. The following year a further law extended this explicitly to divorcées.[24] In Morocco, women's groups had continuing reservations about the circumstances in which a woman's remarriage will cause her custody to lapse under the new law. The 2004 law allows a mother to keep custody of her children if she marries someone who is neither a *mahram* nor the '*shar'i* representative' (*na'ib shar'i*) of the ward in certain circumstances, including if she is the child's *na'ib shar'i*, if the ward is aged seven or below or would suffer harm from being separated from her, or – in resonance with the UAE law – if the ward has 'a disability or condition making custody difficult except for the mother'. Such a marriage to a non-*mahram* by a female custodian who is not the mother of the ward disqualifies her from custody unless she herself is the *shar'i* representative.[25] Certain Moroccan women's groups had advocated the removal of discrimination against women in this, through allowing the male or female custodian to retain custody in the event of re-marriage, provided the ward is not injured; an alternative proposal was to raise the age at which custody would end in such circumstances to fifteen.[26]

Another area of the codes that has tended to remain consistent is the different rules applying to the non-Muslim custodian of Muslim children. Here, the texts tend to set shorter periods of custody – particularly if the custodian is not the mother – or not to allow the extension of the statutory period, sometimes subjecting this to the best interest of the child; they may explicitly allow for custody to be terminated if it is established that she is bring-ing the child up to believe in a different faith.[27] The established *fiqh* princi-ple is that the children of a Muslim man are Muslim and are to be brought up as Muslims.[28] As already noted, one of the provisions in the International Convention on the Rights of the Child to which several Arab states have made explicit reservations is Article 14:

a) States Parties shall respect the right of the child to freedom of thought, conscience and religion;

b) States Parties shall respect the rights and duties of the parents and, when applicable, legal guardians, to provide direction to the child in the exercise of his or her right in a manner consistent with the evolving capacities of the child.[29]

General reservations against the implementation of any CRC provision per-ceived to be 'incompatible with the Islamic *shari'a'* can be called upon by other states in the region to support an interpretation of this provision that disallows apostasy (the leaving of the religion of Islam) or the bringing up of the child of a Muslim father in any other religion, or indeed without the re-ligion of Islam. Hence, in the event of a dispute, a court may consider a Mus-lim family upbringing to be in the best interest of the child of a Muslim father. The Mauritanian law specifically requires the non-Muslim custodian to 'live in a Muslim environment'.[30]

This and other aspects of the rules on child custody in Muslim family laws in the Arab states (and indeed elsewhere) are among the factors observed as obstructing the application by them and to them of the Hague Convention on Child Abduction.[31] The Convention establishes the mutual principle, among states parties who were members of the original Hague Conference on Child Abduction, of the prompt return of a child (under sixteen) habitu-ally resident in one state party who has been wrongfully taken to or held in another state party – the obvious examples are children snatched by one par-ent from the other's custody and taken abroad, or not returned from an agreed holiday.[32] Like most other Muslim majority states,[33] Arab states do not appear to consider the Hague Convention as a useful remedy to the prob-lem of international (especially inter-parental or inter-familial) child abduc-tion. No Arab state was a member of the original 1980 Conference. Those states acceding who were not original members do not automatically achieve mutual standing with the existing membership: each existing state party must individually agree this treaty relationship with the newly acceding state. No Arab state has yet acceded. Carol Bruch notes that at least part of the reason for the unusual arrangements for subsequent accessions was the existence of 'religious laws and secular customs that were markedly different from the laws and practices in most countries then members of the Hague Conference'. She is at pains to point out that it is not only 'Islamic countries' that are intended in such an assumption,[34] but it is clear that custody rules such as those considered here pose challenges to both the legislatures and the executives of different states already parties to the Convention, just as the assumptions and approaches underlying the Convention pose challenges to the legislatures and executives of Arab states. In the matter of accepting new accessions, Bruch observes that 'countries are free to consider matters such as the likelihood, for whatever reason, that courts of an acceding nation may fail to return children as required by the Child Abduction Convention'.[35] In regard to the exception clause included in the Convention, which allows states parties to decline to return a child in the event the court considers this would endanger his or her fundamental rights and freedoms, Bruch notes:

> Religious courts and religious laws raise specific issues, human rights concerns among them, that may prompt other countries to refuse a treaty relationship or may give the courts pause about returning children. Some of these focus on gender-based custody, travel, and support rules.[36]

Some of the custody rules appear to be less amenable to change than others. Where the laws have developed to increase statutory recognition of a mother's role (particular a Muslim mother) in regard to her minor children, these changes have generally provoked fewer jurisprudential and popular objections than those in other areas; there are fewer textual arguments to be made, and the concept of 'best interest' resonated with the *fiqh* emphasis on the custody rules as protecting the rights of the child at different points of his or her life. More practically perhaps, some studies have shown that many men are unlikely to want to assume the legal burdens of custody, particularly if their former wives (and their families) are in effect providing for them as well as bringing them up. Hoodfar for example notes that in Egypt 'among low-income communities men rarely demand custody of their children (especially daughters) except when they intend to punish the mother'.[37] Mir-Hosseini, writing about Morocco in the early 1990s, similarly notes that challenges by fathers to the custody rights of their former wives are very rare, particularly compared to the large proportion of claims submitted by women for custody payments. At the same time, custody rights, and the guardian's financial obligations towards his children, play a substantial role in divorce negotiations and out-of-court settlements; *khul'* divorces negotiated out of court may involve women undertaking to maintain the children in place of the father, while in other cases, the 'exchange' for a *khul'* may include the wife waiving her custody rights. While the statutory laws disallow the latter type of agreements, the fact that some women continue to make them may be indicative of the pressures brought to bear by the husband in agreeing to the divorce, or those presented by a particular socio-economic situation, which might include pressure from the wife's family in consideration of the likely prospects for remarriage of a single woman with young children.[38]

Paternity and adoption

The rules governing paternity and the legal affiliation of a child to her or his father (and thus the establishment of the child's paternal *nasab* or lineage) and those governing adoption continue to present challenges to those seeking modifications of the traditional rules related to parents and children. Concerning the former, attention focuses on the obstacles that remain in law to establishing the paternity of children born to women not in a recognised or provable marital relationship with the biological father. Established *fiqh* principles assume that 'the child is [affiliated] to the conjugal bed' and award legitimate filiation to the husband of the woman who has given birth to the child, unless it is otherwise proven through, notably, the traditional process of *li'an*, where the man denies on oath that the child is his and the woman denies his allegation and the process results in a final divorce between the couple with paternity not established. Beyond this, the rules require that the child is not only born but also conceived in the framework of marriage or of what the couple believed to be a marriage; this is also linked to the criminalisation of sexual relations outside such frameworks. The jurists thus looked to minimum and maximum periods of gestation to uphold or undermine the presumption of legitimacy of children born to a married couple. While there was generally consensus on the minimum period of gestation at six months, the jurists differed as to the maximum. A child born to a married woman after six months of her marriage and up to a set period after its termination, according to the school, would be recognised as the legitimate offspring of the woman's husband. In some cases, notably the Maliki tradition, where the doctrine of the 'sleeping foetus' informed the jurists' positions,[39] the maximum period of gestation might be several years; in others, one or two years. These rules can be seen to be protective both of the mother and of the child, extending the presumption of legitimate filiation beyond the standard term to cover any possible exceptions. Traditional rules also presume the legitimate filiation of a child born to spouses in an irregular marriage, even though the marriage itself must be dissolved. Failing the presumption of paternity through a known marriage, paternity (and indeed maternity for a child of unknown parentage) can also be established by acknowledgement, providing certain conditions of feasibility are met, and 'shar'i evidence'.

Among the rules of Muslim family law introduced in different Arab states in the twentieth century were limits to the maximum period of gestation, introducing a one-year rule either as a substantive rule or as a rule of procedure – that is, that after such a period, courts would not hear claims to establish paternity or claims by a divorced woman for maintenance during her 'idda period on the grounds she remained pregnant from her divorcer.[40] As well as citing an individual view in the body of traditional Sunni *fiqh* for this development from the classical rules, legislators in Arab states have referred to the medical consensus in support. While relying on scientific consensus to limit the period of maximum gestation recognised in law, which removed the assumption of legitimate filiation that worked in exceptional cases to the benefit of women and children, legislatures have been somewhat slower to introduce other scientific methods now available to establish paternity.

Part of the reason for this is the difference made in the laws between a father's paternity and a child's 'lineage' (*nasab*). If paternity is a biological fact, 'lineage' denotes the legally established filiation of the child to the parents and the subsequent establishment of legal rights and claims. In the case of the mother, *nasab* is established by the fact of her giving birth to the child. For the father, on the other hand, the laws generally require proof of an established *shar'i* relationship between the parents (*al-firash*, the 'conjugal bed') and 'this is the fundamental one [i.e. relationship] because the child follows his [/her] father in *nasab*'.[41] In the traditional system, and generally today, biological pa-

143

ternity alone does not give rise to the father's legal and financial responsibilities towards his child; biological maternity, on the other hand, gives rise to a mother's duties to her child whether the child was born in or out of a recognised marital relationship. This brings in the matter of statutory rules for the recognition of marriages. In general, the establishment of paternity and *nasab* is an exception to rules that might otherwise exclude state recognition of rights and claims arising from a marriage not conforming with the procedures legislated as mandatory by the state. In an undocumented and unregistered marriage, for example, the couple may decide to regularise their status in regard to the central authorities when the time comes to register children from the marriage; the principle generally holds that establishing lineage works to establish the marriage, rather than having to establish the formalities of the marriage in order to establish lineage.[42] However, serious problems arise when one party, usually the man, denies the existence of the marriage, and the woman is unable to prove it to the satisfaction of the state.

In 2005 these problems were illustrated in Egypt in a high-profile case covered extensively in the national (and some international) press, involving the attempt by set designer Hind al-Hinawi to establish the paternity of her daughter to actor and television presenter Ahmad al-Fishawi. Al-Hinawi claimed that al-Fishawi, a married man, had married her secretly in an *'urfi* marriage and had kept the copies of the contract, rather than giving her one; he admitted having had a sexual relationship with her but denied the *'urfi* marriage which would have established the child's *nasab* to him. The case was widely covered in Egypt *inter alia* because of the personalities involved, al-Hinawi's unusual step in going public with the issue, and her family's strong support of her.[43] It provoked more discussions on the dangers to women of *'urfi* marriage, particularly in securing recognition of her child's status when the man is denying the marriage. Attention also focussed on al-Fishawi's refusal to undergo a DNA test to settle the question of paternity. Commentators on the case noted government statistics of some 14,000 similar cases pending at the Egyptian courts, while activists were cited as suggesting the figure was much higher ('closer to a million').[44]

In Morocco, commentators similarly report social and legal stigma attaching to women having children outside marriage, or outside what the courts recognise as a marriage, as well as growing attention to the problem of abandoned children. Advocacy by women's and child rights activists produced the inclusion in the 2004 family code of a provision that has been used to empower the court to impose DNA testing on a man in certain circumstances of disputed paternity. This is the case when pregnancy results from sexual relations in a relationship where the offer and acceptance of marriage have been made but the contract (due to 'overwhelming circumstances') has not been formally documented as required under the law to establish marriage, and the man is denying responsibility for the pregnancy; in such circumstances, 'recourse may be had to all lawful (shar'i) means to establish nasab'.[45] This appears to address the problem of 'fatiha' marriages in Morocco not formalised by a marriage deed.[46] However, for such an order to be made, the law requires that the 'engagement' of the couple was known to their respective families and approved where necessary by the woman's guardian. Women's rights activists argue that the requirement of a more or less 'formal' engagement obstructs access to this remedy; it is reported that in the course of one year (August 2005-August 2006) the courts imposed only two paternity tests. The cost, born by the woman, is also considered prohibitive, at some $ 350 US. Nevertheless, the existence of the provision is reported also to serve to strengthen attempts to persuade men to voluntarily take paternity tests, and activists insist that the legal reforms are 'not for nothing'.[47]

In the arguments for the need to establish nasab (rather than only biological paternity), references are made not only to the range of rights and responsibilities that arise to individuals through filiation but also to the wider societal context. The following passage is from the Explanatory Memorandum to the 2005 UAE law, explaining the reasoning behind the position taken in the law in regard to nasab from the father, according to which nasab is established 'by the conjugal bed (al-firash), by acknowledgement, by [shar'i] evidence, or by scientific methods where the conjugal bed is established'. [48]

This article refers to establishing paternity through modern scientific methods such as DNA testing, which are scientific means of establishing the definite relationship between the child and his [/her] father; but in order not to make a mockery of the issues involved in establishment of paternity, by making it a matter simply of establishing this relationship through a medical test, the article has linked its ruling [on the permissibility of DNA testing] to the existence of the conjugal bed in accordance with article 90.[49] This is to prevent what has happened in a number of cases, with sperm being taken from a man and implanted into a woman without there being any shar'i tie between them. Then medical tests establish the paternal relationship, while it is not possible for the child to be attributed to the father in terms of lineage (*nasab*) in such circumstances. These means have developed in our time, and now there are laboratories and sperm banks. [...] And there are several criminal cases involving such matters. [...] And if we were to allow *nasab* to be established in such cases, it would be problematic in regard for example to inheritance, and the impediment of affinity. And the woman might be married to another man, so lineage is mixed and corruption appears.[50]

Here, the need to properly assign lineage is linked to the entitlements of those related by *nasab* to proportions of each other's estate under the law of succession, and to the rules prohibiting marriage between a range of persons related through *nasab* and through marriage. The concerns raised at the prospect of 'mixing lineage' move from the more traditional requirement of a 'conjugal bed' and lawful sexual relations to new reproductive technologies in so far as the latter involve sperm (or eggs) provided by third parties. In Libya, when Mu'ammar Qadhafi embarked on a high-profile process of the 'Islamisation' of criminal law, Mayer notes that the first piece of legislation introduced was a prohibition on artificial insemination and explains that 'artificial insemination threatens to undermine the reliability of certain distinctive presumptions regarding *nasab*'.[51] More recently in Egypt, Martha Inhorn notes that despite approval of *in vitro* fertilisation treatment and other related processes in medical approaches to marital infertility:

> all forms·of so-called 'third party donation' – of sperm, eggs, embryos or wombs (as in surrogacy) – are strictly forbidden, for reasons having to do with the privileging of marriage, 'pure lineage' and the 'natural' biological ties between parents and their offspring. Viewing the al-Azhar *fatwa* as authoritative, Egyptian IVF patients explain that sperm, egg or embryo donation leads to a 'mixture of relations.' Such mixing severs blood ties between parents and their offspring; confuses issues of paternity, descent, and inheritance; and leads to potentially incestuous marriages of the children of unknown eggs or sperm donors. Thus, for Egyptian women with infertile husbands, the thought of using donor sperm from a 'bank' is simply reprehensible and is tantamount in their minds to committing *zina*, or adultery. [52]

Coming back to family law, a new provision introduced in the 2005 Algerian amendments specifically permits artificial insemination, under similar rules: that the marriage is lawful, both spouses consent, and the procedure is carried out with the sperm of the husband and the eggs of the wife 'to the exclusion of any other person'.[53]

Unsurprisingly, similar preoccupations with the 'mixing of lineage' can be seen to underlie the general prohibition on adoption which is, furthermore, generally considered to be based in Quranic texts. In her insightful examination of how the different rules on *nasab* and adoption work to affect 'out-of-wedlock' children in Morocco, the main focus of Jamila Bargach (2000) is on social practice, and the stigma frequently attaching to children of unrecognised *nasab*. In an explanation of the theory behind the rules, however, she considers the reasons behind the juristic aversion to 'fictive kinship ties':

> In all classical texts of *fiqh*, children born out-of-wedlock [...] are entitled to all the rights and duties of a Muslim since the notion of *taqwa* (piety, among many other meanings) is what characterizes a Muslim and not his/her lineage (*nasab*) or wealth (*hasab*). These *fiqh* texts equally comment on the prohibition of plain adoption in the Qur'an (what is known as the 'Zaid incident', Sura 33:4-5) as one aiming to foster, generally speaking, a social order built on truth. Truth implies here the prohibition of fictive kinship ties that may not only alienate those legally entitled heirs but that could also lead to future incestuous relations deemed to be potentially destructive of communal cohesion because they could possibly lead to a *fitna* (disorder, chaos). (2002 a).

In their reservations to the Convention on the Rights of the Child, a number of Arab states refer explicitly to the provisions on adoption,[54] and more general reservations referring to 'the Islamic *shari'a*' would also presumably include this institution. Egypt's statement here seeks to place its reservation in a wider framework, declining to apply the article:

> Since the Islamic *shari'a* is one of the fundamental sources of legislation in Egyptian positive law and because the *shari'a*, in enjoining the provision of every means of protection and care for children by numerous ways and means, does not include among these ways and means the system of adoption existing in certain other bodies of positive law.[55]

The CRC refers explicitly to the major Islamic institutional structure for the care of a child 'temporarily or permanently deprived of his or her family en-

vironment', by including '*kafalah* of Islamic law' along with reference to fos-
ter placement and adoption.[56] A contract of *kafala* may be drawn up with the
parents or parent of the child or with the public guardian appointed to the
care of children of unknown parentage, depending on the circumstances.
Broadly speaking, *kafala* is a system of care that allows a child to be looked
after and brought up in a family not his or her own, with similar rights of
maintenance, education and so on that pertain to minors but without key attributes of *nasab*. That is, the child does not take the family's name, and does
not acquire the proportionate inheritance entitlements automatically ac-
cruing to kin, although he or she may receive bequests from the third of the
estate which is exempted from the system of fixed family entitlements. The
institution is treated as a matter of civil contract rather than of family law;
the personal status codes generally confine themselves to stating that adoption is prohibited.

In this matter as in others, Tunisia is an exception, with a 1958 law permitting and regulating adoption as well as institutionalising public guardianship and *kafala*. In its time, the Somali family code also explicitly allowed legal
adoption giving rise to identical parent-child rights and responsibilities as
those pertaining in biological parentage.[57] In Egypt, radio slots encourage
women without children to engage in the *kafala* of children without parents.
Elsewhere, Algeria has seen probably the most active discussions regarding
adoption. The 1984 law included a separate section regulating *kafala*, but re-
iterating the prohibition on adoption.[58] In 1997, Mitchell described *kafala* as
an 'inadequate solution to the problem of abandoned illegitimate children'[59]
who may include orphans from the violence dating from the 1990s, children
born of rape, or children born otherwise to unmarried mothers facing social
sanctions including rejection by their families; the 2005 amendments did not
address the issue. Those supporting the legalisation of adoption as in Tunisia
may argue that whatever the theory and religious injunction, a child born
out of marriage is often socially stigmatised and that the state effectively per-
petuates this condition through not providing families with the choice of
adoption, which would entitle them to give the child their name and present
him or her to the public as kin. Dargouth-Medimegh[60] finds that Tunisia's legislation on adoption is one point where Tunisian family law 'breaks with its
Muslim law sources'; the jurisprudential (and apparent social) consensus on
its prohibition and on the rules of *nasab* mean that it is not a legislative model
that has yet been followed elsewhere in the region.

Overview

The laws on child custody continue to be gendered across the region, with Tunisia the only state that has dropped from its statutory law the assumption that the mother is the 'natural custodian' of her children, although not the premise that the father is the 'natural guardian'. The extension of a mother's statutory custody periods across much of the region, combined with the inclusion of the 'best interest' principle, generally provide courts with grounds to forestall malicious custody claims raised by a father or other relatives on the simple expiry of a set age limit. Less immediate are remedies for the socio-economic pressures on divorced women with children, particularly those without adequate accommodation and income whose birth families are unwilling or unable to take them and their children into their home. In addition, the persistence of the 'deadline' of the end of a mother's custody remains a major issue for many divorced women where the laws have not substantially extended these terms, or where there is fear that the courts will draw on gendered assumptions to conclude that the child's best interest will be not served by remaining with the mother. Less than efficient procedures of ensuring a father's maintenance payments for his children and their custodian (including for accommodation) generate specific pressures on divorced women and their families. Naila Hamadah considers that the underlying assumptions of the rules stand against social practice and potentially empower the undeserving:

> in practice, the children of a broken marriage stay with their mothers, but the ruling of man-made Islamic law places a powerful weapon in the hands of the worst of men, the ones who are vindictive towards their ex-wives and negligent toward the welfare of their children.[61]

Commentators see the combination of developments on custody and guardianship as tending to the further statutory recognition and promotion of the family as constituted by the conjugal unit (even if dissolved) away from the extended family, particularly where the laws assign certain functions and obligations of guardianship to the mother. Certain of the laws go some way to addressing the criticism that the basic script presents the mother 'in the same category as a carer, a nurse; the underlying assumption is that the child belongs to the father, its care being only temporarily entrusted to the wife'.[62] Women's rights activists continue to work for the expansion of the mother's authorities as guardian alongside the father, and for more efficient guarantees of social support. However, there are also some suggestions that as in certain aspects of rules on the marital relationship, the laws show a certain asymmetry in the development of the spouses' respective rights and obligations towards their children. Dennerlein (1999: 132) for example notes that as the Algerian reforms in 1984 privileged the ties of the nuclear family at the expense of the extended agnatic family, 'the duties of mothers vis-à-vis their children have thereby been extended, without necessarily granting them more rights'.[63]

For their part, children in many states of the region are explicitly addressed, in terms of their rights, by laws issued following different states' ratifications of the Convention on the Rights of the Child. The 2004 Moroccan law incorporates in the duties of parents responsibilities regarding child health and development which invoke determinedly contemporary interpretations of the entitlements of childhood as included in the traditional parenting responsibilities assigned by Islamic law. In different parts of the region there is considerable civil society and quasi-governmental activity around such issues as education rights, health, environment, development and early marriage. Considerable socio-economic challenges remain, and the lived reality of children in many states of the region, as elsewhere, mean that statutory protection may often be more aspirational than immediately accessible. In addition, children born outside marital relationships that are legally registered or can otherwise be established, absent recognition by their biological father, acquire no legally enforceable rights of care, maintenance or family affiliation in his regard, and are additionally at risk of social stigma, despite injunctions to the contrary, due to the social (as well as legal) value placed on lawful lineage (*nasab*).

11 Concluding Comment

Since the promulgation of the first national codes of Muslim personal status in Arab states in the 1950s,[1] the context and debates on codification and reforms of existing codifications have changed significantly. The changes reflect the different political developments since that time, including the growing influence of 'Islamist' movements since the 1970s, the international context of trans-national civil society networks and funding for domestic women's rights advocacy, and interventions by third-party states under the framework of international human rights and in the current focus on 'democratisation' in the Arab region. Domestically in many states, there has been a growth in the type and range of women's organisations, many of which focus at least in part on family law matters. Several states have also, more recently, established national commissions on women along with national commissions on human rights, and as noted during the course of this study, changes in court structure and procedural regulations are bringing in experts from professional disciplines beyond the law at various stages of the process. Regional patterns can be discerned in the approaches of the Maghreb states (particularly Morocco, Tunisia, Algeria), to a certain extent in parts of the Mashreq (Jordan and Syria) and in the Gulf codifications of Oman, Kuwait, UAE and Qatar. Egypt continues to provide 'model' provisions, if not model legislative instruments, that may be taken up elsewhere. The conduct of judges and other court officials (such as notaries) in the application of the law – and the critical significance of procedural rules – draw increasing attention from activists and academics as well as legislatures and policy-makers.

The considerable legislative activity by Arab states in the third phase of Muslim family law reform in the last quarter of a century, and particularly the promulgation of first-time codifications, new laws or significant amendments since the late 1990s, has been characterised by greater public involvement and galvanization than was the case in the 1950s. Observers and researchers in contemporary developments may focus as much on Muslim personal status law as a site for political involvement of organised Islamist movements and of women's movements as on the substance of the law. For example, Egyptian researcher Essam Fawzy, having analysed the context, content and public reaction to the 2000 law, concludes that 'perhaps more important' than the particular provisions of the law was the fact that 'the new law was a product of battles and balances between dynamic groups in society'. He continues:

> this was the first time that this principle became clear for all to see [...] [T]he widespread understanding, through direct experience, that it is possible to change the law through such pressure, and that the law itself is neither sacrosanct nor impossible to change opens the possibility for women to organize themselves for advocacy towards new gains.[2]

A further characteristic of contemporary debates is the trans-national mobilisation of rights-based groups and networks in reviewing and commenting on legislative developments in Muslim personal status law, a product of the greater prominence and influence of international human rights law and activism as well as the growth of the international women's rights movement. In their turn, such interventions have themselves recently become the subject of academic scrutiny, with a 2006 article by Naz Mordizadeh examining the approach of international human rights organisations (notably Amnesty International and Human Rights Watch) to violations of human rights law arising from implementation of particular provisions of 'shari'a-based' Muslim personal status laws and/or criminal law in different countries.[3] As noted in the introductory section of this study, interventions by women's rights and social rights activists invoke international human rights instruments to which the particular state is party, and the general principles contained therein, while (mostly) situating their advocacy within the broad framework of shar'i values and social justice principles, sometimes supported by more detailed jurisprudential arguments challenging the dominant articulations of fiqh. Advocacy for a 'secular' civil law is rarer, although made in different contexts, whether because of the current domestic social and political contexts, the personal conviction of the advocates for change, or a combination of both. In Lebanon, a draft optional civil code to regulate personal status affairs for those choosing to opt out of Lebanon's complex sectarian regulatory system was the subject of lively debate in the late 1990s

152

before being shelved after the opposition of different religious and political leaders was mobilised against the proponents' argument that such a law would be to the benefit of Lebanon's national unity.[4] In Palestine, a survey in 2000 asked respondents whether they would support the right of individuals to marry under civil law provided that this did not affect the right of others to marry under *shari'a*-based personal status law; fewer women (21%) than men (26%) said that they would, and Palestinian scholar Rema Hammami's observation is that:

> While this is a significant one-quarter of males and one-fifth of females surveyed, the overall impression from the responses is the profound commitment to *shari'a* as the basis for family law by both, but especially by women.[5]

Hammami's investigation, through the survey, was aimed at probing beneath the general (what she calls 'doxic')[6] commitment to *shari'a* to examine the practical and experience-based needs and wants that underlie the broad concept of '*shari'a*' – an investigation that she argues is possible in the Palestinian West Bank and Gaza because of the 'surprisingly innocuous nature of polling' there: for political reasons connected with the 'peace process', 'Palestinians in the West Bank and Gaza have since the 1990s become one of the most polled populations, if not in the world, certainly in the Middle East'.[7] The survey revealed, *inter alia*, a gender gap in the level of satisfaction with the day-to-day operation of the courts, with more female than male respondents dissatisfied,[8] and on a more general question women holding that the courts were more supportive of men's rights than of women – although as Hammami notes, the response probably referred to 'rights' in the context of the codified law.[9] Comparing the results of this survey with earlier polls, Hammami finds a growth in support for the principle of reform of *shari'a*-based Muslim personal status law, suggesting the impact of a major awareness-raising and advocacy campaign coordinated in the intervening years by a women's rights organisation, the Women's Centre for Legal Aid and Counselling. Here, the survey showed that some 20% more women than men wanted more rights to be given to women in family law as and when addressed by a Palestinian legislature.[10] Overall, a substantive majority of both female and male respondents agreed that 'family law should respond to changes and new needs in Palestinian society'.[11] In other words, there is a majority commitment to the *shar'i* postulate, and also a majority perception that *shari'a*-based family law can and should change to accommodate societal developments and needs.

Following up these questions, respondents were asked 'who should reform the law?' Here, there was no overall majority for any of the suggested responses: the most support came for 'the society should vote', followed by *shar'i* judges, then the Palestinian Legislative Council, and then the President. Hammami argues that putting these responses together 'suggests the degree to which democratic and inclusive decision-making is an orthodoxy within Palestinian society' and continues:

> It also attests the degree to which personal status law is viewed as simultaneously of religion and about it, but is also seen as needing to function in relation to society, the state and political institutions. Such dispositions represent an opportunity for the development of a unified Palestinian personal status law through a process which is based on public debate and inclusion rather than one in which the law is marked off as an area for religious specialists with no accountability to members of the society whose lives it will frame.[12]

Unlike certain *shar'i* figures in Bahrain, as discussed in Chapter 2, the Palestinian *shar'i* establishment does not express concern at the prospect of parliamentary control over the promulgation of a Muslim personal status law. The *Qadi al-Qudah* has overseen a prolonged drafting and consultation process which has resulted in the submission of a draft to the legislative body, but there are also other drafts from other quarters. Short of similar public opinion surveys elsewhere, Palestinian public opinion cannot be taken as reflective of broader currents in the region, but certainly the public debate in Bahrain and those in Egypt, Morocco, Algeria and elsewhere indicate that greater participation and more broadly inclusive political processes are regarded by many as legitimate fora for the advocacy and negotiation of the particular content of a 'shari'a-based' Muslim personal status law.

It remains to be noted that, differing and changing conceptions of 'the family' notwithstanding, the heterosexual conjugal unit addressed by the codifications remains in general the only legally-recognised framework for sexual relations, and in many states other sites of sexual activity are criminalized. Proposals for a re-scripting of the legal texts on the Muslim family on points such as these tend to be made on the bases of international norms rather than from within the dominant framework of *shar'i* postulates. On sex and gender, some very contemporary questions immediately invoke traditional rules. It is in the context of inheritance cases, for example, that courts may be called on to consider the implications of gender re-assignment or transsexual surgery. Baudouin Dupret has considered Egyptian inheritance claims in cases where one of the recipients of a fixed proportionate share of inheritance has subsequently undergone transsexual surgery; Skovgaard-Petersen tracks the story of Sally, an Egyptian medical student who underwent surgery and experienced a range of obstacles to re-registering for the medical degree as a female, with cases in the administrative courts and a *fatwa* from the Mufti seeking to evaluate the circumstances in which such surgery is 'lawful'.[13]

More generally, however, as already noted, the invocation of *shari'a* by state legislatures in relation to Muslim family law is contested within a political context by actors both opposing and proposing particular representations of *shari'a* in the codes, in a 'relationship with the norm' that may seem to fit Dupret's description as 'highly strategic in nature'.[14] The use of the term 'strategic' here invokes the selection of particular norms and the timing of their invocation rather than a questioning of the unknowable commitment to those norms by individual actors. On different sides of these debates, there is criticism of the state rhetoric that purposefully obscures the political authority and choices central to the formulation of the codes and the regulation of the family and the position of women within it. These choices are highly significant in the options and remedies available to women within the family and at court, and despite reservations about the limits of state law, there seems every prospect that women's rights activists (and other constituencies) will continue to invest considerable effort in law-focussed advocacy. It is a sign of the changed times in which the third phase of Muslim family law reform in Arab states is taking place that this advocacy is as much the subject of academic consideration as the substance of the laws themselves.

List of Statutes Cited[1]

Algeria
- Law no.84-11 of 9 June 1984 containing the Law of the Family
- Ordinance no. 05-02 of 27 February 2005 amending and completing Law no.84-11 on the Law of the Family

Egypt
- Law no.25 of 1920 concerning maintenance and certain provisions of personal status, *Official Gazette* no.61 of 15 July 1920
- Law no.25 of 1929 on certain provisions of personal status, *Official Gazette* no.27 of 25 March 1929
- Law no.44 of 1979 amending certain provisions of personal status, *Official Gazette* 21 June 1979
- Law no.100 of 1985 amending certain provisions of personal status, *Official Gazette* no.27 of 3 July 1985
- Law no.1/2000 regulating certain litigation procedures in personal status, *Official Gazette* no.4 of 22 January 2000.
- Law no.10 of 2004 establishing Family Courts, *Official Gazette* no.12 Judicial Year 47, 18 March 2004.

Iraq
- Law no.188/1959, Law of Personal Status, *Official Gazette* no.280 of 30 December 1959.
- Law no.11 1963 (first amendment to the law of personal status) *Official Gazette* 785 of 31 March 1963
- Law no.21/1978 (second amendment to the law of personal status) *Official Gazette* 2639 of 20 February 1978
- Law no. 57/1980 (fourth amendment to the law of personal status) *Official Gazette* 2766 of 31 March 1980
- Law no.189/1980 (sixth amendment to the law of personal status) *Official Gazette* no.2804 of 24 November 1980
- Law no. 125/1981 *Official Gazette* 2863 of 21 December 1981
- Law no. 77 of 1983 regarding the right of the divorced wife to accommodation *Official Gazette* 2952 of 8 August 1983 p.589, as amended by law no. 27/1988 *Official Gazette* no.3190 of 22 February 1988 p.170.
- Revolutionary Command Resolution 1357/1984 (9 December 1984)

- Law no.51/1985 (ninth amendment to the law of personal status) *Official Gazette* 3052 of 1 July 1985
- Law no.5/1986 (tenth amendment to the law of personal status) 188/1959 *Official Gazette* 3081 of 20 January 1986 p.35
- Law no. 65/1986 (eleventh amendment to the law of personal status) 188/1959 *Official Gazette* 3105 of 7 July 1986 p.415
- Revolutionary Command Council decision no. 1708 *Official Gazette* 2865 of 4 January 1982
- Revolutionary Command Council decision no.147 *Official Gazette* 2870 of 8 February 1982.
- Revolutionary Command Council decision 1529 of 1985, *Official Gazette* 3881 of 20 January 1986 p.36
- Law no.90/1987 (twelfth amendment to the law of personal status)amending the Law of Personal Status *Official Gazette* 3167 of 14 September 1987 p.582
- Law 106/1987 (thirteenth amendment to the law of personal status) *Official Gazette* 3176 16 November 1987 p.830
- Revolutionary Command Council Resolution no.127/1999 of 24 July 1999
- Law no.19/1999 (sixteenth amendment to the law of personal status)
- Law no.22/1999 (seventeenth amendment to the law of personal status)

Jordan
- Law no 92 of 1951, Law of Family Rights, *Official Gazette* no. 1081 of 16 August 1951
- Law no.61 of 1976, Law of Personal Status, *Official Gazette* no.2668 of 1 December 1976.
- Temporary Law no.82/2001 amending the Law of Personal Status, *Official Gazette* no.4524 of 31 December 2001, 5998.
- Directive (ta'limat) of the *Qadi al-Qudah* in accordance with Article 2 of Temporary Law no.82/2001, *Official Gazette* no.4530 of 30 January 2002

Kuwait
- Law no 51/1984 as amended by law no.29/2004.

Libya
- Law no.177/1972 on the Protection of Certain Rights of Women in Marriage and Divorce for Injury and Khul', *Official Gazette* no.61 of 23 December 1972.
- Law no.18/1973 OG 15 16 April 1973 amending law 177/1972
- Law no.10/1984 Regarding Marriage and Divorce and the Effects thereof, *Official Gazette* no.16 of 3 June 1984, 640.
- Law no.175 of 7 December 1972 (on the prohibition of artificial insemination)

Mauritania
- Code of Personal Status 2001 (text in *Horizons* newspaper no.3020, 9 August 2001)

Morocco

- Ordinance no.1-57-343 of 22 November 1957 implementing books I and II of the law of personal status, *Official Gazette* no.13-2354 of 6 December 1957, 2632.
- Ordinance implementing law no. 1-93-347 of 10 September 1993, *Official Gazette* no.12-4222 of 29 September 1993, 1833.
- Law no.70-03 on the Family Code, Ordinance no. 1.04.22 of 3 February 2004, *Official Gazette* no.5184 of 5 February 2004 417.
- Joint Decision of the Minister of Justice and the Minister of Health no.347-04 of 2 March 2004 on the pre-nuptial medical certificate, *Official Gazette* no.5192 of 4 March 2004.

Oman

- Sultanic Ordinance no.32/1997 on the promulgation of the Law of Personal Status, *Official Gazette* no.601 of 15 June 1997.

Qatar

- Regulation of *Shar'i* Procedure issued by the *Shari'a* Courts Presidency, no.106 of 5 September 1997
- Amiri Decree no.22 regarding the Law of the Family, 29 June 2006, *Official Gazette* no.8 of 28 August 2006.[2]

Palestine

- Decision of the *Qadi al-Qudah* no.78/1995 of 25 December 1995 regarding the minimum age of marriage in the Gaza Strip *shari'a* courts
- *Qadi al-Qudah*'s Administrative Directive no. 15/1366 of 12 September 1999 regarding the division of estates (inheritance portions)
- *Qadi al-Qudah*'s Administrative Directive no.15/481 of 15 April 2000 regarding marriage registration procedures
- *Qadi al-Qudah*'s Administrative Directive no.15/711 of 11 May 2000 regarding medical tests before marriage
- *Qadi al-Qudah*'s Administrative Directive no. 15/1358 of 11 November 2000 regarding deeds of the acknowledgement of marriage
- Law of the Maintenance Fund, no. 6 of 2005 (26 May 2005) *Official Gazette* no.55, June 2005.
- Draft Law of Personal Status 2005

Somalia

- Law of Personal Status no.23 of 11 January 1975, *Official Gazette* no.1, appendix 3 of 8 March 1975

Sudan

- Law of Personal Status for Muslims, law no.42/1991, *Official Gazette* no.1554 of 25 July 1991

Syria

- Law of Personal Status law no.95/1953, Official Gazette no.63 of 8 October 1953, 4783; as amended by:
- Law no.34/1975 (31 December 1975), Official Gazette no.3, 21 January 1976, 111; and Law no.18/2003.

Tunisia

- Order no.13/1956 on the promulgation of the Code of Personal Status, *Official Gazette* no.66 of 17 August 1956.
- Law no.27/1958 of 4 March 1958 on Public Guardianship, *Kafala* and Adoption, *Official Gazette* no.19 of 7 March 1958.
- Law no. 1/1964 of 21 February 1964 approving decree no.1/1964 of 20 February 1964
- Law no.46/1964 regarding pre-nuptial medical certificates, *Official Gazette* of 3 November 1964 p.1483.
- Law no.7/1981 of 18 February 1981 amending certain provisions of the code of personal status
- Law no.74/1993 of 12 July 1993 amending certain provisions of the code of personal status

United Arab Emirates

- Federal Law no.28 of 2005 on Personal Status of 19 November 2005, *Official Gazette* no.439 (35th year) November 2005
- Law no.21 of 1997 on the Limitation of Dower in the Marriage Contract and its expenses
- Law no.12 of 1973 on the Limitation of Dower in the Marriage Contract, *Official Gazette* no.12 of 3 August 1973

Yemen

- PDRY Law of the Family, law no.1/1974 *Official Gazette* no.9 of 28 February 1974
- PDRY Ministerial decision no.98/1974 for the purposes of articles 11, 29 and 30 of the law of the Family, *Official Gazette* no.51 of 19/12/74
- PDRY Ministerial Decision no.35/1975 regarding marriage during the *'idda* of revocable *talaq* no.35 of 1975, *Official Gazette* no.19 10 May 1975
- YAR Facilitation of Marriage Law 1976 law
- YAR Law no.3/1978 law of the Family, 8 January 1978.
- Law no.20/1992 regarding Personal Status, *Official Gazette* 6.3 of 31 March 1992
- Law no.27/1998 amending certain provisions of the law of personal status no.20/1992, *Official Gazette* no.22 of 30 November 1998
- Law no.24/1999 amending certain provisions of the law of personal status no.20/1992, *Official Gazette* no.7 of 15 April 1999

Selected Statutory Provisions

1. Marriage Guardianship and Capacity[1]

Algeria 1984 as amended 2005[2]

Article 7: Capacity for marriage is valid at nineteen years for the man and the woman. However, the judge can permit a marriage before this by reason of a benefit or a necessity, if it is established that the two parties are fit for marriage.

Article 11: The major woman concludes her own contract of marriage in the presence of her *wali* who is her father or a relative or any other person of her choice. Without prejudice to the above article 7, the marriage of the minor is contracted by the *wali* or then by a relative. The judge is the guardian for the person who has none.

Article 13: It is forbidden for the *wali*, whether he be the father or someone else, to compel in marriage the minor person under his guardianship just as he cannot marry this person without their consent.

Egypt 2000

Article 17: Claims arising from a contract of marriage shall not be heard if the wife is aged less than sixteen years (solar) or the husband under years (solar) at the time the claim is raised.

In the event of denial, claims arising from a contract of marriage (in cases following 1st August 1931) shall not be heard unless the marriage is established by official document. Nevertheless, claims for judicial divorce or dissolution, according to circumstance, shall be heard [by the court] to the exclusion of other [claims] if the marriage is established by any written document.

Iraq 1959 as amended 1978 and 1987

Article 7 (1): Conditions of capacity for marriage are being of sound mind and having completed eighteen years.

Article 8 (1): If a person who has not completed his fifteenth year wishes to get married, the *qadi* may permit him to do so if he establishes his capacity and physical ability, after the approval of his *shar'i* guardian. If the guardian refuses, then the *qadi* shall ask him to give his permission within a set period of time, and he if he does not object or his objection is misplaced, then the *qadi* shall permit the person's marriage.

Article 8 (2):[3] The *qadi* may permit the marriage of a person who has reached his fifteenth year if there is a pressing necessity requiring this. The granting of permission for this is conditional on the party having reached *shar'i* puberty and having the physical capacity.

Article 9 (1): Nobody, whether a relative or anyone else, is allowed to coerce any person, male or female, into marriage without their consent; a contract of marriage by coercion is voided provided consummation has not occurred. Nor may any relative or other person prevent someone of capacity from getting married, in accordance with the terms of this law.

Article 40: Either spouse may seek judicial divorce if (4) the marriage took place outside court by way of coercion and has been consummated.

Jordan 1976 as amended 2001

Article 5: Capacity for marriage requires that the fiancé and the fiancée are sane and have both completed their eighteenth year by the solar calendar. The *qadi* may permit the marriage of a person below this age if the person has completed their fifteenth year and such a marriage holds a benefit on grounds to be specified in directives/guidelines to be issued by the *Qadi al-Qudah*.

Article 13: The consent of the guardian is not a condition in the marriage of a previously married woman who is of sound mind and over eighteen years of age.

Directive of the *Qadi al-Qudah* 2002: the judge may permit marriage under the age of full capacity on the following conditions:

- that the fiancé is the 'equal'[4] of the fiancée in the sense of being able to pay her maintenance and prompt dower;
- that the marriage prevents an existing cause of corruption or avoids the loss of an established benefit;
- that the *qadi* ascertains the fiancée's consent and choice and that the marriage is in her interest; and that the benefit of marriage is established by medical report if one of the couple is insane or mentally incompetent;
- that the contract is concluded with the consent of the guardian in accordance with articles 6 and 12 of the JLPS: and
- that a record be drawn up setting out the *qadi*'s inquiry into the said bases relied upon to permit the marriage, and on the basis of this record a deed of permission for the marriage shall be drawn up in accordance with proper procedure.

Kuwait 1984

Article 29:

a) The guardian in the marriage of a virgin who is between the age of puberty and twenty-five years is a male agnate according to the order of succession, and if no agnate exists, guardianship transfers to the judge. This provision applies to an insane or feeble-minded person, whether male or female.

b) It is stipulated that the guardian and the person who is the subject of the guardianship be in agreement.

Article 30: A woman who has been previously married or who has attained twenty-five years of age has freedom of choice in her marriage. She shall not however make her own contract: this shall be done by her guardian. (Amended in 2004 to allow an exception for a previously married woman to ask the judge to conclude her re-marriage to her former husband).

Article 31: If the guardian prevents the marriage, she is entitled to bring the matter before a judge for him to order or not to order marriage. The same applies if there is more than one guardian and they are of equal status, whether they jointly prevent her marriage or they disagree.

Libya 1984

Article 6:

a) The requirements of capacity for marriage are reason and puberty.

b) Capacity for marriage is achieved at reaching the age of twenty.

c) The court may permit marriage before this age is reached for an interest or necessity that it shall evaluate, after the consent of the guardian.

Article 8:

a) The guardian is not allowed to force the young man or woman into marriage against their will

b) Similarly, the guardian is not allowed to prevent his female ward from marrying the person she wishes to be her husband.

Article 9: Validity of the contract of marriage requires the consensus of views of the guardian and the ward. If the entitled guardian prevents the ward from marrying the person the ward wishes to marry, the ward may take the matter to court to permit the marriage if the court finds this appropriate.

Mauritania 2001

Article 9: Guardianship is exercised in the interest of the woman. The woman of legal majority may not be married without her own consent and the presence of her guardian. The silence of the 'young girl'⁵ constitutes consent.

Article 10: The guardian must be male, sane, of legal majority, and Muslim if the woman is Muslim.

Article 12: The guardian may mandate another person to conclude the marriage in his place. A woman who is the *wasi* or *kafil* must delegate a man to carry out this task in her place. In both cases the person mandated shall fulfil the conditions in article 10 above.

Morocco 2004[6]

Article 19: Capacity for marriage is completed for the young man and woman with the capacity of reason at eighteen years by the solar calendar.

Article 20: The family judge charged with concluding marriages may permit the marriage of a young man and woman below the age of capacity stipulated in article 19 in a reasoned report setting out the benefit and the reasons justifying such a marriage, after hearing the parents of the minor or his[/her] *shar'i* representative (*na'ib shar'i*) and making use of medical expertise or a social investigation. The report responding to an application for the marriage of a minor is not open to appeal.

Article 21: The marriage of a minor is suspended on the consent of his[/her] *shar'i* representative. This is given by the latter's signature with the minor on the application for permission for marriage, and his presence at the conclusion of the contract. If the *shar'i* representative refuses to give consent, the family judge charged with the marriage shall decide the matter.

Article 24: Guardianship is the right of the woman; the woman of legal majority exercises it according to her choice and her interest.

Article 25: The woman of legal majority may contract her marriage herself, or delegate this to her father or one of her relatives.

Oman 1997

Article 10:

a) If a person who has not completed their eighteenth year seeks to marry and his [/her] guardian refuses to marry him, then he may take the matter to the judge.

b) The judge shall set a time limit during which the guardian shall come to give his statement, and if he does not come or his objection is misplaced then the *qadi* shall marry the person.

c) Bearing in mind the terms of paragraph (b) of this article, a person who has not completed his eighteenth year may be married only with the permission of the judge and after the investigation of the interest [to be served by the marriage].

Article 12: If the closer guardian is absent or of unknown whereabouts and cannot be contacted or vetos [the marriage], then guardianship is transferred to the next [guardian] in line with the permission of the *qadi*.

Article 19: The woman's guardian undertakes her contract of marriage with her consent.

Qatar 2006

Article 28: The woman's guardian carries out her marriage contract with her consent.

Article 29: Marriage is concluded with the permission of the *qadi* by the guardianship of the more distant guardian in the following two cases:

1) If the closer guardian obstructs the woman, or there are a number of guardians in the same level of relationship, and they all veto or they differ.

2) If the closer guardian is absent, and the judge considers that waiting for his opinion will result in the loss of a benefit in the marriage.

Sudan 1991

Article 34: 1) The guardian shall marry the female who has reached puberty, with her permission and agreement to the husband and the dower; her word is accepted regarding having reached puberty, unless appearance belies it.

2) The acceptance of the major *bikr* (virgin) is binding, explicitly or implicitly, if her guardian contracts her in marriage without her permission and then informs her of the contract.

Article 36: If the guardian stops maintaining his female ward for a whole year, without excuse, while being lawfully obliged to do it, his guardianship over her lapses.

Article 37: 1) If the guardian refuses to marry his ward then she may ask the judge to marry her,

2) The judge may permit the marriage of the woman who petitions him if he finds it established that her guardian is refusing to marry her without *shar'i* justification.

Article 40: 1) The marriage of the insane person, the mentally incompetent person, or the discriminating [minor] shall be contracted only by the guardian, after the appearance of a prevailing benefit.

2) The age of discrimination is reached at the age of ten.

3) The guardian of a discriminating [minor] female shall not contract her in marriage except with the permission of the *qadi*, for a prevailing benefit, on the condition of the husband's *kafa'a* and a proper dower.

Syria 1953 (1975)

Article 15: 1) Capacity for marriage requires reason and puberty.

Article 16: The male reaches capacity for marriage with the completion of his eighteenth year, and the female with the completion of her seventeenth year.

Article 18: If the male adolescent claims [to have reached] puberty after completing his fifteenth year or the female her thirteenth, and they petition to be married, the *qadi* shall permit it if the truth of their claim and their bodily capacity are apparent to him.

Article 19: If the engaged couple are not suited in age, and there is no interest [to be realised] through this marriage, the *qadi* is allowed to not permit it.

Article 20: If a mature girl who has attained seventeen years wishes to be married, the judge shall ask her guardian to express his opinion within a time limit which he shall stipulate, and if he does not object or if his objection is not worthy of consideration, the judge shall give permission for her marriage on condition of equality of social status.

Tunisia 1956 as amended 1964 and 1993

Article 5: Both spouses shall be free of *shari* impediments and in addition anyone who has not reached the age of twenty for men and seventeen for women shall not be allowed to conclude a contract of marriage. The conclusion of a contract of marriage below the set age requires special permission from the judge. This permission shall be given only for grave reasons and in the interests of a clear benefit to the spouses.

Article 6: The marriage of a minor requires the agreement of the guardian and the mother. If the guardian or the mother refuses to agree, and the minor insists on his/her desire [to be married], the matter shall be raised with the judge. Permission to marry may not be appealed in any manner.

Article 9: The husband and the wife may undertake their own marriage or may appoint whom they like [as a *wakil*]. The guardian likewise has the right to appoint a *wakil*.

UAE 2005

Article 39: The guardian of the woman who has reached puberty shall conclude her contract of marriage with her consent, and the notary shall have her sign the contract. A contract without a guardian is voided, and if consummation has occurred, the couple are divorced, and paternity of the child is established.

Yemen 1992 as amended 1998 and 1999

Article 7: Conditions for the validity of marriage are: 2) the offer of what customarily means marriage is made by the guardian of the female being contracted [...]

Article 15: The contract concluded for a minor female by her guardian is valid. The person to whom she is contracted in marriage may not consummate the marriage, nor does she move to live with him, until after she is ready for intercourse, even if she is over fifteen years old. The contract of a minor male is valid only if his interest [in this marriage] is established.

Article 18 (2): If the woman's guardian is vetoing [her marriage], the *qadi* shall order him to marry her, and if he refuses, the *qadi* shall order the next closest guardian in line and then the next after him to marry her, and if there are no other guardians or they all refuse to marry her, then the *qadi* shall marry her to an equal for a proper dower.

Article 30: Every marriage that fulfils the pillars and conditions set out above is valid even if not followed by consummation, and all the effects of marriage stipulated in this law arise from the time of its conclusion, so long as it is not suspended. A suspended marriage is one that is suspended for the consent of the person who holds the consent [...] as for the contract concluded for the minor and the insane, the effects of this contract arise from the time of contract and they may dissolve it upon [the minor] reaching puberty and [the insane person] recovering.

2. Polygyny[7]

Algeria 1984 as amended 2005[8]

Article 8: It is permitted to contract marriage with more than one wife within the limits of the *shari'a* if there is justified motivation and the conditions and intention of equitable treatment. The husband shall inform the existing wife and the future wife, and shall present a request for authorisation of the marriage to the head of the court in the jurisdiction of the marital home. The president of the court may authorise the new marriage if he establishes their consent and finds that the husband has proven the justified reason and his ability to provide equitable treatment and the necessary conditions for conjugal life.

Article 8 *bis* In case of deception, each wife may lay an action for divorce against the husband.

Article 8 *bis* (1) The new marriage is dissolved before consummation if the husband has not obtained the judge's authorisation as per the conditions in article 8 above.

Egypt 1929 as amended 1985

Article 11 *bis*: The husband shall confirm his social status in the marriage document, and if he is [already] married, he shall set out in the statement the name of the wife or wives to whom he is already married and their places of residence. The notary shall notify existing wives of the new marriage by registered letter with recorded delivery.

A wife whose husband takes a second wife may petition for divorce from him if she is affected by some material or mental harm of a kind which would make it impossible for a couple such as they to continue living together, even if she has not stipulated in the contract that he will not marry another woman while married to her.

If the judge is unable to reconcile them, he shall rule for a final *talaq*. The wife's right to petition for divorce on these grounds lapses upon the expiry of one year after the date of her knowledge of the other marriage, unless she has agreed to it explicitly or implicitly. Her right to petition for divorce shall be renewed whenever he marries another woman.

If the new wife was not aware that [her husband] was [already] married and it subsequently transpires that he is, she likewise has the right to petition for divorce.

Iraq 1959 as amended 1980

Article 3 (4): Marriage to more than one woman shall not be permitted except with the permission of a judge. For such permission to be given, the following two conditions must be fulfilled:

a) the husband must have the financial ability to support more than one wife

167

b) there must be some lawful benefit.

(5) If a lack of equity between the wives is feared, polygyny shall not be permitted; the assessment of this shall be left to the judge.

(6) Any man who makes a marriage contract with more than one woman in breach of the provisions of paragraphs 4 and 5 shall be punished by a prison sentence which shall not exceed one year or by a fine not exceeding one hundred dinars or both.

(7) The terms of article 3(4) shall not apply where the women intended in marriage is a widow.[9]

Jordan 1976 as amended 2001

Article 40: A man who has more than one wife shall be obliged to treat them equally and equitably, and he shall not be entitled to accommodate them in a single dwelling except with their consent.

Article 6 *bis* a)[10] Before carrying out the contract for a polygynous marriage, the *qadi* shall ascertain the following:

1) the husband's financial ability to pay the dower and maintenance; and

2) that the second wife is informed that the husband is (already) married

b) The court shall notify the first wife of the polygynous contract after it has been concluded.

Mauritania 2001

Article 45: It is permitted to contract marriage with more than one wife if the conditions and intention of equity are met and after prior notification of the former and the future wife having stipulated monogamy.

Morocco 2004[11]

Article 40: Polygyny is prohibited if there is fear of lack of justice between the wives, and likewise prohibited if there is a stipulation from the wife against her husband marrying another wife [while married to her].

Article 41: The court shall not permit polygyny:

– If the exceptional objective justification is not proven to it;

– If the man seeking [permission] does not have sufficient resources to provide for two families and guarantee all rights of maintenance, accommodation and equality in all aspects of life.

Article 42: If there is no stipulation prohibiting polygyny, the person wishing [to undertake a polygynous marriage] shall seek permission from the court. The application shall include an explanation of the exceptional reasons justifying it, and shall attach a report of his material situation.

Article 43: The court shall summon to appear the wife of the man who wishes to undertake a polygynous union. If she is notified in person and does not appear, or refuses to accept the summons, the court shall send a court usher with a written notice informing her that if she does not attend the session on the date specified in the notice then the husband's application shall be considered in her absence. The application can also be considered in the absence of the woman whose husband wishes to marry another wife if the Public Prosecutor is unable' to reach a locality or residence from where she may be summoned. If the reason that it is not possible to reach the wife to summon her to appear arises from the husband providing, with ill intention, an incorrect address or alteration in the wife's name, the husband shall be liable to the penalty specified in section 361 of the Criminal Code, this on application of the injured wife.

Article 44: The discussion shall take place in the consulting room in the presence of the two parties, and they shall be heard in a situation of mediation and reconciliation, after examinations of the facts and presentation of the required statements. The court may permit polygyny in an argued report not open to any appeal if it finds an exceptional objective justification to be established, and if the legal conditions are met, while constraining it with conditions to the benefit of the existing wife and their children.

Article 45: If during the discussions it is established to the court that the marital relationship cannot continue, and the wife whose husband desires a polygynous union insists on seeking divorce, the court shall specify an amount to cover payment of all the rights of the wife and children.

The husband shall deposit the set sum within a deadline of not more than seven days. The court shall issue a ruling for judicial divorce (*tatliq*) when the deposit is made, and this ruling shall not be open to any appeal in so far as it ends the marital relationship.

Failure to deposit the said amount within the set deadline shall be considered a withdrawal of the application for permission to undertake a polygynous union. If the husband insists on seeking permission for polygyny, and the existing wife does not agree, but does not seek divorce, the court shall automatically apply the framework of discord (*shiqaq*) set out in articles 94-97 hereunder.

Article 46: In the event that permission for polygyny is granted, the contract shall not be concluded with the woman until after she has been notified by the *qadi* that the man who wishes to marry her is married to another, and after she has consented to that.

Qatar 2006

Article 14: Capacity for marriage requires rational capacity and puberty.

In the event of marriage to another woman, the documenter shall ascertain that the wife has knowledge of the husband's financial circumstances if the husband's situation suggests that financial ability is not in place. The documenter may not refuse to document the contract if both parties wish to conclude it. In all cases the wife or wives shall be informed of this marriage after it has been documented.

Syria 1953 as amended 1975

Article 17: A judge may refuse permission for a man who is already married to take another wife unless he has a lawful justification and is capable of providing maintenance for both.

Tunisia 1956 as amended 1958, 1964[12]

Article 18: 1) Polygyny is prohibited.

2) Any man who marries while he is already married before the bond of his previous marriage is dissolved shall be punished by one year in jail and by a fine in the amount of 240,000 francs or by one of the two penalties. This shall apply even if the new marriage is not contracted in accordance with the provisions of the law.

Article 21: An irregular marriage is one that is accompanied by a condition contradicting the essence of the contract, or is concluded regardless of the terms of [...] article 18 of this law... If criminal proceedings arise in application of article 8 of this law, then the crime and the irregularity of the marriage shall be ruled on in one judgement.

Spouses who continue to live together despite the declaration as to the irregularity of their marriage shall be liable to six months' imprisonment.[...]

Yemen 1992 as amended 1998:[13]

Article 12: A man is allowed up to four wives provided the following is realised:

1. that he has the ability to be equitable and if not, then one;
2. that the husband has the capacity to provide [for the wife];
3. that the woman is notified that the man is married to another woman.

3. The Marital Relationship[14]

Algeria 1984 as amended 2005

Article 36: the obligations of the two spouses are as follows:

1. to safeguard conjugal ties and the duties of their life together
2. cohabitation in harmony and mutual respect and in kindness
3. jointly contribute to protecting the interests of the family, and to the protection and sound education of the children
4. joint effort in managing family matters and in spacing births
5. respecting their respective parents and relatives and visiting them
6. preserving the bonds of family and good relationships with parents and kinsmen
7. Each spouse has the right to visit and to have visit their parents and relatives according to convention.[15]

Article 37: Each spouse retains their own property. At the same time, the two spouses may, in the marriage deed or by another authentic deed, agree upon the community of goods acquired during the marriage and determine the proportions returning to each of them.

Article 78: The husband shall provide maintenance for his wife, in accordance with the provisions of articles 78, 79 and 80 of this law, from the date of the consummation of the marriage or if she is in need thereof, on the basis of evidence.[16]

Egypt 1920 as amended 1985

Article 1: The husband is obliged to maintain the wife from the date of the valid contract if she delivers herself to him, even if only legally,[17] and even if she is wealthy or is of a different religion to him.

The wife's illness does not prevent her entitlement to maintenance.

Maintenance comprises food, clothing, accommodation, the cost of [medical] treatment and other matters required in law.

Maintenance is not an obligation for the wife if she becomes an apostate, or voluntarily declines to submit herself to her husband without right, or is forced to do this by some reason not from the husband's part, or if she goes out without the permission of her husband.

The wife's maintenance shall not be held to lapse by reason of her going out of the marital home without the consent of her husband in such circumstances as are generally endorsed, whether by legal text or in custom or by reason of necessity, nor her going out to legitimate work, provided that it does not transpire that she is abusing this right, or that her exercise thereof is contrary to family interests and her husband has asked her to refrain from it.

Law no. 25/1929 as amended 1985:

Article 11 bis 2: If the wife refuses to obey her husband without right, marital maintenance ceases from the date of her refusal.

Her refusal shall be considered to be without right if she does not return to the marital home after the husband has called upon her to return by a notification via the notary [delivered] to her person or to a person delegating for her. The husband must identify the [marital] home in this notification.

The wife is entitled to object to this before the first instance court within thirty days from the date of the notification. She shall set out in the text of her objection the shar'i reasons on which she is relying in her refusal to obey him. Failing this her objection shall be ruled not acceptable.

The cessation of her maintenance is calculated from the date of the end of the objection period if she does not object [within this period].

When considering the objection, or based on a petition from one of the spouses, the court shall intervene to end the dispute between them by reconciliation, with the continuation of the marriage and harmonious cohabitation. But if it becomes clear that the dispute is chronic and the wife petitions for judicial divorce, then the court shall take the arbitration measures set out in articles 7 to 11 of this Law.

Iraq 1959 as amended 1980

Article 25

1. The wife is not due maintenance in the following situations:
a. if she leaves her husband's home without permission and without *shar'i* reason
b. if she is imprisoned for a crime or a debt
c. if she refuses to travel with her husband without *shar'i* reason.
2.[18] The wife shall not be bound to obey her husband, and shall not be considered disobedient (*nashiz*), if the husband is arbitrary in his demand for obedience, intending to injure or oppress her. In particular, the following shall be considered by way of injury or oppression:
a. the husband failing to prepare for his wife a *shar'i* home that is appropriate to the two spouses' social and economic status
b. if the *shar'i* home that is prepared is far from the wife's place of work such as to make it impossible for her to reconcile her domestic and employment commitments
c. if the furnishings prepared for the *shar'i* home do not belong to the husband
d. if the wife is suffering an illness that prevents her obeying her husband.
3. The court shall give long consideration in issuing a ruling for the disobedience of the wife, in order to understand the reasons for her refusal to obey her husband.
4. The court shall rule on the wife's *nushuz* [only] after having expended its utmost efforts in removing the causes that prevent her obedience.
5. *Nushuz* is considered a reason for judicial divorce, in the following manner [...]
Article 33: The wife's obedience is not due the husband in any matter contradicting the rulings of the *shari'a*, and the judge can award her maintenance.

Jordanian Law of Personal Status 1976 as amended 2001:

Article 37: After receiving the immediate portion of the dower, the wife shall obey her husband and live in his lawful home and shall move with him to any place the husband wishes, even if this is outside the Kingdom, provided that it is a safe place for her and that there is no condition in the [marriage] contract requiring otherwise. If she withholds obedience, her right to maintenance shall be forfeit.
Article 39: The husband shall be obliged to make conjugal life with his wife agreeable and to treat her in a proper manner, and the wife shall obey her husband in matters which are lawful.
Article 67: Maintenance to the wife shall be incumbent upon the husband from the time of the valid contract, even where there is a difference of religion, and even if she is living in her family's house, unless he asks her to move and she refuses

without lawful right. She shall have the right to refuse if the husband has not paid the prompt dower or if he has not prepared a lawful home for her.

Article 68:[19] A wife who works outside the home shall be entitled to maintenance on two conditions: a) that her work is legitimate; and b) that her husband consents to the work, explicitly or implicitly; he may go back on his consent only for a legitimate reason and without thereby causing harm to the wife.

Article 69: If the wife is disobedient, she shall not be entitled to maintenance. A 'disobedient' wife is one who leaves the matrimonial home without lawful justification or who refuses to allow the husband to enter her house prior to his asking her to move to another house. Lawful justification for her leaving the home shall include harm caused to her by the husband through beating or by ill-treatment.

Kuwaiti Personal Status Law 1984

Article 87: a) If the wife refuses to move to the matrimonial home without justification or prevents the husband from cohabiting with her in her home, provided that he has not prevented her moving (to the marital home), her right to maintenance shall be forfeit for the duration of her refusal which is established by the court.

b) A wife's violation of her marital duties shall not be established except by her refusal to abide by a final judgment for her to show compliance.

c) Her refusal shall be justified if the husband is not faithful to her, if he does not pay the prompt dower, or does not provide a lawful dwelling, or if he does not provide maintenance and it is not possible to implement a ruling for maintenance because he has no apparent funds.

Article 88: It shall not be permissible for a judgment for obedience to be imposed on the wife by force.

Article 89: It shall not be considered to be a violation of matrimonial duties for a wife to go out for any lawful purpose, nor for any permitted work, provided her work does not conflict with the interests of the family.

Article 90: A wife shall move with her husband, unless the court finds that there is benefit in her not moving.

Libya 1984

Article 17: The wife is entitled [to the following] from her husband:

a) maintenance and its effects within the limits of the capacity of the husband and his ability, according to the provisions of this law;

b) not usurping her private property; she may dispose of it as she wishes;

c) not causing her physical or mental injury;

Article 18: The husband is entitled [to the following] from his wife:

a) maintenance and its effects where the husband is needy and the wife is wealthy, in accordance with the provisions of this law;

b) concern for the husband's repose and his emotional and mental stability;

c) supervising the conjugal home, organising its affairs and looking after it;

d) custody of her children from him and looking after them, and breastfeeding them if there is no obstacle health-wise.

Article 23: The wife's maintenance is obligatory on the husband with means from the date of the valid contract. The wife with means shall be obliged to maintain her husband and her children from him for the period of his incapacity. Maintenance shall be assessed according to the financial position of the person bound to provide it at the time of it being imposed.

Article 73:

b) Rulings of *nushuz* issued before this law are abrogated, and are considered as if they never were.

Mauritania 2001

Article 55: A valid marriage gives rise to all its effects and establishes the following rights and duties:

1. maintenance and accommodation
2. preservation of honour, the duty of faithfulness, help and assistance.

Article 56: The husband is the head of the family. He exercises this function in the interest of the family. The wife gives her help to the husband in the management of the family.

Article 57: The wife may, subject to the prescriptions of the *shari'a*, exercise any profession outside the conjugal home.

Article 58: The wife disposes freely of her personal property. The husband may supervise her management only in the matter of a gift taking up more than a third of her property.

Article 150: The wife's right to a ruling for maintenance ceases (3) by *nushuz*.

Morocco 2004

Article 51:[20] Mutual rights and duties of the spouses:

1. *shar'i* cohabitation with the consequent requirements of conjugal relations, justice and equality in the case of polygyny, the fidelity and integrity of each to the other with virtue and the preservation of honour and looking after their offspring;
2. good conjugal relations, mutual respect, affection and concern, and looking after the interest of the family;
3. the wife bears with her husband the responsibility of managing and looking after the affairs of the house and the children;
4. consultation in the taking of decisions in regard to the management of the affairs of the family and the children and family planning;
5. respect and good treatment by each of the other's parents and *mahrams*, visiting them and having them to visit as is customary
6. mutual inheritance rights.

Article 52: If one of the spouses persists in violating the duties set out in the previous article, the other party may petition for implementation of what is due, or have recourse to the dispute framework set out in articles 94-97 below.

Article 53: If one of the spouses puts the other out of the marital home without justification, the Public Prosecutor shall intervene in order to promptly restore the wronged spouse to the marital home, taking the [necessary] measures to guarantee [his or her] safety and protection.

Article 49: Each spouse has an estate separate from the other. However, the spouses may, in the framework of management of property acquired during the marriage, agree on its investment and distribution. Such agreement shall be in a written document separate from the marriage contract. The notaries shall inform the spouses of this option at the time of their marriage. In the absence of any such agreement, general rules of evidence shall be applied with regard to the work of each spouse, the efforts they have put in and the burdens they have carried in order to develop the property of the family.

Oman 1997

Article 36: The spouses' mutual rights and responsibilities are:
1. lawful sexual enjoyment of each spouse with the other such as is permitted by the *shariʿa;*
2. the fidelity of each to the other;
3. *sharʿi* cohabitation;
4. good treatment, mutual respect and affection, and preserving the family interest;
5. caring for children and bringing them up in such a manner as ensures their sound development;
6. the respect of each of them for the parents and close relatives of the other.

Article 37: The wife's rights vis-à-vis her husband are:
1. maintenance;
2. permission to visit her parents and close relatives (*mahrams*) and to have them visit her in accordance with custom;
3. keeping her family name;
4. not usurping her personal property; she has the right to dispose of it freely;
5. not injuring her physically or mentally;
6. equitable treatment between her and other wives, if the husband has more than one.

Article 38: The husband's rights vis-à-vis his wife are:
1. caring for him and obeying him in accordance with custom in view of his being head of the family;
2. managing the house and organising its affairs, and looking after its contents;
3. looking after his children from her, and breastfeeding them if there is nothing preventing that.

Article 54: No maintenance is due the wife in the following situations:

1. if she withholds herself from her husband, or refuses to move to the conjugal home without *shar'i* reason;
2. if she leaves the conjugal home without *shar'i* reason;
3. if she prevents the husband from entering the conjugal home without *shar'i* reason;
4. if she refuses to travel with her husband without *shar'i* reason.

Qatar 2006

Article 55: A valid marriage gives rise to rights that are shared between the spouses, and to rights particular to each of them, in accordance with the provisions of this law.

Article 56: Rights that are shared between the spouses are:

1. sexual enjoyment by each of the other in a *shar'i* manner;
2. fidelity of each to the other;
3. *shar'i* cohabitation;
4. good treatment, mutual respect and affection and looking after the family interest;
5. caring for the children and bringing them up in such a manner as to ensure their sound development;
6. the respect of each for the other's parents and relatives.

Article 57: The wife's rights vis-à-vis her husband are:

1. dower;
2. *shar'i* maintenance;
3. being allowed to visit her parents and close relatives (*mahrams*) and having them visit her, in accordance with custom;
4. not usurping her personal property;
5. not injuring her physically or mentally;
6. justice between her and other wives if the husband is married to more than one.

Article 58: The rights of the husband vis-à-vis his wife are:

1. caring for him and obeying him in accordance with custom;
2. looking after herself and his property;
3. managing the house and organising its affairs;
4. looking after his children from her and breastfeeding them if there is no *shar'i* obstacle.

Article 68: The husband shall give his wife the opportunity to complete her education to the end of the mandatory period and shall facilitate her pursuit of university education inside the country, in so far as this does not conflict with her family duties.

Article 69: The wife shall be considered *nashiz* and not entitled to maintenance in the following situations:

1. if she refuses herself to her husband, or refuses to move to the conjugal home without *shar'i* reason;
2. if she leaves the conjugal home without *shar'i* reason;
3. if she prevents the husband entering the conjugal home without *shar'i* reason;
4. if she refuses to migrate with her husband or travels without his permission;
5. if she goes out to work without the approval of her husband, so long as the husband is not being arbitrary in forbidding her.

Sudan 1991

Article 51: The wife's rights against her husband are:

a) maintenance;
b) being allowed to visit her parents and *mahrams*, and having them to visit her in accordance with custom;
c) [the husband] not doing [the following]:
   1) usurping her private property;
   2) injuring her physically or mentally.
d) justice between her and other wives if the husband has more than one.

Article 52: The husband's rights against his wife are:

a) caring for him and obeying him as is customary;
b) looking after herself and his property.

Article 75: No maintenance is due the wife in any of the following cases:

a) her refusal to move to the marital home, without *shar'i* reason;
b) leaving the marital home without *shar'i* reason;
c) preventing the husband from entering the marital home, without *shar'i* reason;
d) working outside the marital home, without her husband's agreement, provided that he is not being arbitrary in his prohibition on her work;
e) her refusal to travel with her husband, without *shar'i* reason;

Article 91: The wife is obliged to obey her husband in matters that do not contradict the law, provided the following conditions are met:

a) that he has paid her prompt dower;
b) that he is to be trusted with her;
c) that he prepares for her a *shar'i* dwelling, provided with the necessary items and among good neighbours.

Article 92: If the wife refuses to obey her husband, her right to maintenance lapses for the period of her refusal.

Article 93: The wife shall be considered disobedient in any of the following cases:

a) her refusal to implement a final [court] ruling for obedience;
b) cases in which she is considered disobedient set out in article 75.

Article 94:

1) A ruling for obedience may not be forcibly implemented against the wife.
2) Rulings for *ta'a* may be implemented twice in the proper ways, according to what the judge considers to be in the spirit of the Islamic *shari'a*, provided that the period between the first and second petitions shall be at least one month.

Article 95: If the wife defends the claim of obedience on the grounds that he has not paid her prompt dower, or has not prepared the dwelling or is not safe [for her to be with] and she sets this out, then if the husband denies this and she is unable to prove it, and he takes the oath at her demand in regard to her defence, then the husband shall be charged with proof, and on establishing his claim he shall be granted the ruling for her obedience.

Syria 1953 as amended 1975

Article 72:

1) Maintenance for the wife shall be obligatory on the husband – even if she is of a different religion – from the time of the valid contract, even if she is living in her family's house, unless the husband has asked her to move and she has refused without right.

3) Her refusal [to move] shall be considered to be with right so long as the husband has not paid the prompt dower or has not prepared a shar*i residence.

Article 73: The wife's right to maintenance lapse if she works outside the house without the permission of her husband.

Article 74: If the wife becomes disobedient, then she is not entitled to maintenance for the period of her disobedience.

Article 75: The disobedient [wife] is she who leaves the conjugal home without shar*i reason or prevents the husband from entering her house before she has asked to be moved to another house.

Tunisia 1956 as amended 1993

Article 23: Each spouse shall treat the other well and avoid injuring the other. The spouses shall fulfill their conjugal duties according to custom and usage. They shall cooperate in running family affairs and bringing up the children and managing their affairs including their education, travel and financial affairs. The husband, as head of the family, shall provide for the maintenance of his spouse and the children according to his means and their circumstances. The wife shall contribute to maintaining the family if she has means.[21]

UAE 2005

Article 54: Mutual rights and duties of the spouses:

1. sexual enjoyment of each spouse of the other as permitted by the shari‘a;
2. shar*i cohabitation;
3. good treatment, mutual respect and affection, and looking after the family interest;
4. caring for the children and bringing them up in such a manner as to ensure their sound development.

Article 55: The rights of the wife against her husband are:

1. maintenance;
2. not being prevented from completing her education;

3. not being prevented from visiting her ascendants, descendants and collaterals and having them visit her in accordance with custom;
4. not usurping her personal property;
5. not injuring her physically or mentally;
6. justice between her and other wives if the husband has more than none.

Article 56: The husband's rights against his wife are:
1. obedience in accordance with custom;
2. managing the house and looking after its contents;
3. breastfeeding his children from her unless there is something preventing this.

Article 71: The wife's maintenance lapses in the following situations:
1. if she withholds herself from her husband or refuses to move to the *shar'i* conjugal home without a *shar'i* reason;
2. if she leaves the conjugal home without *shar'i* reason;
3. if she prevents the husband from entering the conjugal home without *shar'i* reason;
4. if she refuses to travel with her husband without a *shar'i* reason;
5. if a court ruling or decision is issued restricting her freedom and is implemented.

Article 72:
1) The wife is permitted to leave the house in circumstances that allow her this according to law or custom or the exigencies of necessity, and this will not be considered as a violation of the obligatory obedience.
2) It will not be considered a violation of obligatory obedience if she goes out to work if she was working when she got married, or if [her husband] consented to her work after the marriage, or if she stipulated this in the contract [of marriage]. The notary shall inquire about this stipulation when drawing up the contract. All this is so long as nothing happens that renders implementation of the stipulation in conflict with the interest of the family.

Article 158: (final paragraph): It is not permitted to execute forcibly a ruling for obedience made against the wife.

Yemen 1992 as amended 1998

Article 40: The husband shall have the right that his wife be obedient to him in that which is for the benefit of the family, and in particular the following:
1. that she should move with him to the matrimonial home, provided that she has not stipulated in the contract that she should remain in her home or in her family's home, in which case she shall be obliged to make it possible for him to live with her and to consummate the marriage;
2. that she should allow him to have lawful sexual intercourse with her;
3. that she obey his instructions and undertake her work in the matrimonial home in the manner of her peers;
4. that she should not leave the matrimonial home except with his permission.

The husband shall not be entitled to prevent his wife from leaving the home for any lawful purpose or for that which is customary, provided this is not a breach of honour or of her duties towards him, in particular she may leave to attend to her property or to go to her agreed upon employment. It shall be considered a lawful justification for a woman to help her elderly parents where they have no one else to help one or both of them other than her.

Article 41: The following are the obligations of the husband towards his wife:

1. that he prepare for her a lawful domicile which befits both of them;
2. that he provide her with maintenance and clothing which befit both of them;
3. that he maintain equity between her and his other wives if he has more than one wife;
4. that he not interfere with her personal property;
5. that he not cause her either material or moral harm.

4. Stipulations

Algeria: 1984 as amended 2005

Article 19: The two spouses may stipulate in the contract of marriage, or in another supplementary contract, any clause they consider useful, notably concerning polygyny and the wife's work,[22] provided that these do not contradict the dispositions of the present law.

Article 35: If the marriage contract is accompanied by a stipulation that contradicts it, the stipulation is voided, and the contract is valid.

Iraq 1959

Article 6

(3): Lawful stipulations made in the contract of marriage are valid and must be fulfilled.

(4): the wife may seek dissolution of the contract if the husband fails to fulfil what she has stipulated in the contract of marriage.

Jordan 1976

Article 19: If a condition is stipulated in the contract that is of benefit to one of the parties, is not inconsistent with the intentions of marriage, does not impose something unlawful and is registered in the contract document, it shall be observed in accordance with the following:

1) if the wife stipulates something to the husband that brings her a benefit that is lawful and does not infringe upon the right of the other, such as if she stipulates that he shall not remove her from her [home] town, or shall not take another wife during their marriage, or that he shall delegate to her the power to divorce herself, this shall be a valid and binding condition, and if the

husband does not fulfil it, the contract shall be dissolved at the application of the wife, and she may claim from him all her matrimonial rights;

2) if the husband stipulates to the wife a condition that brings him a lawful benefit and does not infringe upon the rights of the other, such as if he stipulates that she shall not go out to work, or that she shall live with him in the area in which he works, this shall be a valid and binding condition, and if the wife does not fulfil it, the contract shall be dissolved at the application of the husband and he shall be exempted from paying her deferred dower and maintenance during the 'idda period;

3) if the contract is constrained by a condition that contradicts the intentions of marriage or imposes something unlawful, such as if one of the spouses stipulates that the other shall not live with him/her, or that they shall not share marital intimacy, or that one of them shall drink alcohol, or shall break off relations with their parents, then the condition is void while the contract remains valid.

Kuwait 1984
Article 40
1) If the contract of marriage is accompanied by a stipulation that conflicts with its basis, the contract is voided.
2) If it is accompanied by a stipulation that does not conflict with its basis, but conflicts with its requirements, or is forbidden in law, then the stipulation is voided, and the contract is valid.
3) If it is accompanied by a stipulation that does not conflict with its basis or its requirements and is not forbidden in law, then the stipulation is valid and must be fulfilled. If it is not fulfilled then the person who made the stipulation has the right to seek judicial dissolution (faskh).
4) The terms of the preceding paragraph shall apply in the case of the lapse of a particular quality stipulated in one of the spouses.

Libya 1984
Article 3:
a) Each of the spouses may insert stipulations in the contract of marriage that do not conflict with the purposes and intentions of marriage.
b) No stipulation shall be considered unless it is explicitly stated in the marriage contract.

Mauritania 2001
Article 28: The wife may stipulate that her husband shall not marry another woman, that he shall not absent himself for more than a given period, that he shall not prevent her from pursuing her studies or from working as well as any other condition not contrary to the permanence of the marriage contract.

Article 29: Partial or total failure by the husband to implement the conditions stipulated by the wife give rise, on the initiative of the latter, to judicial dissolution of the marriage and a gift of consolation (*mut‘a*) the value of which is at the discretion of the judge.

Morocco 2004

Article 47: All stipulations are binding except stipulations that contradict the terms and objectives of the marriage contract and legal rules; these stipulations are void while the contract remains valid.

Article 99: Failure to respect any condition in the marriage contract constitutes injury justifying a petition for divorce.

Oman 1997

Article 5:

e) The spouses shall fulfil their stipulations, apart from a stipulation that renders the prohibited lawful or the lawful prohibited.

f) No stipulation shall be considered unless it is explicitly stipulated in the marriage contract.

g) In the event the stipulation is violated, the injured spouse has the right to seek judicial divorce.

Qatar 2006

Article 53: If the contract of marriage is accompanied by a stipulation that contradicts its basis, the contract is voided.

If it is accompanied by a stipulation that does not contradict its basis but contradicts the requirements of the contract, or is forbidden in law, then the condition is voided, but the contract is valid.

If it is accompanied by a stipulation that contradicts neither the basis nor the requirements of the contract, the stipulation is valid and shall be fulfilled. If it is not fulfilled, the person who made the stipulation has the right to seek judicial dissolution.

Article 54: The right of judicial dissolution lapses if the one so entitled waives it explicitly or implicitly.

Sudan 1991

Article 42:

1) The spouses shall abide by their stipulations, except for a stipulation that renders what is lawful prohibited or what is prohibited lawful.

2) If the contract is accompanied by a stipulation that contradicts its purpose or intentions, then the stipulation is void and the contract valid, apart from the stipulation of a time limit which voids the contract.

3) No stipulation shall be considered unless it is explicitly stated in the contract of marriage.

Syria 1953 as amended 1975

Article 14: 1) If the contract of marriage is constrained by a condition contradicting its *shar'i* regulation or its intentions, obliging something that is forbidden, then the condition is void, and the contract is valid.

2) If it is constrained by a stipulation that requires a benefit to the woman that is not forbidden in law and does not affect the rights of others and does not constrain the freedom of the husband in his lawful personal affairs, the stipulation is valid and binding.

3) If the woman stipulates something in the contract of marriage that constrains the freedom of the husband in his personal affairs, or affects the rights of others, then the stipulation is valid but not binding on the husband, and if he does not fulfil it, then the wife who made the stipulation may seek dissolution of the marriage.

Tunisia 1956

Article 11: Spouses may insert stipulations in the marriage contract. Non-fulfilment or contravention of a stipulation gives rise to the possibility of a petition for dissolution through *talaq*. No rights to compensation arise from the divorce if it takes place before consummation.

UAE

Article 20:

1. Spouses shall fulfil their stipulations, apart from a stipulation that makes what is prohibited (*haram*) lawful (*halal*) or makes lawful what is prohibited.
2. If a stipulation is made that contradicts the basis of the contract of marriage, the contract is voided.
3. If the stipulation does not conflict with the basis of the contract but conflicts with its requirements or is prohibited by law, then the stipulation is voided, and the contract is valid.
4. If a stipulation is made that does not conflict with the basis of the contract nor with its requirements, and is not prohibited by law, then the stipulation is valid and shall be fulfilled. If the person to whom the stipulation is made violates it, then the person who made the stipulation is entitled to seek judicial dissolution, whether this be from the side of the wife or the husband; the husband shall be exempt from paying the maintenance for the *'idda* period if the violation is from the part of the wife.
5. If one of the spouses stipulates that the other shall have a particular quality and the opposite transpires, then the person who made the stipulation shall be entitled to seek judicial dissolution.
6. In the event of denial, no stipulation shall be considered unless it is written in the documented contract of marriage.
7. The right of dissolution lapses if waived by the person so entitled, or by explicit or implicit consent to the violation. The passage of one year after the

occurrence of the violation with the stipulating party's knowledge thereof shall be considered implicit consent, and similarly with [the right to] final *talaq*.

Yemen 1992 as amended 1998:
Article 7(5): [..] every stipulation not related to a lawful objective of one of the spouses or contradicting the contract shall be abrogated.

5. Judicial *Khulᶜ* and comparable divorce provisions

Algeria 1984 as amended 2005[23]
Article 54: The wife may separate from her husband, without the latter's consent, for the payment of a sum by way of *khulᶜ*. In the event of disagreement on the remuneration, the judge shall order the payment of a sum of not more than the value of the proper dower at the date of the ruling.

Egypt Law no.1/2000
Article 20: The spouses may agree between themselves on *khulᶜ*. If they do not agree, and the wife submits a claim seeking *khulᶜ*, and she ransoms herself and divorces herself[24] from her husband by waiving all her *sharᶜi* financial rights and returns to him the dower that he gave her, the court shall rule for her divorce against him. The court shall rule for the divorce for *khulᶜ* only after attempting to achieve a reconciliation (*sulh*) between the spouses and charging two arbiters with constant endeavour to effect a reconciliation between them, during a period of not more than three months, in the manner set out in Articles 18(2) and 19(1) and (2) of this law; and after the wife has explicitly stated that she loathes life with her husband and that there is no way for their married life to continue, and that she is afraid that she will not [be able to] live within the limits of Allah because of this loathing [that she has for her husband].
It shall not be valid for the consideration of *khulᶜ* to be the waiving [by the wife] of [her entitlement to] custody of children [from the marriage] or their maintenance or any other of their rights.
In all cases, the *khulᶜ* gives rise to a final *talaq*.
In all cases, the ruling shall not be open to any form of appeal.

Jordan 1976 as amended 2001[25]
Article 126
b) Before consummation of valid seclusion (*khalwa*), the wife may petition the *qadi* for judicial divorce from her husband if she is prepared to return such dower as she has received from him and other expenses of marriage that the husband has incurred. The husband may choose to receive these costs in cash or in kind [i.e. the items or their value] and if the husband refuses to divorce her, the *qadi*

shall dissolve the contract after the return of the dower and expenses is
guaranteed.

c) After consummation or *khalwa*, the spouses may agree together on *khul*. If they
do not agree and the wife petitions the court for a *khul*, setting out by explicit
affirmation that she loathes life with her husband and that there is no way for
their married life to continue, and that she is afraid that she will not [be able
to] live within the limits ordained by Allah because of this loathing, and she
'ransoms' herself by waiving all her marital rights and divorces her husband
and returns to him the dower she received from him, the court shall attempt
reconciliation between them [the spouses]. If it is unable [to effect
reconciliation] it shall send two arbitrators to pursue efforts at reconciliation
for a period of not more than thirty days. If reconciliation is not achieved, the
court shall rule for her final divorce from him.

Libya 1984
Article 49:
a) Either spouse may retract the offer of *mukhala'a*[26] before the response of the
other.
b) If the retraction is from the side of the husband by way of stubbornness
(*ta'annutan*), then the judge shall rule for *mukhala'a* for an appropriate exchange.
c) If the court ascertains that the wife is [financially] unable, it may rule for the
payment of the exchange to be postponed until such time as she is able [to pay
it].

Mauritania 2001
Article 92: Repudiation (*talaq*) for compensation to the husband given by the wife
or her representative or for renunciation of a right that she has against the
husband is valid. The compensation must be lawful. In the event of irregularity
of the *khul*, the repudiation is valid, and the husband is not entitled to
anything.
Article 93: If it is proven to the court that the wife initiated the repudiation for
compensation solely to remove herself from prejudice arising from abuse or
from ill-treatment, then the repudiation is effective, and the compensation is
returned. The same applies if the wife is a minor or prodigal.

Qatar 2006
Article 122: If the spouses fail to agree on *khul*, the court shall attempt to reconcile
them and for this purpose shall delegate two arbitrators to undertake
reconciliation efforts for a period of not more than six months. If the two
arbitrators do not arrive at reconciliation [of the spouses] and the wife seeks
khul in exchange for her renunciation of all her *shar'i* financial rights, and
returns to him the dower that he gave her, the court shall rule for their divorce.

Sudan 1991

Article 170: The disobedient wife may petition for judicial divorce for a ransom (*fidiya*) in accordance with the following conditions:

a) that the disobedience is established in a judicial ruling;
b) that one year has passed on the disobedience at the time the claim papers are submitted;
c) that the petition sets out the material exchange for the divorce by which she shall be bound, in items or in cash;
d) that she shall set out in her claim that she is unable to perform the rights that her husband has in her regard, and that she has been injured by remaining married to him, along with the waiving of her rights against him.

Article 171: If the husband acknowledges the claim for judicial divorce for ransom, and consents to the proposed ransom, he shall be ordered to cause the *talaq* to occur himself, and if he refuses, the judge shall perform it.

Article 172: If the husband acknowledges the claim for judicial divorce for a ransom, but does not agree to the divorce, and does not set out a legitimate interest in the continuation of his marriage tie to her; or if he consents to the divorce but does not agree to the amount of the ransom, then the judge shall send two arbitrators in accordance with articles 163-168 as it is a situation of dispute.

Article 173: If the husband denies the claim for judicial divorce for ransom in [all] its details, the wife shall be charged with establishing it through confronting him, and if she establishes it then he shall be ordered to undertake the *talaq*, and if he refuses, then the court shall send two arbitrators as it is a situation of dispute.

Tunisia 1956 as amended 1981

Article 31: Divorce shall be decreed:

1. by mutual consent of the two spouses;
2. based on the application of one of the spouses on grounds of injury;
3. based on the desire of the husband to establish *talaq* or the application of the wife.
   Compensation shall be awarded to the spouse who is injured for the material and mental prejudice arising from the divorce in the two cases set out in the second and third paragraphs above.

UAE 2005

Article 110:

1) *Khul'* is a contract between the two spouses in which they agree to terminate the contract of marriage for an exchange paid by the wife or another person.
2) Whatever may be validly specified as dower may be validly specified as the exchange for *khul'*; it is not valid to agree on waiving the maintenance or custody of children.

3) If the exchange for the *khul*ʿ is not valid, the *khul*ʿ occurs, and the husband is entitled to the dower.
4) *Khul*ʿ is judicial dissolution (*faskh*).
5) In exception to the terms of paragraph (1) of this article, if the refusal from the husband's part is arbitrary, and it is feared that they will not live in the limits of God, the judge shall rule on *khul*ʿ for an appropriate exchange.

6. Compensation for injurious/arbitrary divorce

Algeria 1984 as amended 2005
Article 52: If the judge establishes that the husband has abused his power of *talaq*, he shall grant the wife reparation for the damage she has suffered.
Article 53 *bis*: The judge who pronounces divorce at the application of the wife can grant her reparations for the damage she has suffered.

Egypt 1920 amended 1985
Article 18 *bis*: If a man divorces his wife without her consent after the marriage has been consummated and for no reason on her part, she shall be entitled, in addition to the maintenance for her ʿ*idda* period, to financial consolation (*mutʿa*) to be assessed as the maintenance for at least two years. Regard shall be had [in the assessment of the award] to the financial situation of the husband, the circumstances of the *talaq* and the length of the marriage. The divorcer may be permitted to pay this in instalments.

Iraq 1959 as amended 1985
Article 39
(3): If the husband divorces his wife and it appears to the court that he was arbitrary in such divorce and that the wife suffered prejudice from this, then the court shall rule, at her petition, for her divorcer to pay compensation (*taʿwid*) appropriate to his financial status and the extent of his arbitariness, in a total sum, provided this shall not exceed her maintenance for a period of two years, in addition to her other established financial rights.

Jordan 1976 as amended 2001[27]
Article 134: If the husband divorces his wife arbitrarily, such as if he divorces her for no good reason, and she applies to the *qadi* for compensation, he shall award her against the man who divorced her compensation (*taʿwid*) of not less than a year's maintenance and not more than three years' maintenance. In imposing it, the situation of the husband, rich or poor, shall be taken into consideration. It shall be paid in a lump sum if the husband is wealthy and in instalments if he is poor. This shall not affect her other matrimonial rights.

Kuwait 1984

Article 65:

e) if a valid marriage is terminated after consummation, the wife is entitled – apart from maintenance for the *'idda* period – to *mut'a* to be assessed so as not to exceed one year's maintenance, according to the situation of the husband, to be paid to her in monthly instalments following the end of her *'idda*, so long as the two parties have not agreed otherwise in terms of amount or method of payment;

f) excepted from the terms of the preceding paragraph are:
    i. divorce for non-payment of maintenance due to the poverty of the husband;
    ii. divorce for injury if the reason was from the wife's part;
    iii. *talaq* with the consent of the wife;
    iv. judicial dissolution (*faskh*) of the marriage at the petition of the wife;
    v. death of one of the spouses.

Libya 1984

Article 51: In the event of *talaq*, the court shall specify the maintenance of the divorced wife during her *'idda*.

If the *talaq* was by reason of the husband, the court shall award *mut'a* according to the financial situation of the divorcer, bearing in mind article 39 of this law [regarding the apportioning of blame by arbitrators].

Mauritania 2001

Article 84: In all cases the wife divorced by *talaq* may approach the court for the rights resulting from the *talaq*, including maintenance and the gift of consolation.

Morocco 2004

Article 84: The wife's entitlements include: deferred dower where there is such, maintenance for the *'idda* period, and *mut'a*. The assessment of the amount of *mut'a* shall take into consideration the duration of the marriage, the financial situation of the husband, the reasons for the *talaq*, and the extent to which the husband was arbitrary in causing it to occur.

Oman 1997

Article 91: The divorcée from a consummated marriage is entitled to *mut'a* according to the wealth of the divorcer.

Qatar 2006

Article 115: Every divorcée is entitled to *mut'a* if the *talaq* is by reason from the husband.

Excepted from the terms of the previous paragraph is divorce for lack of maintenance by reason of the husband's poverty.

Mut'a shall be calculated in view of the wealth of the divorcer and the situation of the divorcée, provided that it shall not exceed three years' maintenance.

Sudan 1991

Article 138: 1) The divorced wife is entitled to *mut'a*, apart from maintenance for the *'idda* period, according to the means of the divorcer, provided this shall not exceed the maintenance for six months.

2) Excepted from the terms of paragraph 1) are the following cases:
   a) judicial divorce for failure to maintain by reason of the husband's impoverishment
   b) judicial divorce for [physical/mental] condition, if the condition is from the side of the wife
   c) divorce by *khul'* or for a ransom, or for property.

Syria 1953 as amended 1975[28]

Article 117: If a man divorces his wife and it appears to the judge that the husband was arbitrary in divorcing her without good reason, and that the wife will suffer distress and poverty from this, the *qadi* may award her compensation (*ta'wid*) against her divorcer according to the case and the extent of arbitrariness, provided this does not exceed the amount of three years' maintenance for her peers, besides maintenance for the *'idda* period. The judge may require the payment to be made in a lump sum or in monthly [instalments] according to the circumstances.

Tunisia 1956 as amended 1981[29]

Article 31 (3) [Divorce shall be ruled for] based on the desire of the husband to establish *talaq* or the application of the wife, and compensation shall be awarded to the spouse who is injured for the material and mental prejudice arising from the divorce in the two cases set out in the second and third paragraphs above.

With regard to the wife, she shall be compensated for material injury by a stipend to be paid after the end of the *'idda* on a monthly basis to the amount on which she is accustomed to living during marital life, including accommodation. This alimony can be reviewed and either increased or decreased according to changes that occur. It shall continue until the woman dies or her social circumstances change, by a new marriage, or by her attaining something that enables her to do without the compensation... Should her divorcer die, the alimony shall be a debt against the estate, to be settled at that time by agreement with the heirs, or by way of [judicial] award of a payment of a lump sum that will take into consideration her age at that time. All this is unless she chooses to have her compensation for material injury paid as one capital lump sum.

UAE 2005

Article 140: If the husband divorces his wife in a valid, consummated marriage by his unilateral wish and without her having asked for this [divorce], she is entitled to *mut'a* besides the maintenance for the *'idda* period according to the circumstances of the husband and not more than the sum of one year's maintenance of her peers. The *qadi* may break the sum into instalments according to the husband's ability to pay, and in assessing the amount shall have regard to the prejudice suffered by the woman.

Yemen Law of Personal Status 1992

Article 71: If a man divorces his wife and it appears to the judge that the husband was arbitrary in divorcing her without good reason, and that the wife will suffer distress and poverty from this, the *qadi* may award her compensation (*ta'wid*) against her divorcer according to the case and the extent of arbitrariness, provided this does not exceed the amount of one year's maintenance for her peers, besides maintenance for the *'idda* period. The judge may require the payment to be made in a lump sum or in monthly [instalments] according to the circumstances.

Notes

Notes Chapter 1

1 The distinctions between usage of *shari'a*, *fiqh*, and 'Islamic law' are the subject of many scholarly and activist interventions and are assumed rather than examined in this paper, as discussed further below.

2 Actors involved in the debates also invoke this image: see El-Cheikh 1998-1999 151. For a relevant social science critique that goes to the practice of the law in Egypt, see Dupret 2006.

3 The 'Book of rules of justice', subsequently translated into English as *The Civil Law of Palestine and Transjordan* (Hooper 1933).

4 Scholars in the region and in the Western academy have paid considerable attention to civil law developments, particularly looking at the work of the jurist 'Abd al-Razzaq Sanhuri and post-Sanhuri civil law codifications in different Arab states. A relatively recent example is al-Zulmi and al-Mahdawi 1999, looking at 'the new fabric' of Islamic jurisprudence in the 1976 Jordanian Civil Code.

5 Yilmaz 2002.

6 Anderson 1976 17

7 Messick 1993; Ahmed 1992; Charrad 2001.

8 Buskens 1999; Dennerlein 1996; Mir-Hosseini 1993; Moors 1995; Shaham 1997; Welchman 2000; Wurth 2000.

9 Moors 1999.

10 See essays in Sonbol (ed) 1996; Buskens 1993; Shehada 2004, 2005; Tucker 1996.

11 Buskens 1993 95.

12 Dennerlein 1999; Sonbol 2004; Stowasser and Abul-Magd 2004.

13 Rosen 1980-1; Shehada 2005.

14 Hijab 1988 52-55; Keddie 2007.

15 Abdo 1997; Abu-Odeh 1997 and 2004 ('Modernizing Muslim Family Law); Bennoune 1995; Buskens 2003; Hatem 1992; Molyneux 1995; Moors 2003; Singerman 2005; Welchman 2003; Wurth 2003, 2005.

16 Hélie-Lucas 1994.

17 Buskens 2003; Eickelman and Anderson 2003.

18 Notably on Somalia (where I have no information on current law or practice, but give texts from the 1975 law for comparative purposes); also the Sudan (from the mid-1990s), Libya (where I have been unable to access the texts of amendments to the 1984 law); Mauritania; and to some extent Iraq (post-1999).

19 Other scholars have examined more closely the various political and civil society movements involved in seeking family law reform in different countries of the region. See for example Brand 1998 and Charrad 2001.

20 The practice or precedent of the Prophet Muhammad, as narrated in the *hadith*, the second material source of law in classical Islamic jurisprudence.

21 This concept is borrowed from Chiba 1986. See Dupret 2006 for the risks that attend scholars approaching personal status laws as primarily 'Islamic' rather than as national codifications.

22 On Lebanon see Shehadeh 1998.

23 For reasons of space, it has not been possible to include other important areas such as the provisions governing child custody or general provisions on divorce.

Notes Chapter 2

1 Much of the work for this chapter was done in preparation for two conferences in which I participated in 2006, the first convened by Amira Sonbol of Georgetown-SFSQ under the title 'Arab Women, past and present: democratisation and participation' in Qatar in March 2006, the second by Birzeit University's Institute of Law under the title 'Legal Reform in the Arab World' in Amman in June 2006. The discussions at both conferences considerably enriched the substance of this chapter.

2 Sonbol 2003 ('Women in Shari'ah Courts') 234.

3 Messick 1993.

4 See Imber 1997 on Ebu Su'ud's circular requiring *qadis* in the Ottoman Empire not to implement the view of Abu Hanafi permitting the marriage of adult women without the consent of their guardians, but rather to follow alternative Hanafi views that agreed with the majority in requiring the guardian's consent.

5 Shehada 2005: see in particular pp. 130-150 on 'codified law and use of discretion by the *Qudah*.'

6 Shehada 2005 268.

7 Shehada 2005 138.

8 I am using 'he' because although there are women judges in unified national court systems in Arab states, to my knowledge there is as yet no female judge in a *shari'a* court system. From a methodological point of view, it might also be noted of course that the judge who performs his functions in this manner might in any case be more disposed to entertain close scrutiny by women researchers in his court, as compared to others who may be less 'protective' or sympathetic towards female petitioners.

9 Moors 1999 155-6.

10 Cited in Jamshir 2005 91.

11 Jamshir 2005 19.

12 *Al-Sharq al-Awsat* 21 May 2003; Jamshir 2005 122.

13 Omani Law of Personal Status 1997, article 281.

14 2006 Law of the Family, article 4.

15 Anderson 1960 545.

16 Mallat 1990 91.

17 On the events around 'resolution 137' in issued in December 2003 see Cole 2007 and comment in *Al-Zaman* newspaper (19 January 2004). The text of Resolution 37 and a short discussion may also be found in ABA ILDP 200, 48-49.

18 See Women Leadership Institute in Iraq 2006 p. 11 on the role of interventions by international groups.

19 Ibid p. 4, including a listing of rights liable to be restricted in the event of abrogation of the Law of Personal Status.

20 Notably the Organisation for Women's Freedom in Iraq; see www.equalityiniraq.com.

21 Sonbol 2003 ('Women in shari'ah courts') 232.

22 See Benyahya 2004; Loukili and Zirari-Devif 2004-2005 206. The latter count eight *'ulama'*, four judges experienced in personal status law, and three women, the latter comprising a physician and professor of medicine, a Supreme Court Counsellor, and a university president.

23 Al-Thani 2006 24. She further reports that criticisms raised in the public debate on the absence of women from the drafting process resulted in the re-constitution of the committee to include a number of women.

24 *Al-Ayyam*, 18 May 2003; Jamshir 2005 119-120.

25 *Al-Wasat*, 28 June 2003; Jamshir 2005 140-145.

26 Article 56 Morocco 1957, article 99 2004.

27 The Ministry of Justice's *Practical Guide to the Code of the Family* was published in 2004.

28 Article 94(1) of the Jordanian Constitution.

29 Mervat Hatem reports that the Egyptian decree was attacked by the left as authoritarian and anti-democratic, by the right as contradicting the *shari'a*, while women found themselves in the particular dilemma of not wanting to support anti-democratic methods in law-making and not wishing to denounce the changes introduced by its terms. Hatem 1992 243. For the moment, the Jordanian amendments remain in place pending the scheduling of a joint session of the two houses. Brown (2002 50) has noted that although many Arab state constitutions similarly grant the executive emergency legislative powers, the Jordanian text is unusual in that rather than requiring the legislature, when re-convened, to give its assent to decrees issued in its absence, it requires that Parliament positively repeal such temporary legislation if it is not to remain valid; 'parliamentary inaction constitutes acquiescence.'

30 Charrad 2001 222. Charrad stresses the point (219) that 'the CPS was not a response from the state to pressures from a women's mass protest movement'.

31 Lazreg 1994 155. See further on Algeria, Bennoune 1995. On women's reactions

in Yemen to the 1992 code, see Molyneux 1995.
32 Hinz 2002 23.

Notes Chapter 3

1 The GCC website describes this document as consultative. It was issued at the 17th session of the Supreme Council of the GCC in accordance with a recommendation from the GCC Justice Ministers, in October 1996. See http://www.gcc-sg.org/prief5.html
2 Moghadam 1994 3.
3 Lazreg 1994 155.
4 Hatem 1992 246.
5 Kandiyoti 1988 278. See the article in full for her examination of the 'most overused' concept of patriarchy.
6 Anderson 1976 195.
7 See for example Mayer 2004.
8 In article 2 of the Convention.
9 Respectively, articles 15 and 16. A number of states have also made reservations to article 9 regarding equal rights to nationality and to the nationality of children.
10 Connors 1996 362.
11 Compare for example the official Egyptian presentation of the introduction of judicial khul' in Law no.1 of 2000, examined in Tadrus 2003, with the presentation of the subject to the Committee by the Egyptian National Council for Women (UN Doc. CEDAW/PSWG/2001/CRP.2/Add.3 23 October 2000). On changes by Libya and Algeria to the wording of reservations to the Convention, see Mayer 1998; and see also Mayer 1995 critiquing the positions of Egypt and Morocco as well as that of the USA, and 2005 for a specific examination of Arab states (including Algeria and Libya) before the CEDAW Committee.
12 Human Rights Watch issued a substantial report on divorce law and practice in Egypt (2004), while Amnesty International's examination of women's rights in countries of the Gulf Cooperation Council includes a section on family law (2005 17-26).
13 The Global Rights group, which has an office in Morocco, has for example placed on-line a complete English language translation of the new Moroccan family law. See www.globalrights.org.
14 Respectively, articles 14, 20 and 21. See generally Paradelle 1999.
15 CRC article 7 on nationality.
16 Loukili and Zirari-Devif 2004-2005 210.
17 For example the 'One Hundred Measures and Provisions for a Maghrebian Egalitarian Codification of Personal Status and Family Law' produced by a collective of North African women's organizations.
18 Daoud 1995 108.
19 See Hajjar 2004 234.

20 Jamshir 2005.

21 'Algeria: A protest against discrimination', *Qantara.de Dialogue with the Islamic World* 7th April 2004 (Martina Sabra, translated by Christina M. White), at http://www.qantara.de (last accessed 25th January 2006).

22 Moosa 2001-2002 4.

23 Kandiyoti 1991 7.

24 Sen 2005 45.

25 An-Nai'm 2002.

26 WLUML 2003 21.

27 Including those of WLUML (www.wluml.org) and the Islamic family law site hosted by the Emory School of Law in the first phase of the project that resulted, *inter alia*, in the publication of the 'global resource book' edited by An-Na'im (2002) (www.law.emory.edu/IFL). The Women's Learning Partnership has a comparative chart of Muslim family laws in the Arab region and elsewhere based on information from the Emory project (www.learningpartnership.org/legislat/family_law.phtml). Regionally, the Arab Women's Forum Arabic website (www.awfarab.org) carried a substantial selection of legal texts and comment through 2004 and 2005 (this site could not be accessed as of late 2006), while many relevant English and Arabic news items and texts are posted on www.amanjordan.org, a site focussed on combating violence against women as a project of Sisterhood is Global Institute(SIGI)/Jordan.

28 On the Egyptian project, see Shaham 1999 and Zulficar and al-Sadda 1996.

29 Al-Sawi and Abu Taj 2000.

30 Hammami 1995; Jad 2004; and see Kandiyoti 1991.

31 El Alami and Hinchcliffe 1996; Anderson 1976; Coulson and Hinchcliffe 1978; Esposito 2001; Hijab 1988; Mahmood 1972, 1995; Nasir 1986, 1990, 1994; Rahman 1980; White 1978.

32 Loukili and Zirari-Devif 2004-2005 211.

33 Wurth 2003 13.

34 Wurth 2003 19.

35 See Cuno 2007 on the 'first phase' in Egypt.

Notes Chapter 4

1 Respectively, articles 3 of the Law promulgating Egyptian Law no. 1 of 2000; 305 Syrian law of Personal Status 1953; and 183 Jordanian Law of Personal Status 1976. There had been a debate in Egypt on the inclusion of an alternative reference to 'the four schools' in the law of 2000. Sudan's 1991 law (article 5) directs the court to the dominant opinion of the Hanafi school in the event of there being no text in the law, while referring to the 'historical sources of the law' in the event of a legal provision needing interpretation or explanation.

2 Article 1 Iraq 1959.

3 Respectively, articles 281 (c) Oman 1997; 74 Libya 1984; 222 Algeria 1984.

4 Article 349 Yemen 1992; 343 Kuwait 1984; 311 Mauritania 2001.

5 Article 400 Morocco 2004.

6 Article 2 Law 28/2005.

7 Article 1 Somalia 1975.

8 Article 3. In the absence of Hanbali text, the court is directed to 'another of the four schools' and failing this to the 'general principles of the Islamic *shari'a*'.

9 Anderson 1958 275. The PDRY 1974 law similarly indicated no residual reference.

10 Ltaief 2005 334.

11 Anderson 1958 269-70. The Somali law also failed to mention this as an impediment to marriage.

12 Press conference of 28 February, Chekir 2000 127

13 Civil Cassation Arret no.3384 of 31 January 1966. Sharif 1997 24 summarises other parts of the ruling.

14 Chekir 2000 286.

15 Chekir 2000 127.

16 Ltaief 2005 339.

17 For case studies among different communities, mostly outside the Middle East, see An-Na'im 2005.

18 El-Cheikh 1998-99 148-149.

19 The Code of Obligations and Contracts. Part of Chekir's arguments revolves around the French text of the TPLS.

20 The specific reference is to the 1962 Convention on Consent to Marriage, Age of Marriage and Registration of Marriages. Chekir 2000 127-129 and 281-285; see also Dargouth-Medimegh 1992 58-61.

21 According to article 51 of the Civil Law of 1992: Wurth 2003 21.

22 Articles 15 and 23 of the YLSP 1992. The previous text in the YAR law (article 20) had validated the guardian's contracting in marriage of a minor female provided that she agree at the time of the marriage procession to the hubsand's house (*zifaf*) and stipulated that there was to be no consummation of the marriage (and no *zifaf*) until the girl had reached at least sixteen (by the lunar calendar), with penal and other sanctions provided for in support.

23 Wurth 2003 21. The 1992 law did not stipulate penal or other sanctions and set no registration requirements for marriage.

24 The 1998 amendments reintroduced specific reference to dissolution at puberty (article 30 of 1992 as amended 1998).

25 See Abu Zahra 1957 332-3, who for his part disapproved of this initiative by certain colleagues.

26 Chamari 1991 66-67.

27 Welchman 2000 271. See also Anderson on Iraq, 1976 221.

28 Loukili and Zirari-Devif 2004-2005 218.

29 Loukili and Zirari-Devif 2004-2005 217, citing a report by the Moroccan

Democratic League for Women's Rights and other organisations.

30 Chemais 1994 133-46, cited in Fawzy 2004 37. This provision was removed in the 1985 law; see further below.

31 Welchman 2000 340-341.

32 Wurth 2003 23-24. See also Fahmi's 1987 ethnographic account from the Cairo court in the 1980s.

33 See Welchman 2003. Before the 1991 codification in Sudan, the Judicial Circulars of the 'Grand *Qadi*' regulated different aspects of Muslim personal status law. Anderson 1976 notes that some of the earliest Egyptian statutory reforms in family were 'on occasion tried out, as it were, in the Sudan' before their adoption in Egyptian law, particularly during the tenure of an Egyptian jurist in the post of 'Grand *Qadi*' (1976 40).

34 See for example Wurth 1995; Welchman 2000 262-3; Shehada 2005. Sudan's code includes as its first-cited general jurisprudential principle 'to accompany the judge's application of the law' the rule that 'reconciliation is permitted between Muslims, except that which permits the prohibited or prohibits the permitted' (article 5).

35 And see Bernard-Maugiron 2005 95 on the provision in the (then) draft law of family courts requiring the Public Attorney's office to attempt reconciliation before passing any divorce petition on to the courts.

36 Bernard-Maugiron 2005 95.

37 Shehada 2005 365.

38 Information published by the Public Relations Department of the Office of the *Qadi al-Qudah* (*al-qada' al-shar'i fi filastin: injazat wa tumuhat*, 2004 7-8).

39 Article 16 Law no.28/2005.

40 Explanatory Memorandum to Law no.28/2005, *Official Gazette* no.439 p.139.

41 Article 5, Law 10/2004. If no application has been made, the court is empowered to order transfer of the claim to the Office rather than ruling not to accept the case (article 9).

42 See also Human Rights Watch 2004 26-28.

Notes Chapter 5

1 Thus, Charrad notes that French insistence on compulsory registration of marriage in Algeria not only assisted French administrative affairs in the country but facilitated colonial control over the population. Charrad 2001 137. See also Lazreg 1994 88.

2 The connection is recognised for example in the UN Convention on Consent to Marriage, Minimum Age to Marriage, and Registration of Marriages (1964).

3 See Cuno 2007; Tucker 1998 71. See also Imber 1997 165-166 on sixteenth-century registration requirements by the Ottomans; and Anderson 1951 ('Contract of marriage') 118-119 on the 1917 Ottoman regulations.

4 Dennerlein (1999 128) for example notes that despite criticism by the nationalist forces in Algeria of French colonial requirements of registration,

the first independent Algerian government 'further regulated registration'. The British carried over the registration requirements accompanying the OLFR 1917 (including associated penal sanctions for non-compliance) into the then Mandatory territories of Palestine and Transjordan, and they also remained in force under the French Mandate in Syria.

5 Zubaida 2003 180.

6 Arabi 2001 (*Studies*) 147-167.

7 *Daily Star*, 'Gulf women enraged over Islamic ruling on strings-free marriage', 26th April 2006 (Hassan Fakih).

8 See www.awfarab.org/page/mrt/2004/lo.htm (last accessed 11 August 2005).

9 Penal sanctions for non-compliance were included explicitly in the first codifications of YAR 1978 (article 11) and PDRY 1974 (article 49) as well as in the unified law of 1992 (article 14), but were removed by the 1998 amendments. Jordan 1951, Somalia 1975 (article 5, with an extended grace period for 'inhabitants of the desert'); Syria 1953 (40(3)). Iraq added penal sanctions to its existing registration requirements in 1978 (article 10(5) of law 1959 as amended by article 4 of law 1978); Mauritania 2001 article 79.

10 For example Syria (1953 article 46) and Iraq (1959 article 10).

11 For example, the Omani law of 1997 (article 6) requires marriage to be 'officially registered' but allows establishment 'by proof or affirmation' in view of 'specific circumstances'; the 2005 UAE law (article 27(1)) has similar wording allowing for establishment by '*shar*ʿi proof'. See also Algeria 1984 article 22; Libya 1984 article 5; Mauritania 2001article 2; Qatar 2006 article 10.

12 Tunisia 1964; Iraq 1959 article 19c (see el-Alami and Hinchcliffe 1996 68 on a 1960 directive from the Ministry of Health); Syria article 40c.

13 Morocco 2004 article 65(4).

14 UAE 2005 article 27(2).

15 Qatar 2006 article 18. Compare Tunisia 1964 article 3, which puts the burden on the medical practitioner rather than on the marriage registrar.

16 Tunisian law of 1956 article 3; the official document is regulated by the Law of Civil Status (law no.3 of 1957); Sharif 1997 20.

17 Article 99 of the Law of Procedure no.78 1931. See Abu Zahra 1957 134 for a jurisprudential justification of this provision based on the requirement of publicity. Paternity of any children from such a marriage could however be established. See below ('Parents and Children') in regard to the difficulties of establishing paternity if the husband denies the marriage. Kuwait's law takes a similar approach while allowing a disputed unregistered marriage to be formally established through a separate successful claim to establish paternity or paternity-related rights (article 92).

18 See Fawzy 2004 42-43.

19 Law 1 of 2000 article 17. Recent concern at the practice of ʿurfi marriage in Palestine is demonstrated in interventions by the Chief Islamic Justice (for example, 'Al-hukm al-sharʿi fi al-zawaj al-ʿurfi', *Al-Hayat* 6 May 2005).

20 See Fawzy 2004 and Zakariya 2003 70.

21 Mir-Hosseini (1993 171) notes that the parties in a mutual acknowledgement procedure bring twelve witnesses to support their claim of marriage in a document known as a *lafif*. She examines some of the motivations for women entering *fatiha* marriages (173-174) and notes that disputed claims to establish the marriage, in her case material, were always raised by the wife, usually after the birth of a child when the need to regularise the marriage and establish paternity arose.

22 Morocco 2004 article 16 and 65-69. Compare previous texts in the law of 1957 article 41 (as amended in 1993), 42 and 43. See Charrad 164-165 on early problems in the implementation of registration procedures on the original law.

23 Ministry of Justice 2004 26-27.

24 Dennerlein 1999 128.

25 Syrian law 1953 article 40(2). Compare Iraq 1959 article 11 which allows mutual acknowledgement and confirmation from a couple to establish an out-of-court marriage provided there are no statutory or *shar'i* impediments.

26 Qatar 2006 article 10; UAE 2005 article 27(1).

27 WLUML 2003 140.

28 Federation of Women's Work, Benyahya 2004 94.

Notes Chapter 6

1 An earlier international instrument committed state parties to taking appropriate measures with a view of 'eliminating completely child marriages and the betrothal of young girls before the age of puberty'. Convention on Consent to Marriage, Minimum Age of Marriage and Registration of Marriages 1962; entered into force in 1964.

2 For an overview of the issues globally, and the relevance of different provisions of the CRC, see UNICEF 2001, 2005, and Somerset 2000.

3 Laws 56/1922 and 78/1931. Article 17 of Law 1/2000. Solar years.

4 These include Kuwait, where puberty is a condition of capacity and a contract may not be registered or confirmed nor any claims of marriage heard until the ages of 17 male and 15 female by the lunar calendar (articles 24(a), 26, 92 and 342). The now repealed Libyan law of 1972 also took this approach. The original Tunisian text of 1956 stipulated actual puberty as well as minimum ages as conditions of capacity, while as amended the text tends more to the procedural approach of prohibiting parties below the set age to carry out a contract of marriage, this being, as discussed above, the only way to establish marriage in Tunisia.

5 Article 15 of Yemeni law 1992 as amended by article 1 of 1999.

6 Article 34.

7 The OLFR 1917 had set minimum ages as 12 males and 9 females, and the age of full capacity at 18 males and 17 females, with marriages below the minimum age irregular and marriage in between the two ages permitted by

the *qadi* if puberty had been reached and the female had her guardian's permission. Articles 4-7.

8 Algeria minimum age 19 males and females (1984 law as amended 2005); Iraq 1959 as amended 1978 capacity at 18, minimum age 15 but see also below for 14 as amended 1987; Jordan 1976 capacity at 16 male and 15 female (lunar) and see below on the 2001 amendments; Kuwait no registration before 16 male and 15 female; Libya 1984 capacity at 20 for both, an increase from its 1972 law at 18 male and 16 female (lunar); Morocco 2004 18 years (solar) for both, this being the age of legal majority and an increase from 15 for the female in the previous law; Oman 1997 capacity at 18 lunar years (legal majority) for both; Qatar 2006 capacity requires actual puberty while documentation of marriage below the ages of 16 for the female and 18 for the male needs the consent of the guardian and the court; Somalia full capacity at 18 males and females, females of 16-18 may marry with the consent of the guardian or the court; Syria 1953 age of capacity 18 male and 17 female, minimum age 15 males and 13 females; Tunisia as amended 1964 age of capacity 20 male and 17 female (age of legal majority at 20), raised from 18 and 15 respectively in the 1956 text; UAE 2005 capacity at puberty with the permission of the judge and the guardian, while puberty is presumed to be reached at 18 lunar years when a party may ask the judge to perform the marriage in the event of veto from the guardian. Mauritania 2001 (article 6) sets capacity for marriage at the age of legal majority, 18 years; a person without capacity may be married by the guardian if there is an evident interest in the marriage, but this appears (article 164) to be intended to apply to persons lacking rational capacity rather than being underage.

9 Algeria 1984 article 7; Iraq 1959 as amended 1987, article 8(2) allowing the judge to permit marriage of a person who has 'reached their fifteenth year' (i.e. is fourteen) if there is a 'pressing need' and provided actual puberty has been reached; Jordan see below; Libya 1984 article 6 provided actual puberty has been reached and a 'benefit or necessity' is established; Morocco 2004 article 20; Oman 1997 article 10 after investigation of the 'benefit'; Somalia 1975 article 16 allowing the judge in cases of 'the utmost necessity' to marry parties below the stipulated ages; Syria see below; Tunisia as amended 1964 article 5 allows marriage to be registered under the set ages for 'grave reasons and a clear benefit'; UAE 2005 the judge may allow marriage from actual puberty to 18 years after investigation of the benefit realised by such marriage (article 30 (2)).

10 Article 4 of law no. 05-02 (2005) amending article 7 of law 84-11 of 1984.

11 Article 43 JLPS; Welchman 2000 116, and 2001. Compare Syrian law (article 40(2)), where parties to a marriage not carried out in accordance with the administrative conditions of the law may establish their marriage without going through these procedures in the event that the wife has given birth or is pregnant. Anderson (1951 ('Contract') 116-117) notes that before the

promulgation of the national law, Syrian courts retrospectively validated marriages contract below the age of full capacity under the OLFR without the required consent of the court provided that the parties had reached puberty. See also Mitchell 1997 on Algerian court practice before the promulgation of the code.

12 Mayer 1980 32.

13 It also evokes the financial factors motivating the marriage of minor females posited by Shaham (with regard to Egypt in the first half of the twentieth century) and Motzki (in seventeenth-century Palestine), including – depending on the circumstances – the desire to transfer the responsibility of a girl's support to her husband, and to preserve the integrity of property within the family. Shaham 1997 45; Motzki 1996 139; and see Tucker 1998 46-47.

14 Morocco 1957 article 12(4); repealed 1993.

15 Should the rape be reported to the legal authorities, a number of states in the region and elsewhere have criminal provisions allowing suspension of the penalty in the event that the perpetrator marries the victim. The assumptions and implications of such measures are challenged by groups working on violence against women, through activities on the ground but also through interventions in an increasingly public debate in the region.

16 See White 1978 55.

17 In Egypt, securing legislation setting the minimum age of marriage at 18 for males and 16 for females was one of the first demands of the Egyptian Feminists' Union; although a procedural law to this effect was issued in 1923, Badran observes that it 'stood to benefit middle- and upper-class girls, giving them a chance to extend their education before marriage' while lower-class and rural families might find the change 'burdensome' (1995 126). She also notes the 'limits of legal reform' demonstrated by the legislative gains secured (128), including complaints of its frustration by doctors willing to falsify ages (126). See also Shaham 1997 58.

18 For example, in regard to Yemen, Wurth (2003 21) notes that while the 1992 law prohibited marriage under fifteen, the prohibition was unenforceable, given the absence of registration requirements and of penalties for non-compliance. The amendment of 1999, while going back in part to the YAR law by removing the minimum age of marriage, failed to reinstitute the penalties in that law that backed up the prohibition of consummation of a marriage before the wife had reached sixteen. Article 20 YAR 1978 also provided for compensation to be paid to the wife as indemnity – according to Wurth, 'compensation to the wife for loss of virginity'. Wurth's material included only one case of a 'sizeable fine' being imposed on the husband and wife's father in accordance with this provision. 2003 14.

19 WLUML 2003 24. See their discussion on the 'complex range of issues' involved in their effort to 'forge a WLUML position' on the age of marriage. The allowance for exceptions is made also in the Convention on Consent to

Marriage, Minimum Age of Marriage and Registration of Marriages, which after requiring the establishment of a minimum age of marriage, provides that no marriage shall be concluded before that age 'except where a competent authority has granted a dispensation as to age, for serious reasons, in the interest of the intending spouses' (article 2).

20 Al-Thani 2006 23-26. There are many points of resonance in her description of the Qatari debates on setting a minimum age of marriage with the Jordanian debates described in the following paragraphs. For 1991 statistics on early marriage in different Gulf states, see Fakhro 1996 258.

21 This requirement had been removed in the 1976 legislation. Welchman 2000 117.

22 Jordanian Civil Code 1976 Article 43(2) sets the age of legal majority at 18 years by the solar calendar for males and females.

23 El-Imam 2000 7-9 on the campaign by the Jordanian Women's Union to raise the age of capacity to 18.

24 Al-Qassim 2000 15.

25 CRC/C/8/Add.4 26 November 1993 para. 1(d).

26 CRC/C/70/Add.4 17 September 1999: appendix para. 42.

27 Article 2 of Temporary Law no.82/2001 amending the Law of Personal Status.

28 *Dir' mufsida qa'ima.*

29 *'Adam tafwit li maslaha muhaqqiqa.* 2002 Directive (*ta'limat*) of the *Qadi al-Qudah* in accordance with Article 2 of Temporary Law no.82/2001.

30 *Al-Dastur* 13 December 2001.

31 *Al-Dastur* 23 December 2001.

32 *Al-Ra'y* 13 October 2001.

33 *Al-Dastur* 7 November 2001.

34 *Al-Ra'y* 20 December 2001.

35 WUNRN via The AGENDA Feminist Media Project, reproduced by Women Living Under Muslim Laws (www.wluml.org/english/news 'Jordan: Rights group launches drive to curb early marriage', last accessed 24 March 2006.

36 Article 9 as amended by article 3 of Law no.21 of 1978. The law also seeks to protect positive choice, prohibiting relatives or others from preventing the marriage of a person of capacity. Penalties for relatives of the first degree are a fine and/or prison for up to three years, for others the maximum is ten years in prison. The law holds a contract of marriage by force to be invalid before consummation, while providing for judicial divorce after consummation on grounds of coercion (article 40(4)).

37 Article 13 of Law 84-11 1984; the 2005 amendments clarifies that this now refers to 'minor wards'.

38 Syria and Jordan; UAE 2005 article 21(2) (where the fiancé is twice as old or more than the fiancée); and previously the PDRY disallowed marriages where there was an age difference of more than twenty years unless the woman was aged 35 or above (article 9).

39 Al-Ghabri, 'Early marriage among girls on the rise', *Yemen Times* 4 May 2006.

40 BBC Online: http://news.bbc.co.uk/1hi/world/middle_east/4437667 last visited 12 April 2005.

41 Including the concern that a guardian so minded could abuse the system of marriage concluded by proxy or delegation. Chekir 2000.

42 ABA ILDP 2005 55.

43 Kuwait article 30; Oman article 19; UAE 2005 article 39; Yemen article 7(2) as amended in 1998. Also included in the Qatari law article 28. This is also implied by the text of the Sudanese code of 1991 (article 34).

44 Article 12(2) 1957, as amended 1993 (article 12(4)), and article 24 2003.

45 *Practical Guide* 2004 31.

46 Dennerlein 1996 131.

47 Article 10 of law 05-02 amending Article 11 of Law 84-11 of 1984. The family guardian continues to conclude the marriage of a female below the age of capacity, and the judge remains the guardian for the woman who has none. Mauritanian law (article 9) requires the presence of the guardian for the marriage of an adult woman.

48 Article 9 of law 05-02 adding article 9 *bis* to the 1984 law; and article 10 amending article 33.

49 Libya article 9.

50 Jordanian law implicitly takes this position: see Welchman 2000 123-132; and see el-Alami 1992 156 on a similar obscurity in the 1957 Moroccan law.

51 Yemen 1992 article 18 as amended 1998.

52 Kuwait 1984 article 30 as amended 2004. The UAE law has a similar provision in article 108, allowing the court to remarry the woman to her first husband if their first marriage was concluded with the consent of the *wali* or by order of the court.

53 Article 39; Explanatory Memorandum p.162.

54 Article 28.

55 Raafat 2001.

56 For example, in Oman and in UAE the factors to be taken into consideration are 'religion and then custom' (Article 20(b) Oman; 22 UAE); in Yemen 1992 'religion and morality' allowing either spouse to seek judicial dissolution in its absence (article 48); Jordanian law holds a husband 'equal' if he is able to pay the prompt dower and the wife's maintenance (1976 article 20); Libya 1984 and Syria 1953 refer to custom (article 14 (c) and 28, respectively). The 2004 Moroccan law requires a 'certificate of *kafa'a*' only in regard to non-Moroccan spouses (article 65(6)) with penalties for deceit in this matter.

57 Syria 1953 (article 27); Jordan 1976 (article 22); Sudan 1991 (article 24), in all cases unless the wife has in the meantime given birth or become pregnant.

58 Compare Mayer's examination of the argument made in the Explanatory Memorandum to the 1972 law: 1980 35.

59 Kandiyoti 1988 275, 278, 283.

60 See Abu Zahra 1957 146.

61 Khadr 1998 134-135; Welchman 2000 363.

62 On the *wasi* (legal guardian appointed by the father on his death) and *kafala*, see below, chapter 10.

63 Article 12.

64 Chekir 2000 134 considers the remaining stipulation that the guardian be a male relative to be 'anachronistic'.

65 Morocco 2004 articles 20, 21, 231, 238. On the other hand, the law does not explicitly include the mother among the persons to whom a woman of full legal majority may delegate the contracting of her marriage, should she choose not to do it in person: this is 'her father or one of her relatives' (in the male form). Article 25.

66 Somalia 1975 article 19.

Notes Chapter 7

1 That is, within the limit of four wives, and in terms of formal jurisprudence.

2 For some statistics and comment on polygyny in different Gulf states, see Fakhro 1996 256, 259.

3 Shahd 2001.

4 Article 18 TLPS 1956.

5 Cited in Anderson 1958 269 and in Chekir 2000 123.

6 Chekir 2000 121.

7 Explanatory Memorandum 187.

8 Ibid 194. This was first included in the OLFR 1917 (Article 38).

9 King Muhammad VI's address at the opening of the parliamentary year, 10 October 2003; extracts published in Benyahya 2004 37-41; at 38.

10 Algeria (art. 8 1984), Iraq (article 3(4)(a)), Jordan (article 6 *bis* added by law of 2001, see below; Libya (art.13 1984); Morocco (art.41 2004); Syria (article 17 1953).

11 Algeria (art. 8 1984), Iraq (article 3(4)(b)); Libya Law no.9/1994; Morocco (art. 41 2004, requiring an 'exceptional, objective justification' which replaced an earlier draft reference to 'necessity' Benyahya 95); Syria (article 17 1953 as amended 1975).

12 Article 6 (*bis*) a) JLPS as inserted by article 3 Jordan 2001.

13 The amended text (article 14) requires the wife 'to be informed' should the husband's circumstances indicate that his finances are not sufficient for a further marriage.

14 Draft Arab law article 31; Article 12 (2) a) and b) of Yemen 1992; article 12(2) as amended 1998. Wurth 2003 19.

15 'Reasons Necessitating the Amendment of the Law of Personal Status', in Atari 2002 14.

16 Article 6 of law no. 05-02 amending article 8 of law no. 84-11 of 1984.
PDRY Law 1974 article 11(a). A subsequent Ministerial Decision (no. 98/1974)

established a wife's refusal to present herself for medical tests to establish her (in)fertility as 'deliberate prejudice' to the husband, entitling him to seek divorce. Compare YAR 1976 articles 7 and 13 regarding the wife's infertility, incurable illness and 'recalcitrance or ill conduct'. In the 1975 Somali code (article 13), infertility and incurable disease were accompanied as exceptional circumstances on the grounds of which polygyny might be permitted by the wife's incurring a prison sentence of more than two years or being absent from home for no acceptable reason for more than a year; in addition, a broader exception was made for 'circumstances dictated by the environment'.

17 Mitchell 1997 201.

18 Badran 1995 128.

19 For example Abu Zahra 1957 104-5.

20 Article 3(7) of ILPS 1953 as amended by law no.189/1980.

21 This argument evokes the circumstances identified as the context of the Quranic legitimation of polygyny.

22 Arabi 2001 (*Studies*) 161.

23 For example, Abu Zahra 1957 104.

24 *The Guardian* 21st January 2004.

25 Oman 1997 articles 37(6) and 59; Kuwait 1984 article 85; Sudan 1991 articles 51 and 79; UAE 2005 articles 55(6) and 77.

26 Iraq 1953 article 3(5). Morocco 1957 article 30(1), and article 40 of law 70.03. Compare Yemen 1992 article 12. See also Anderson 1960 (on Iraq) 549 for a comparison of the Iraq and Moroccan provisions written at the time of their promulgation, in particular criticising the 'invidious task' of prediction thus placed on Iraqi judges. The Algerian law after its amendment in 2005 continues to require (article 8) that the husband have 'the intention of equity'.

27 Morocco 1957 article 30 and as amended 1993. Anderson 1958.

28 Morocco 2004 article 43; Egypt 1929 as amended 1985, article 11 *bis*. See also Algeria 1984 article 8.

29 *Jordan Times* 29 June 2004. Article 6 *bis* b) as added in Article 3 of the 2001 law. See also the previous discussion of the UAE draft proposing registration procedures for *misyar* marriages that explicitly excluded (in the explanation of 'limited publicity') the notification of the husband's existing wife.

30 Article 12 1992 law as amended 1998.

31 See www.awfarab.org/page/qt/2004/pl.htm. Article 14 of the 2006 law includes this requirement.

32 Law no. 9/1994: el-Alem 1994 233.

33 Morocco 2004 articles 40 and 42. By contrast, the 2001 Mauritanian law (article 45) makes notification of a polygynous marriage mandatory only in the event that the future or existing wife has stipulated monogamy, presumably on the grounds that this gives the objecting wife the option to activate the stipulation. No requirement is made of notification of wives who have not inserted such stipulations.

34 Text of the 1979 legislation in Badran 1981 200. The Somali code of 1975 had
   already taken this position, allowing a woman to seek divorce if her husband
   had been granted permission by the court to marry another wife, unless she
   has children from the marriage (article 43(2)).
35 Explanatory Memorandum to Law no.44/1979, in Badran 1981 212-213.
36 Chemais 1996 74.
37 For a summary of the arguments made for and against this part of the 1979
   legislation, see Najjar 1988 328-331.
38 Egypt 1929 as amended 1985 article 11 *bis*.
39 Morocco 1957 article 30 and 2004 article 45. The King's speech to parliament
   presenting the draft law did make the connection with injury: speech of 10
   October 2003 in Benyahya 2004 38.
40 Articles 8 and 53(6)of the 1984 law; article 8 *bis*, 8 *bis* (1) and 53(6) according to
   the 2005 amendments.
41 Algeria 1984 article 8; ILPS 1959 article 40(5) as amended by Law no. 21/1978.
   The PDRY law (article 29(2)) allowed a woman to seek divorce when her
   husband married another wife in accordance with the conditions set in the
   law.
42 Explanatory Memorandum to the Syrian Law of Personal Status 1953, in 'Atari
   2002 53. See further below.
43 Iraq 1959 article 13, amended 1963. Anderson 1976 64.
44 Tunisia 1956 article 21; Anderson 1958 (TLPS) 268-269.
45 Article 21 as amended by law no.1/1964 of 21 February 1964; al-Sharif 1997 41-
   43. Anderson 1960 (Iraq) 550 note 31. Children from such a marriage however
   retain legal filiation to the father: see below. This was also the position taken
   in the 1975 Somali law: article 22(3)c); the code actually listed such marriages
   as void.
46 Law no. 9/1994, el-Alem 1994 233.
47 PDRY Ministerial Decision no. 35 of 10/5/75.
48 Iraqi Revolutionary Command Council decision no. 147 of 1982.
49 Hinz 2002 23. Hinz also notes the significance of the head of state's personal
   interest in this matter; Barger 2002 38 also remarks on Qaddafi's interest in
   constraining the institution.
50 Different views in the debate are presented at
   www.awfarab.org/pages/eg/2004/h.htm
51 Proposals from Printemps d'Egalité and the Federation of Women's Work,
   Benyahya 2004 89, 95.
52 Al-Haq 1995 52.
53 WLUML 2003 24.

Notes Chapter 8
1 Abu-Odeh 2005; Sonbol 1998; Mir-Hosseini 2003.
2 See Kandiyoti 1988.

3 As explained by Libya in its report to CEDAW 1999 48. See Chekir 2000 145 and Welchman 2000 212. The text of the Somali law was an exception, explicitly providing for women to inherit equally with men in accordance with statements of the revolution (article 158). Anderson (1976 192), writing shortly after the Somali law was promulgated, noted demonstrations against this provision being met with harsh action by the authorities. He also observed that Somali customary law 'commonly denies women any right of inheritance whatever' and that it was possible that this too was implicated in the protests, rather than 'Islamic orthodoxy' alone.

4 WLUML 2003 22; see their discussion on 217-221. See Hammami and Johnson 1999 330-331 on this discussion in Palestine; Badran 1995 134 on Egypt in the early twentieth century.

5 Abu-Odeh 2004 ('Egyptian feminism') 205.

6 'Reasons Necessitating Amendments to the Law of Personal Status', in 'Atari 2002 14-15.

7 Revolutionary Command Council resolution no. 127/1999. On the other hand, a law of the same year inserted a limit of one year on maintenance arrears that a wife could claim from her husband, a move that elsewhere has been seen to negatively impact the wife's negotiating position. Article 24 (1) as amended by law no.19/1999.

8 UAE 2005 article 49, Explanatory Memorandum p.180. The reference is to Law no. 21 of 1997 on the Limitation of Dower in Marriage, article 1 of which is cited here as establishing 20,000 dirhems as the maximum prompt dower and 30,000 as the maximum deferred. The 1997 law replaced earlier legislation including a 1973 Law on the Limitation of Dower in Marriage.

9 Somalia 1975; UAE 1973; Tunisian Decree of 1941 (see Chekir 2000 119); YAR 1976. See also PDRY 1974.

10 Molyneux 1995 423; and see Wurth 2003 13 on the YAR legislative attempt to limit dower having 'largely failed'. Dahlgren 2005 137-140 examines the reactions of differently placed Adeni women to the dower limitation, and some ways in which it was avoided. The YAR law also sought to regulate the considerable customary sums associated with marriage but separate from dower; compare also article 2 of the Somali law.

11 Sharif 1997 29. Article 12 as amended in 1993.

12 Articles 26 and 28.

13 Badran 1995 139-140.

14 Lazreg 1994 181-182 and see 183-184 as to why women are motivated to demand dower even in circumstances where they do not stand in need of it.

15 Wing 1994 188-189.

16 Chekir 2000 141; Mir-Hosseini 1993 32. See also Lamia Shehadeh 1998 515.

17 WLUML 2003 22. For contesting and intersecting arguments on dower in specific context, see Dahlgren 2005.

18 Wynn 1996; Hoodfar 1996; Moors 1995.

19 Moors 1995 121-125; and see also Wurth 2003 13

20 Moors 1999 154. On the 'token dower' in Tunis, see Dargouth-Medimegh 1992 76; and Sharif 1997 18.

21 Moors 1995.

22 Somalia (1975) article 33(2); and see article 4 where the definition of marriage describes 'a contract between a man and a woman equal in rights and responsibilities' while 'the husband is considered the head of the family by virtue of the law'. See further below on the issue of the 'head of the family' elsewhere.

23 Welchman 2000 380; Wurth 2005 292-293; Shehada 2004 71; Hammami and Johnson 1999 330-331.

24 Iraqi Revolutionary Command decisions 252 and 1239 of 1980. On Egypt, see Fawzy 2004 70 (and also on the debate as to the utility of imprisoning defaulting husbands). In Palestine the Maintenance Fund Law was approved by the legislature on 7 April 2005 and signed by President Mahmud Abbas on 26 April 2005. Tunisia established such a fund in a 1993 law: Chekir 2000 144.

25 Sharif 1997 47. On the 'unusual' *fiqh* position to which a wife's financial obligations might be attributed, see Abu Zahra 1957 145 and Anderson 1958 276.

26 Article 23 1956 as amended 1993. See Sharif 1997 47.

27 Dargouth-Medimegh 1992 54. Compare Anderson 1958 270, who found that the original text on maintenance 'corresponds closely with the parallel provisions in the Turkish Code and the code of the Turkish Cypriots, based as they both are on the Swiss Code'.

28 Chekir 2000 130-131.

29 Chekir 2000 132.

30 Sharif 1997 55.

31 Libya 1984 articles 73(b), 18 and 23. A 1973 amendment to the previous law had made specific reference to rulings for obedience, *nushuz* or the lapse of maintenance rights (article 19 *bis* 1).

32 Unless she did not know of his impoverishment before the marriage. Article 40. The Omani code (artice 109 c)) also disallows a wealthy wife to seek divorce from an impoverished husband. See also discussion in Dennerlein 1999.

33 See Abu-Odeh 2004 ('Modernizing') 118: 'husband no longer spares wife's purse.'

34 Article 24 Tunisia; article 17 b) Libya.

35 Sharif 1997 63.

36 Law no. 08.01 of 9 November 1998; Chekir 2000 131.

37 Article 49 of the 2004 Moroccan law; article 10 of Algerian law 2005 amending article 37 of the 1984 law.

38 Mir-Hosseini 1993 126, 194. One comment on this provision referred specifically to women's domestic labour: Benyahya 2004 89 (proposals of Printemps d'Egalité). The UAE 2005 law (article 62(1)) similarly emphasises the

spouses' independent property rights but specifically allows either spouse to retrieve their share from a joint enterprise in 'property development or building a home' on termination of the marriage. The terms of the provision suggests that this relates only to financial investment.

39 Ministry of Justice (Morocco) 2004, 45.

40 Loukili and Zirari-Devif 2004-2005 217.

41 Algerian law no. 05-02 2005 article 10 amending article 36 of the 1984 law; Moroccan Law no.70-03 of 2004 article 51.

42 Articles 194 and 195. The provision in the 1984 Algerian law (article 37(1)) requiring the husband to maintain his wife and providing for its lapse (where the parallel French text of the law published by the Ministry of Justice translates *nushuz* as 'abandoning the conjugal dwelling') was removed by the 2005 amendments. A later provision however (article 74) also obliging the husband to maintain his wife was left intact.

43 Egypt 1920 as amended 1985 article 1; Jordan 1979 as amended 2001 article 68; Kuwait 1984 article 89; Mauritania 2001 article 57; Qatar 2006 article 69(5); Syria article 73; Sudan article 75(d); UAE 2005 article 72(2); Yemen 1992 as amended 1998 article 98.

44 See Welchman 2000 223-230. The 2001 amendments introduced some of these considerations into the statutory law (article 5 amending article 68).

45 Iraq 1959 article 25(2) b) inserted by law 57/1980. However, in 1984 the Revolutionary Command Council suspended application of this clause to husbands in military or security service 'for so long as the war lasts' (resolution 1357 of 9 December 1984).

46 Egypt article 1 of law no. 25/1920 as amended by law 100/1985 and article 11 *bis* (2) of law 25/1929 as amended by law 100/1985; Kuwait 87; Sudan articles 75 and 91-95; Syria article 75; Jordan 1976 article 37; Iraq article 25(1); Mauritania article 150; Oman article 54; UAE article 71; Yemen article 152.

47 For example Jordan 1976 article 37 (modified from 1951 article 33); Egypt 1967 by ministerial order, and by omission from subsequent laws; Kuwait 1984 explicitly in article 88 and Sudan 1991 likewise in article 94(1); UAE (see further below) article 158. See Welchman 2000 232; Badran 1995 131 on early protests in Egypt; and see Dargouth-Medimegh on Tunisia.

48 Wurth 2003 28 and generally 2005. In Syria, the Arab Women's Forum reports an intervention to the legislature by a human rights group concerned at the granting, in a draft civil procedure law, of complete discretion to the judge in selecting the method of enforcement of 'house of obedience' rulings, and arguing that by contrast the personal status law does not permit the use of force: see www.awfarab.org/page/sr/2004/T.htm.

49 UAE 2005 articles 54, 55, 56; Explanatory Memorandum 186-88.

50 UAE 2005 article 158; Explanatory Memorandum 268 and 100.

51 Abu Odeh 2004 ('Modernizing') 90.

52 Dennerlein 1999 132. Algeria articles 19 and 35; Iraq article 6(3); Jordan article

19; Kuwait article 40; Libya article 3; Mauritania article 28; Morocco 2004 articles 47 and 99; Oman article 5; Qatar article 53; Sudan article 42; Syria article 14; Tunisia article 11; UAE article 20; Yemen article 7. See below on the potential impact in the 2004 Moroccan law of a stipulation against polygyny.

53 Sonbol 1998 291; Shaham 1999 464; Dennerlein 1999 125 in regard to Morocco.

54 See Shaham 1999.

55 Zulficar and al-Sadda 1996; Shaham 1999; Singerman 2005. See also Federation of Women's Work in Benyahya 2004 98. Iran's marriage contract includes detailed stipulations which must be signed by both parties; printed stipulations also appear in the standardised forms in other Muslim majority countries such as Bangladesh and Pakistan.

56 Khadr 1998 137.

57 Jamshir 2005 140-145.

58 Welchman 2000 163-168; Fawzy 2004 86; Wynn 1996 115-117. Shaham 1999 464 found stipulations regarding a woman's work in informal documents in Egypt in the first half of the twentieth century. Sonbol 1998 291 found that stipulations were a 'normal part of marriage contracts' in Egypt under the Ottomans, with 'the most usual condition' being that a man not marry a second wife. Welchman 2000 163-168; Fawzy 2004 86; Wynn 1996 115-117.

59 Wynn 1996 115. A study among Egyptian university students carried out during the course of the campaign for the new marriage contract document found that the least favoured stipulation was that granting the wife the unconditional power to divorce herself: Zulficar and al-Sadda 1996 251-259; Welchman 2000 268-272.

60 Speech by King Muhammad VI to parliament 10 October 2003; Benyahya 2004 39. See Chapter Nine in regard to Jordan's claim that wives have equal access to divorce.

61 Mir-Hosseini 1993 86.

62 Wynn 1996 115; Arabi 2001 157; see also al-Dimashqi 2002.

63 Explanatory Memorandum to the UAE Law, 139; article 20(3).

64 Dr Husna al-Qunay'ir notes that the term 'zawaj al-frand' 'comes from the words "boyfriend" and "girlfriend" used in the West'. Al-Riyad, 30th April 2006. Two other 'modern forms of marriage' were ruled unlawful by the Assembly, those with conditions relating to reproduction and divorce.

65 Daily Star, 'Gulf women enraged over Islamic ruling on strings-free marriage!' (Hassan Fakih) 26th April 2006. The discussions were not limited to the Gulf; see for example the Jordanian women's magazine al-Muslima no. 4 of July 2006 (Wala' Marwan).

66 Reuters 24th July 2006 (Sohail Karam).

67 Al-Riyad 22nd January 2006, 'Opening the file of women divorced from misyar marriages'.

68 Daily Star 26th April 2006 (Hassan Fakih).

69 Al-Riyad 27th April 2006 (Hanan Hassan Atallah).

70 *Al-Riyad* 30th April 2006 (Dr Husna al-Qunay'ir).

71 *Al-Watan* 3rd May 2006 (Maram Abdulrahman Makkawi).

72 *Reuters* 24th July 2006 'Saudis turn to '*misyar*' marriage to beat inflation' (Sohail Karam).

73 This structuring is also of course apparent in the West, with the difference that sexual relations outside marriage are generally more accepted socially as well as legally.

Notes Chapter 9

1 Some of the codes use the term *mukhala'a* rather than *khul'*.

2 Depending on the particular divorce agreement, this may be registered as 'talaq in exchange for a general renunciation', but mostly the texts use the term *khul'* or *mukhala'a* in addressing the procedure, even if the default consideration is renunciation of remaining rights (*mubara'a*). See further below.

3 Variations of this terminology occur, indicating different requirements or implications; see Wurth 2003 on the Yemeni categorisation of *talaq* and *faskh*, the latter being judicial divorce or dissolution. Compare Somali usage in the code of 1975.

4 A revocable *talaq* does not end the marriage unless the wife's waiting period (*'idda*) expires without the husband revoking his *talaq*. The standard *'idda* following divorce is three menstrual cycles, or until childbirth if the divorcée is pregnant; the traditional rules, reflected in modern codifications, do not require the wife's consent to the husband's revocation of his *talaq*.

5 The third of three *talaq*s occasions what is called the 'greater finality' (*baynuna kubra*), ending the marriage irrevocably with immediate effect and disallowing the spouses from re-marrying unless and until the woman has been married to another man, widowed or divorced from him and completed the *'idda* period from that marriage.

6 The last provision in Yemen's 1992 law was reversed in the 1998 amendment to article 65. Wurth 2003 26. The amendments also revalidated divorce by implicit expression where accompanied by intention, whereas the 1992 law had referred only to explicit expression of *talaq*: article 58. Omani law (article 85) also appears to validate conditional *talaq*.

7 Coulson and Hinchcliffe 1978 42.

8 Fakhro 1996 259.

9 Moors 1999 155-6.

10 See on this in regard to Egypt Shaham 1997.

11 With differences sometimes between refusal and inability to pay.

12 UAE 2005 article 114 (4). Explanatory Memorandum 221. The Memorandum also emphasises that the right to seek divorce in these circumstances pertains to the spouse who is not suffering from the contagious condition, not to the spouse who is.

13 Iraq 1959 article 40(2) as amended 1981; Algeria article 53(7). UAE 2005 article

114 (3).

14 Yemen 1992 article 55; Iraq 1959 as amended 1986.

15 Iraq 1959 article 43 (5).

16 UAE 2005 article 114(2).

17 Decisions 1529/1985 and 1708 of 1982.

18 Similar rules apply if the husband takes the option of divorcing his wife in these circumstances, although he is not limited by the two-year rule. Article 25(5)) of Iraqi law 1959 as amended law 57/1980.

19 Sudan 1991 articles 170-173 on divorce for *fidiya* (literally a 'ransom' or 'redemption'); see further below.

20 See for Palestinian case material from the West Bank on this, Welchman 2000 283-292. Examples of the application of this article include the wife supporting her claim of injury with evidence from the regular courts where the husband had been convicted and sentenced to prison for physical assault on his wife. The law applicable in Gaza however does allow for divorce on the establishment of injury.

21 Kuwait 1984 article 127 as amended 2004. The court itself is still required to attempt reconciliation of the spouses. A similar position is taken in the UAE law (article 117), in Mauritania (article 102) and in Qatar (article 129).

22 Chemais 1996 63; Hijab 1988 19. See Chapter 2 regarding the definition of 'injury' in the 2004 Moroccan law. Kuwaiti law (article 126) uses the relative wording in an article allowing both spouses to apply for divorce on grounds of injury.

23 On attitudes to domestic violence, see for example Fawzy 2004 and Hajjar 2004; compare Hammami 2004 139 whose respondents held the husband's physical abuse of his wife to be the third most acceptable reason for divorce (after the husband being a 'political collaborator' and the husband's mental illness).

24 Hajjar 2004 245.

25 See for example al-Gabali 2003 39-40; Zakariya 2003 51; Soliman and Salah 2003 13; Fahmi 1987 19.

26 Welchman 2000 247-251. In three West Bank courts in 1965, 1975 and 1985, deeds of *talaq* or *khulʿ* accounted for 90% of all recorded divorces, and of these the overall proportion was 40% *talaq* to 60% *khulʿ* (or more accurately *mubara'a*, as only in a few cases was a sum of money, possibly constituting all or part of the prompt dower, also paid by the wife). Later research in a wider set of courts in the West Bank and Gaza in the 1990s showed an overall proportion of 72% divorce for renunciation, to 28% unilateral *talaq*. The proportions were highest in regard to divorce before consummation of the marriage, where 92% of the deeds involved a renunciation in return for the *talaq*.

27 Shaham 1997 107.

28 Article 20 Law no.1/2000. See above on the period of mandatory reconciliation attempts by the judge. See Welchman 2004 (Egypt) on the law and the debates

and observations on its implementation, and Singerman 2005 on the advocacy
campaign.

29 Tadrus 2003 86-88.

30 For an examination of interpretations of this concept in the Qur'an 4:34 see
Stowasser 1998, and see further review by Fawzy 2004.

31 Tadrus 2003 89-95.

32 Constitutional case no. 201 for the 23rd Judicial Year, *Official Gazette* no. 52 of 26
December 2002.

33 Sonneveld 2006 51. On 'women divorcing at will,' see Arabi 2001.

34 This cartoon (in *al-Dustur* 14 September 2003) showed a man on his knees
holding onto the hem of his wife's skirt as she storms into the *shari'a* court
clutching a *khul'* paper in her hand. The husband is shaking and sweating with
a sticking plaster on his temple; the wife wears a tight sleeveless top and high
heels, her skirt just below her knees. The man is saying 'Imm Mahjoub, you've
got to understand, I asked you to take off your gown, not to divorce me by
khul' (*ana talabat minnik tikhla'i li mish tikhla'ini*). The caption is a play on words,
with the root *khala'a* from which *khul'* is taken having the meaning of to take
off (as in clothes) – scholars thus often explain the *khul'* divorce as a wife
'taking off' her husband as she would take off her gown. Cartoon by Imad
Mahjoub: see www.mahjoob.com.

35 CEDAW/PSWG/2001/I/CRP.2/Add.3 23 October 2000; page 4, on Question 3.
Article 16 of the Convention on the Elimination of All Forms of Discrimination
Against Women concerns equality in marriage and at its dissolution.

36 CEDAW/PSWG/2001/I/CRP.2/Add.3 23 October 2000; page 4, on Question 3.
Article 16 of the Convention on the Elimination of All Forms of Discrimination
Against Women concerns equality in marriage and at its dissolution.

37 Zakariya 2003 52. See Welchman 2004 (Egypt) and Soliman and Salah 2003.

38 See notably Human Rights Watch 2004.

39 El-Alami 2000 135; Arabi 2001 ('The dawning') 171.

40 UN Doc. CEDAW/C/JOR/1 10 November 1997 page 24.

41 Ibid page 26.

42 Temporary Law No. 82 of 2001 article 6 amending article 126 of 1976 law.

43 Judge 'Awad Hussein Rawajbah, 'Waraqa fi mashru'iyyat da'wa al-zawja al-
iftiraq li'l-iftida' al-musamma bi'l-khul' qada'iyan' (Paper on the legitimacy of a
claim by the wife for separation for a ransom, known as judicial *khul'*),
Department of the *Qadi al-Qudah*, 17 August 2003.

44 Compare interview with Shaykh 'Esam 'Arabiyyat, the Director of *Shari'a* Courts
in the Office of the *Qadi al-Qudah*, countering 'those who oppose the law on the
grounds that it contradicts the *shari'a*' with the principle that 'it is permitted
(*mubah*) so long as the aim is to remove injury'. *Al-Dustur* 14 September 2003.
A lecturer in religion (*usul al-din*) was similarly quoted as noting that 'both *talaq*
and *khul'* are forbidden (*haram*) if done as an injustice, but both are permitted
when carried out justly'. *Al-Ra'y* 28 August 2003.

45 In regard to this last reference, he pointed out briefly that the complaints made about *khulʿ* during the programme concerned flaws in application and the length of procedures (i.e. rather than the availability of the procedure itself).

46 'Maʿrakat ʿal-khulʿ'. *Al-Dustur* 31 August 2003. Memorandum by Deputy Taysir al-Fityani.

47 In the second defeat for the personal status law amendments in 2004, Islamic Action Front deputies were reported as saying that 'women who initiate divorce proceedings under this law are often women of comfort and leisure who don't care about their families'.*The Jordan Times*, 29 June 2004 (Rana Husseini).

48 For a critique of this argument, see Hamadeh 1996 337-338.

49 *Al-Dustur* 1 September 2003. Roundtable convened by Nayef al-Mhaisen. Participants were, respectively, Deputy Nariman al-Rusan, Deputy Mahmud al-Kharabsheh, Judge Dr. Wasif al-Bakri and Advocate Ratib al-Zhahir.

50 Advocate and activist Asma Khadr was quoted as giving figures of of 135 terminations by *khulʿ* in 2002 compared to 9000 by *talaq*. *Al-Dustur* 14 September 2003. Figures also given in the paper cite 561 petitions for *khulʿ* lodged in the courts during 2002, of which 135 resulted in divorce and 173 were dropped. The details were 324 cases lodged in Amman, 119 in Zarqa and 47 in Irbid.

51 *Al-Hadath* 15 February 2003.

52 Article 14 of law no. 05-02 of 2005 amending article 54 of the 1984 law.

53 See also 'New divorce law should not be abused, say national women' http://www.gulfnews.com/Articles/NationNF.asp?ArticleID=172794. A report in *al-Quds al-ʿArabi* on the other hand reported only a provision for consensual *khulʿ* (14 July 2005).

54 Article 110 of the 2005 law; Explanatory Memorandum pp.226-228.

55 Qatar article 122. There has been some opposition to this proposed provision: see www.awfarab/page/qt/2004/pl.htm (last accessed 13 August 2005).

56 See interventions in Benyahya 2004 86 and 102. The Moroccan law (article 120) refers the wife to the procedures on 'dispute' in the event that the husband refuses to agree to a *khulʿ* settlement. It does allow the court to rule for *khulʿ* in the event that the spouses agree on the principle of *khulʿ* but disagree on the terms (article 120). This is also the case for example in Algeria (article 54). The previous Moroccan law (article 56) allowed for arbitrators to investigate *shiqaq* in the event that the wife had petitioned for divorce on grounds of harm, had failed to prove her husband's harm of her and had then renewed her petition for divorce. Some activists had suggested in regard to the new provisions that the court not be empowered to order additional compensation to be paid by either spouses, out of concern for women's ability to make payment.

57 Loukili and Zirari-Devif 2004-2005 209. Articles 94-97.

58 Mauritanian Law of the Family 2001 article 92.

59 Wurth 2003 14, noting a 1952 Cassation Court ruling to this effect. Yemen 1992 article 54 (reproducing YAR 1978 article 52).

60 Sudan 1991 article 170. This textual requirement of the submission recalls the Egyptian *khul‘* provision, while the provision overall is closer to the Iraqi procedure noted above, although potentially financially more costly to the wife. The woman is also required to specify in her claim the 'exchange' that she proposes to provide to the husband, and to waive all her remaining rights. The Sudanese procedure is available to a woman declared disobedient a year or more previous to her divorce claim. If the husband disputes the claim as a whole, the judge will transfer the matter to arbiters in the standard procedure that may result in divorce.

61 Iraq 1959 article 43(2) as amended in 1978; less absolutely, Oman article 108 and compare article 116 of the draft Unified Arab Personal Status Law. The 2006 Qatar also includes this (article 136).

62 Article 123; Explanatory Memorandum p.239.

63 Libya 1972 article 14(b). Mayer 1978 42-43.

64 Libya 1984 article 49(b) and (c); the latter clause regarding deferral of payment had been added to the 1972 law by a 1973 amendment. The UAE law of 2005 uses the same language in regard to the husband's 'obstinacy'.

65 For example, Morocco 2004 117 (and previously article 63 1957). Chemais 1996 66 found Egyptian judges to include as 'injury' giving grounds for divorce the exertion of pressure on a woman to give up her rights during divorce proceedings. Somewhat akin to the Mauritanian provision noted above, Kuwaiti law (article 116) makes it an explicit requirement that the wife's *khul‘* be her choice, without coercion or injury, if the husband is to be entitled to the compensation.

66 Article 48c).

67 On this role of the Egyptian court under the law of 2000, and the developments it represents to previous Egyptian legislation, see Bernard-Maugiron 2005.

68 For example in Syria, the 1975 amendments (article 88) require the court to delay registering a *talaq* or *khul‘* for a specified period in the hope that reconciliation will occur and it will be dropped, with the help of the court if necessary.

69 JLPS article 101; Yemen 1992 article 348.

70 Jordan 1951 article 77; Welchman 2000 258-261.

71 Welchman 2000 258. On the third *talaq*, see *supra* note 5.

72 Coulson and Hinchcliffe 1978 42-43. Iraq 1959 article 39.

73 Algeria (article 49; the 2005 amendments added further recording requirements on the the court); Libya (article 28; and Hinz 2002 22 reports that a 1994 amendment suspended the validity of a *talaq* on court recognition).

74 Dennerlein 1999 130-131.

75 This position was also taken up in the Somali and South Yemeni codes. Tunisia

article 30. See Sharif 1997 75 and Anderson 1976 60 and 1958 (Tunis) 271-2 (in which he considers opposition to this provision at the time). The PDRY and Somali codes allowed *talaq* only by court permission after mandatory processes of mediation by popular (PDRY) or reconciliation (Somalia) committees, but unlike Tunisia did not institute a procedure for a wife to apply for 'no fault' divorce. The PDRY law allowed the court to rule for a *talaq* only where it was convinced that there were 'reasons necessitating the *talaq* that had made the continuation of married life and conjugal harmony impossible' (article 25). Like the Somali law (article 43(1)), the PDRY law provided a list of grounds on which either spouse could apply for divorce, similar to those mostly available only to the wife under other laws in the region, such as lack of maintenance and absence. Coulson and Hinchcliffe 1978 44 held that the law's position on *talaq* put the PDRY, together with Iran, 'in the forefront of law reform in this sphere'.

76 Article 5 *bis* of Law No. 25 of 1929 as amended by Law No. 44 of 1979, with criminal penalties for violation.

77 Article 5 *bis* of Law No. 25 of 1929 as amended by Law No.100 of 1985.

78 See Najjar 1988 320-323 on the parliamentary debates on this issue.

79 Article 21 of Law no. 1 of 2000. Also of interest is Article 22, which allows the wife the right to establish by any means of proof her husband's revocation of his *talaq* of her (and thus her resumption of status as his wife), while disallowing claims of revocation by the husband, in the event of her denial, unless he had informed her of the revocation by official document within certain time periods.

80 Fawzy 2004 table 1.24.

81 A provision repeated in Law no.1 of 2000 in Article 17. Mallat 1990 85 notes this same argument being made in the early 1960s by a prominent Shi'i jurist in Iraq, criticising the 1959 Iraqi family law for not requiring witnesses for the validity of a *talaq*.

82 Explanatory Memorandum to the Draft Law Regulating Conditions and Procedures of Litigation in Personal Status Matters, Appendix to the Record, 22nd Session, 16 January 2000, 100-101.

83 Article 78 2004: '*Talaq* is the dissolution of the conjugal covenant, exercised by the husband and the wife, each according to their conditions, under the scrutiny of the judiciary and in accordance with the provisions of this law.'

84 Moroccan Ministry of Justice 2004 62.

85 Morocco 2004 articles 83-87. Morocco 1957 article 48 as amended 1993 had already required a *talaq* to be registered. See Mir-Hosseini (1993 84-96) on practice under the original law and specifically on 'divorce dues' contested in court following the husband's registration of his *talaq* with a notary, at the time without court procedure.

86 Buskens 2003 82.

87 Unlike Sunni law, Ithna'ashiri (Ja'afari) Shi'i law requires two witnesses to a

talaq for it to be valid.

88 UAE article 106; Explanatory Memorandum 223.

89 In Egypt, before statutory legislation on the subject was introduced (first in 1979), some courts were awarding compensation to divorced women while others would not. Abu Zahra 1957 332-333.

90 See for example Abu Zahra 1957 333-334.

91 The Syrian 1953 Explanatory Memorandum noted that such compensation was recommended in *fiqh* and that 'the ruler may order the recommended to the permitted if there is a lawful benefit'. 'Atari 2002 9. These arguments were echoed in the Jordanian note on the 1976 law which introduced this institution into statutory law, and were explored in more depth in Egypt in explanations of the 1979 and 1985 legislation. Some of the texts (such as in Egypt and Morocco) maintain the term *mut'a* while Syria and Jordan use the term *ta'wid* (compensation).

92 See, variously, Algeria 1984 article 53 *bis* as amended 2005; Egypt law no.25/1920 as amended by law no.100/1985 article 18 *bis*; Iraq 1959 article 39 as amended 1985; Jordan 1976 article 134 (maximum amount increased and a minimum introduced in the 2001 temporary legislation); Kuwait article 165; Libya article 51; Mauritania 2001 article 84; Morocco 2004 article 84 (and 1957 article 60, also amended 1993); Oman article 91; Sudan 1991 article 138(1); Syria 1953 article 117 (maximum amount increased 1975); UAE 2005 article 140; Yemen 1992 article 71 (unchanged in 1998; the text is a word for word reproduction of the original 1953 Syrian text, without the increase made by the Syrians in 1975).

93 In Jordan, al-'Arabi 1984 59 case no 19859/1978; and 'Amr 1990 44 case no. 20245/1978. In Syria Appellate decision 508/511 of 16/11/67 in Dahi 1978 169; compare decision 167/171 of 29/4/65 with similar content. Compare in Tunisia: 'Effecting a divorce without reason is legal evidence of arbitrariness giving the other party the right to seek compensation.' Civil appellate decision (Tunis) 57872 of 24/6/65, in al-Sharif 1997 97.

94 In Jordan, a maximum award of the equivalent of one year's maintenance was set in the 1976 law; the 2001 amendments made this the minimum and revised the maximum to three years, in line with Syria's increase of its maximum in 1975.

95 See Welchman 2000 337-351.

96 Decision 642/619 of 11/2/72, in Dahi 1978 note 46, at 168.

97 Decision 304 of 21/6/70 in Dahi 1978 172.

98 Decision 345 17/11/60; in Dahi 1978 171.

99 Decision 45 of 7/2/58; Dahi 1978 171.

100 Kashbur 1996 345-346, and note 167 citing Rashid Mashqa'a in an article in *al-'Ilm* newspaper of 24/7/93.

101 El-'Alami 2000 59, note 13. The case citation is Cairo Court of Appeal dispute 105/180 Muhammad A. v. Nabila A.

102 As summarised by Najjar 1988 332-333. See earlier on this Abu Zahra 1957 note 1, 335.

103 El-'Alami 2000 note 28, at 57 and note 7, referring to Court of Appeal decision no. 422 of judicial year 106, Ahmad A. v. Soraya A.

104 Algeria article 53 *bis*, adding to article 52; Kuwait 1984 article 165; Qatar 2006 article 115.

105 The PDRY and Somali codes took similar although more limited positions, holding that where the court found the divorce to be the fault of the husband, he could be ordered to pay up to a year's maintenance to his former wife, while if she was found at fault, she could be ordered to pay him up to the amount of her dower (articles 30 and 44, respectively).

106 Article 31 of 1956 as modified in 1981. In all cases the judge is required to seek to reconcile the spouses; article 32 to this effect has been amended several times, each time expanding this duty of the court, and in 1993 introducing the institution of the 'family judge' for this purpose; the family judge is empowered to call upon the assistance of those considered helpful in this regard, which Sharif 1997 110 observes implies the principle of the 'family mediator' who 'is normally a specialist in sociology, psychology or counselling'.

107 Dargouth-Medimegh 1992. Chekir and Dargouth-Medimegh use the French 'divorce caprice'.

108 Specific elements to consider in assessing the amount to be awarded were detailed as including the length of the marriage, whether or not the couple had children, the psychological distress caused by the divorce including grief and pain and the general loss of married life, lessened prospects for remarriage for the spouse claiming compensation, and the age of the parties. Civil Appellate decision Tunis 58223 30/11/65; al-Sharif 1997 98.

109 Chamari 1991 66-67.

110 Dargouth-Medimegh 1992 57 takes a similar view. Chekir 2000 143-144 is concerned that it maintains a relationship between the ex-spouses that might perpetuate the authority of men and the dependence of women.

111 Chamari 1991 68.

112 Civil Appellate decision nos. 38013/1994, 16890/1987, 22695/1989 and 1487 (Susa)/1990: al-Sharif 1997 84, 104, 105.

113 Welchman 2000 349-350.

114 Mitchell 1997 201-202. Husbands might argue injury by reason of the wife's *nushuz*, particularly in the event that she has left the marital home or is otherwise refusing to cohabit. The latter is also an argument made by husbands in Tunisia: al-Sharif 1997 97.

115 Law no. 77/1983. A later amendment (law 27/1988) suggests that husbands were finding ways of avoiding this requirement, notably by transferring title of property to a third person; the amendment gives the divorcée the same rights 'even if her husband gifted the house or apartment owned by him to someone else before divorcing her'.

116 See ruling 21305/1980 in al-'Arabi 1984 115.

117 Article 52 1984. See Dennerlein 1999 132. Article 72 as amended 2005.

118 Najjar 1988 323, 335. See also Wurth 2003 16 on the impact of the housing shortage in Aden leading to courts dividing the marital home between the divorced couple 'who were thus forced to continue to live together, separated by a hastily erected wall or curtain'.

119 Article 18 *bis* 3 of law no.25/1929 as amended 1985.

120 See Jamshir 2005 98-102.

Notes Chapter 10

1 Meriwether 1996 225.

2 Meriwether 1996 228. This finding was particularly the case in 'non-elite families'.

3 Mauritania's code makes a break here, providing that the 'exercise of custody is not remunerated' (article 127).

4 Algeria 1984 (article 65, not amended in 2005) daughters to the age of capacity for marriage and sons to ten with extension possible to sixteen if the mother has not remarried, and interest of child to be observed in all cases; Egypt sons till they reach ten and daughters twelve, with the court empowered to extend till fifteen for sons and until the daughter marries; Iraq (article 57 as amended 1978) until ten, with extension to fifteen in the interest of the ward, at which point the ward may choose with whom to live; Jordan 1976 to puberty; Kuwait (article 193) to puberty for sons and until the daughter consummates her marriage; Mauritania 2001 (article 126) daughter to the consummation of her marriage and son to his legal majority (at eighteen), while the judge can order the male child to be transferred to his father at the age of seven if the boy's interest so requires; Morocco 2004 until the age of legal majority, with the ward choosing with whom to live from the age of fifteen (article 166); Libya a son until puberty, a daughter until she consummates her marriage (article 62); Oman (article 129) sons until seven, daughters until puberty unless the court decides otherwise in their interest; Somalia (articles 64, 69), daughters to fifteen and sons to ten with extension possible to eighteen (legal majority); Sudan (article 115) sons to seven, daughters to nine, with extensions possible till the son reaches puberty and the daughter consummates her marriage); Syria (articles 146 and 147 as amended 2003) sons to thirteen and daughters to fifteen (previously, from 1975 to nine and eleven) with the court allowed to place them with their mother until they reach legal majority (*rushd*) or the daughter marries if the guardian is other than the father or if the father is not to be trusted with them; Yemen 1992 (article 140) sons to nine, daughters to twelve unless the judge decides otherwise in their best interests, and with the choice going to the child when of an 'independent age'. Qatar 2006 (article 173) provides for *hadana* to end at thirteen for the son and fifteen for the daughter, unless the *qadi* rules in the interest of the ward for an extension to fifteen for

the son and consummation of her marriage for the daughter, or unless the *qadi* gives the choice to the ward.

5 www.gulfnews.com/Articles/NationNF.asp?ArticleID=172793 (last accessed 9 August 2005).

6 Qatar 2006 (article 173) contains a similar provision, as does Morocco's new law (article 175 (2)).

7 UAE 2005 article 156.

8 Explanatory Memorandum 256.

9 In the West Bank, the law assigns custody to 'the mother who devoted herself to the custody and upbringing of her children' until they reach puberty (JLPS 1976 article 162); in the Gaza Strip, the *qadi* may allow women to maintain custody after the ages of seven for the boy and nine for the girl as under traditional Hanafi law until the ages of nine and eleven, respectively, if their interests so require (Law of Family Rights 1954, article 118). A draft Palestinian text (2006, articles 205, 206), which has the support of the *Qadi al-Qudah*, grants standard custody rights to the mother up to the age of physical puberty or the age of fifteen solar years, 'whichever is greater', while 'the mother who has devoted herself to the custody and upbringing of her children' can have her custody over her children extended to the age of legal majority at eighteen.

10 *Al-Quds* 22 November 2005.

11 For example Syria (article 139(2)) as amended 1975; Yemen article 140; and Egyptian and Jordanian court practice.

12 Morocco 2004 articles 165 and 172; Oman 131. Iraq issued Instructions for the establishment of Popular Committees to feed into custody decisions in accordance with the 1978 reforms.

13 For example, Algeria article 76; Libya article 71; Morocco 2004 199 (this was already established in article 129 of the 1957 law); Tunisia 1956 article 47; Yemen 1992 as amended 1998 article 157. By comparison, Jordan's law requires the mother who is able to pay for her children's medical treatment and education to do so if the father is unable but allows her to reclaim these expenses from him when it becomes possible (article 170). See on the earlier laws Anderson 1976 144.

14 Syria 1953 article 173 as amended 1975, and articles 170 and 21; Algeria 1984 articles 87, 63; Tunisia article 154 as amended 1981, 67 as amended 1993, and 8; Morocco 1957 article 148 as amended 1993, article 11, article 12 (3). A 1980 Iraq law (no.78/1980) identifies the guardian as first the father, then the court, while the court is instructed to give the mother precedence over others in its appointment of a *wasi* to administer the affairs of the minor after the death of the father. Somalia (1975 article 82) provided that financial guardianship over a minor ward was the prerogative of 'the father and the mother and then the grandfather'. The Omani and UAE laws retain the role of the father or closest male agate as the guardian in all matters, although he is allowed to appoint a *wasi* to guardianship over property (UAE articles 181, 188).

15 Article 87 as amended 2005.

16 Morocco 2004 article 173; this article sets out the requirements to be fulfilled by the custodian in a mostly gender-neutral fashion, no longer requiring a male custodian to be able to call on a woman to undertake the functions of custody. The gendering of the rules continues in regard to the re-marriage of a female (but not male) custodian.

17 Qatari Law of the Family 2006, article 170.

18 Algeria (article 64 as amended 2005); Iraq (article 57(7) as amended 1978); Morocco 2004 (article 171); Oman (article 130); Somalia (article 64); UAE (article 146). The Qatari law also puts the father after the mother, with the paternal before the maternal grandmother (article 169). Libyan law (article 62) puts the father as the third presumed entitled to custody after the mother and maternal grandmother. In Algeria under the original 1984 text, the father came after the mother, maternal grandmother and maternal aunt.

19 Tunisia articles 67 (as amended 1966 by law no. 49 of 3 June 1966) and 58. Compare Sudan 1991 article 113(b)1).

20 See Abu-Odeh 2004 (Vanderbilt).

21 A *mahram* is a person in such a degree of relationship that they are prohibited from marrying the ward (assuming they are of different sexes). The most obvious candidate here would be the father's brother, who is prohibited from marrying his brother's daughters but allowed to marry his brother's widow.

22 Algeria article 66; Jordan article 155; Kuwait article 191; Libya article 65; Mauritania article 130; Morocco 2004 article 175; Oman article 127; Sudan article 113(a)2); Syria article 138; Tunisia article 58; UAE article 144(1). Amendments to Iraqi law (laws 65/1986 and 106/1987) discounted the mother's remarriage as *per se* causing the lapse of custody, while allowing the court to decide whether the ward's interest lies with being placed with the mother or the father; where the father is dead, a mother's remarriage to an Iraq national is no bar to her custody rights unless the child is injured by this circumstance. Yemeni law is less explicit on this point. The Somali code (articles 64 and 67) allowed a mother who had remarried to retain custody if the children's father agreed and removed the general lapse of custody in the event of remarriage to a non-relative by a widowed mother. Qatar 2006 article 168. Jamshir 2005 39 records the head of the Bahraini Women's Association calling for a Bahraini personal status law to allow mothers to retain custody in the event of remarriage.

23 For example, Algeria article 68; Libya 66; Kuwait article 191; Tunisia article 58 as amended 1981.

24 Laws no. 65/1986 and no. 106/1987. The first amendment also allowed the mother in a new marriage to seek divorce in the event that her new husband broke his undertaking to look after the child.

25 Articles 173, 174, 175.

26 See Benyahya 2004 87, 103.

27 Kuwait article 192 (non-Muslim custody ends in all cases at age 7); Libya article 64 (the 'kitabiyya' mother is entitled to custody of her Muslim children so long as it does not transpire that she is bringing them up in a religion different to that of their Muslim father); Oman article 128 (custody of non-Muslim ends at age 7 for boys and puberty for girls unless the qadi decides otherwise in the interest of the ward); Sudan article 114 (2) (if the ward is the child of a Muslim father and the custodian of a different religion, her custody ends when the ward is five years old, or when there is fear that she is raising the ward in a religion different to that of the father); Tunisia article 59 (custody of a non-Muslim other than the mother ends at 5 unless there is a fear that the ward is taking up a different religion before that); UAE (article 145, mother of a different religion to lose custody of her child unless the qadi decides otherwise in the interest of the child, and in all cases for her custody to end when the child is 5). The Qatari family law allows a non-Muslim mother to have custody until the child is 7, provided she is not an apostate from Islam, and unless there is fear that the ward is acquiring a different religion (article 175). Algeria is less explicit on this issue in the code; article 62 defines custody as 'looking after and educating the child and bringing him up in the religion of his father[...]' and requires that the custodian 'must be capable of doing this'.

28 I am referring to the father here because, as already discussed, the marriage of a Muslim woman to a non-Muslim man is not recognised in the Muslim family law codes under examination here.

29 Explicit interpretative declarations or reservations made to this article by: Algeria, Djibouti, Iraq, Jordan, Morocco, Oman, Syria, UAE.

30 Law of Personal Status 2001 article 122 (7).

31 The Hague Convention on the Civil Aspects of International Child Abduction (1980).

32 Subject to an exception (article 20) in the event that the child's return to their country of habitual residence would endanger their fundamental rights and freedoms.

33 Turkey is a party to the Hague Convention. Outside the Middle East, so are Turkmenistan and Uzbekistan.

34 She includes for example a case from Israel (a member of the original Hague Conference) where Spain refused to return a child on the grounds that the Israeli courts had awarded the husband custody on the grounds that it understood that the mother had been 'disobedient' rather than on consideration of the child's best interest. Bruch 2000-2001 50, 53.

35 Ibid, 51.

36 Ibid, 52.

37 Hoodfar 1996 125.

38 Mir-Hosseini 1993 151; Welchman 2000 279; Moors 1995 211; Layish 1975 159.

39 For a contemporary consideration of this doctrine in society, see Jansen 2000.

40 Or indeed had simply not 'seen blood three times' and thus terminated the

waiting period. In large part, the setting of limits of maximum *'idda* period (initiated in the OLFR 1917) can be attributed to a desire to set an end to 'excessive maintenance demands' by women who might be prepared to perjure themselves in order to secure continuing financial support from their former husbands long beyond that envisaged by the jurists. This is an example of modern changes to the classical rules that did not necessarily work to the advantage of women.

41 Explanatory Memorandum to the 2005 UAE law, 200.

42 See for example Kuwait 1984 article 92, and case law in Syria ('Atari 2002 128 citing Cassation Court decisions from the 1960s).

43 Heba Saleh ('Paternity scandal divides Egypt') reported that in such situations 'the normal remedy is to have an abortion in silence'. (www.news.bbc.co.uk/hi/world/middle_east/4295911/stm)

44 IRIN, 'Egypt: landmark paternity case highlights dangers of *'urfi* marriage' at http://www.wluml.org, 13 June 2006 (retrieved 26 August 2006). Hind al-Hinawi was eventually successful, with a Cairo appeals court ruling in her favour after she brought witnesses to establish his paternity.

45 Article 156. The official guide to the new law adds nothing to the legal text in this regard.

46 As such it was welcomed by activists: Femmes Du Maroc (2004: 25) sets the article in this context and notes the wider range of legal proofs available to the court in establishing paternity and the law's provision of five years' delay before enforcing the new registration requirements.

47 'Morocco: women's advocates push men to recognise paternity', 23 August 2006 at http://www.wluml.org (retrieved 26 August 2006); including interview with Aicha Ech-Chenna, founder of the Casablanca-based organisation Feminine Solidarity that works with single mothers. Ech-Chenna is also reported as noting that although sex outside marriage is criminalised in Morocco, 'no single mother has been prosecuted under the law for over ten years'.

48 Article 89.

49 This article says that the child's lineage from his mother is proven by the birth; that the child's filiation to the husband in the marriage is established provided the minimum period of gestation (180 days) has expired since the marriage contract, and it has not been proven that it was impossible for the spouses to have met; in the case of an irregular marriage the period runs from the date of consummation.

50 Explanatory memorandum to the UAE Code of Personal Status 2005 200-201.

51 Mayer 1980 290.

52 Inhorn 2002.

53 Article 45 *bis* of Law no. 11 of 1984 as amended 2005.

54 Djibouti, Egypt, Jordan, Kuwait, Oman, Syria, UAE.

55 The reservation by Kuwait points up another concern relating to adoption: that

it might lead to a Muslim child abandoning Islam.

56 Article 20.

57 Somalia 1975 articles 10-114.

58 Respectively, articles 116-125, and article 46, unchanged in the 2005 amendments.

59 Mitchell 1997 203-204.

60 Dargouth-Medimegh 1992 57.

61 Hamadeh 1996 344.

62 Mir-Hosseini 1993 147; and see Fardia al-Naqqash cited in Najjar 1988 335.

63 See also Dennerlein 1999 140, and Abu Odeh 2004 ('Modernizing'). Compare for example Libyan law.

Notes Chapter 11

1 As noted at the beginning of the study, the Egyptian laws of the 1920s (and indeed 1940s on succession) were extremely influential in the region but did not (and do not) represent a unified 'code' of Muslim personal status as legislated elsewhere.

2 Fawzy 2004 91. By comparison, see Hamadeh's critique of what she calls the 'authoritarian discourse of silence' (1996).

3 Mordizadeh 2006

4 El-Cheikh 1998-1999.

5 Hammami 2004 141.

6 Following Bourdieu 1979, Hammami 2004 34 explains 'doxa' as follows: 'Doxa stands for aspects of tradition and culture which are so internalised that they exist as unquestionable commonsense beliefs and dispositions. Clearly, for many shari'a is a doxa – in this case assumed to be an unquestionable good that even the everyday negative experiences of the law and courts cannot undermine.'

7 Ibid 126.

8 In the West Bank, 31% of females and 8% of men reported themselves 'dissatisfied', in the Gaza Strip 18% and 4%, respectively. Hammami 2004 136 table II.7.

9 Ibid 137.

10 An overall total of 62% of female respondents and 41% of males said they would like to see more rights given to women in the applicable family law. Hammami 2004 140.

11 Loc cit. A total of 84% of male and 88% of female respondents agreed.

12 Ibid 142-143.

13 Dupret 2002; Skovgaard-Petersen 1997.

14 Dupret 1999 139.

Notes List of Statutes Cited

1 This List of Statutes has been included for ease of reference to the legislative

instruments cited in the text. In a few cases, it has not been possible to ascertain the official publication details.

2 Details from al-Thani 2006 4.

Notes Selected Statutory Provisions

1 The selected provisions translated here do not include the full texts on ages of capacity for marriage, as these have been indicated in the body of the text. For reasons of space it has also not been possible to include all the provisions regarding the guardian's right to challenge a marriage on the grounds of *kafa'a*.

2 Original text 1984:
  - Article 7: Capacity for marriage is valid at twenty-one years completed for the man and eighteen years completed for the woman. The judge can permit a marriage before that by reason of a benefit or a necessity.
  - Article 9: Marriage is contracted by the consent of the future spouses in the presence of the marriage guardian and two witnesses and with the establishing of a dower.
  - Article 11: The contracting of the marriage of a woman is the duty of her marriage guardian who shall be either her father or one of her close male relatives. The judge shall be the marriage guardian for a person who has no marriage guardian.
  - Article 12: The marriage guardian may not prevent the person under his guardianship from contracting marriage if she wishes to do so and if this is beneficial to her. Where the guardian opposes the marriage the judge may authorise it subject to the provisions of Article 9 of this law. A father may, however, oppose the marriage of his daughter who is a virgin if this is in the interest of the daughter.
  - Article 13: It is forbidden for a marriage guardian, whether he be the father or any other person, to compel a person under his guardianship to marry, just as he may not give her in marriage without her consent.

3 Inserted 1987. The original law set sixteen years completed as the minimum age of capacity; the 1978 amendment took this down to fifteen, and a further exception was made possible by the 1987 amendment.

4 From *kafa'a*.

5 La jeune fille. I do not have access to an Arabic text of the law in order the check the meaning in the original Arabic; it could mean a female below the age of legal majority, or a virgin married for the first time.

6 Original 1957 text Article 12:
  1. Guardianship is the right of the woman, and the guardian shall not contract her marriage unless she authorises him to do so, except in the case of *ijbar* (compulsion) specified hereafter.
  2. A woman shall not make the contract herself but shall authorise her guardian to contract her marriage.

3. A woman shall appoint a male agent whom she authorises to contract the marriage of her ward.

4. It shall not be permitted for a guardian, even if he is the father, to compel his daughter who is of age, even if she is a virgin, to marry, except with her permission and consent, unless it is feared that the woman will fall into immorality in which case the judge has the right to compel her to marry in order that she be under the marital authority of a husband of equal status who will take care of her.

Amended 1993 to read:

1. Guardianship is the right of the woman, and the guardian shall not contract her marriage unless she authorizes him to do so.

2. A woman shall authorize her guardian to contract her marriage.

3. A woman of the age of legal majority who has no father may contract her own marriage, or appoint whom she chooses of her guardians [for this purpose].

7 The selected provisions in this section illustrate constraints on polygyny additional to those contemplated in the traditional rules and included in the codes, notably the right to equitable treatment with co-wives and not to share accommodation with a co-wife. These rules are included in the statutory instruments in Kuwait and Oman as well as in the other codifications.

8 Original text 1984: Article 8: It is permitted to contract marriage with more than one wife within the limits of the *shariʿa* if the reason is justified and if the conditions and the intention of maintaining equity are met and after prior notification to existing and future wives. Any of these may instigate legal action against the husband in case of harm or to petition for divorce in the case of lack of consent.

9 This clause was inserted in 1980.

10 Added in 2001.

11 Text in *Mudawwana* 1957 as amended 1993: Article 30: 1) The first wife shall be advised that her husband intends to marry a second wife.
2) The wife may stipulate that her husband shall not marry another wife, or else she has the right to choose [to leave the marriage].
3) Marriage may not be contracted with a second wife unless she has been informed that the man who wishes to marry her is already married to another woman.

12 The second paragraph was an expansion on the original 1956 text through a 1958 explanatory law; there are three further paragraphs regarding various penalties added in 1964, not translated here.

13 Original text 1992 Article 12:

1. A man shall be permitted to marry up to four wives provided he has the ability to treat them equitably, otherwise only one.

2. He may make a contract with another wife upon fulfilment of the following conditions:

    a. that there is some lawful benefit

    b. that the husband has the financial capacity to support more than one wife

    c. that the woman is informed that the man who wishes to marry her is married to someone else

    d. that a wife is informed that her husband wishes to marry another wife.

14 The selected provisions here focus on the issue of 'obedience', the wife's right to work, and mutual rights and duties. For lack of space, I have not included the more standard texts in many of the laws regarding the provision of the marital home, dower, and the details of maintenance.

15 Original text 1984 Article 36: The obligations of the two spouses are as follows:

    1. to protect the conjugal bonds and the duties of their life together;

    2. to contribute jointly to the preservation of the interests of the family, and to the protection of the children and their sound education;

    3. to preserve the bonds of family and good relationships with parents and kinsmen.

Article 37: The husband is required to:

    1. provide maintenance for the wife within the limits of his ability, except from such time as it is established that she has abandoned the matrimonial home

    2. act with complete equity towards his wives if he has more than one.

Article 38:

The wife has the right to:

    – visit those of her relatives who are within the degree within which marriage is prohibited and to receive them in accordance with custom and convention

    – dispose freely of her property.

Article 39:

The wife is required:

    1. to obey her husband and to accord him the respect due to his position as head of the family

    2. to suckle her offspring if she is able to do so and to bring them up

    3. to respect the parents and family of her husband.

16 Unlike the other two articles translated above, article 74 was not amended in 2005. The three other articles to which article 74 refers concern what maintenance has to include, how it is to be assessed and a limit on arrears that may be awarded, of not more than one year prior to the claim being filed at court.

17 The translation of this phrase is borrowed from el-Alami and Hinchcliffe 1996 52.

18 Inserted 1980.

19 Amended 2001. Original 1976 text: No maintenance is due the wife who works outside the house without the consent of her husband.

20 The equivalent provisions in the 1957 law read as follows:

Article 34: Reciprocal rights and duties of the spouses are:

1. *shari* cohabitation;
2. good relations, mutual respect and affection and the preservation of the family interest;
3. mutual inheritance rights of the spouses;
4. family rights such as the paternity of children and the impediment of affinity.

Article 35: The wife's rights from her husband are:

1. *shari* maintenance including food, clothing, medical treatment and accommodation;
2. justice and equality if the man is married to more than one [wife];
3. being allowed to visit her family and have them visit her in accordance with convention;
4. full freedom in disposing of her property without the supervision of the husband; the husband has no guardianship over the property of his wife.

Article 36: The husband's rights from his wife are:

1. the wife's preservation of herself and her chastity;
2. the wife's obedience to her husband in accordance with convention;
3. breastfeeding her children if she is able;
4. supervising the house and organising its affairs;
5. respecting the husband's parents and relatives in accordance with convention.

21 Original text of article 23: The husband shall treat his wife well and make their conjugal life pleasant and shall refrain from harming her. He shall maintain her and his children from her in accordance with his circumstances and hers with regard to the matters generally involved in maintenance. The wife shall participate in supporting the family if she has money. The wife shall pay heed to her husband in consideration of his being head of the family and obey him in that which he tells her to do in these rights and shall fulfil her marital duties as required by custom and convention.

22 This phrase inserted in 2005.

23 Original text: The wife may separate from her husband for an agreed upon sum; if nothing is agreed upon, then the judge shall order the payment of a sum of not more than the value of the proper dower at the time of the ruling.

24 The verb form is *khala'at*, from the same root as *khul'*.

25 The two paragraphs translated here were inserted in 2001.

26 This is another form from the same root as *khul'* and bearing the same meaning.

27 The original 1976 text allowed for a maximum of one year's maintenance and gave no minimum.

28 The original 1953 text set a maximum of one year's maintenance.

29 Final paragraph added by the 1981 amendment.

Glossary of Arabic Terms

The meanings given to the terms below are related to their use in personal status law and in the discussions in this study. Some of the terms also carry other meanings in other contexts and usage.

bikr	virgin (used to distinguish the status of a woman at marriage from that of *thayyib*, see below)
bulugh	puberty
faskh	judicial dissolution of marriage
fatiha	used in Morocco to refer to an unregistered marriage
firash	the (conjugal) bed; used in maxims such as 'the child belongs to the marriage bed' (*al-walad li'l-firash*)
fidiya	ransom; used in some countries (for example Sudan) to indicate a form of divorce whereby the wife 'ransoms' herself with a consideration
fiqh	(Islamic) jurisprudence: broadly, used here to refer to the body of rulings on matters of law worked out by the Muslim jurists and contained in the voluminous writings of the various schools of law
fitna	subversion, chaos, disorder
hadith	textual report of a practice or precedent of the Prophet Muhammad, collections of which constitute the second material source of Islamic law in classical jurisprudential theory
halal	lawful, permitted (under the *shari'a*)
haram	unlawful, prohibited (under the *shari'a*)
hasab	wealth or standing
'idda	the waiting period that must be observed by a woman following her divorce, before she is allowed to marry again (normally three menstrual cycles or until childbirth if the divorcée is pregnant; for a widow, four months and ten days)
idrar	harm, prejudice
ijbar	coercion, compulsion
ijtihad	interpretation; from the root meaning 'effort', the term is usually employed to indicate the efforts exerted by a jurist in working out a ruling of law on a particular point through consulting the source texts, rather than through relying on existing rulings of jurists

kafala (kafil)	sponsorship, tutelage; used to indicate a system of child care that does not admit certain rules of adoption such as giving the ward the family name of the sponsors/carers. The *kafil* is the sponsor, the person undertaking *kafala* of a ward
karahiya	hatred or aversion; used to indicate grounds for judicial divorce at the petition of the wife in some countries, notably Yemen
khiyar al-bulugh	the 'option of puberty', whereby a person married below puberty has the right to repudiate the marriage on reaching puberty
khalwa	seclusion; used to describe a situation where a man and woman have been secluded together in such a manner as to give rise to the presumption of consummation of a marriage
khul'	divorce by the husband in return for remuneration by the wife
li'an	a divorce procedure involving a series of oaths by husband and wife regarding the paternity of a child from the marriage
madhhab	school of law
mahr	dower
mahram	a family member of a degree of relationship that prohibits marriage to a *mahram* of the other sex
misyar	a modern form of marriage that normally involves the husband not providing accommodation for the wife, and a system of 'visits' rather than cohabitation
mut'a	monetary compensation paid by the ex-husband to a divorced wife; sometimes translated as 'gift of consolation'; some of the laws use this word while others use *ta'wid* (see below)
na'ib shar'i	the '*shar'i* representative' of a legal minor
nasab	lineage (usually denoting patri-lineage)
nizami	regular or statutory; used of the 'regular' court system which is separate in some countries from the *shari'a* courts and other religious courts
niza' wa shiqaq	discord and strife, grounds for judicial divorce
nashiz	disobedient (see *nushuz*)
nushuz	disobedience; used in some laws to describe the situation of the wife who has been formally held to be disobedient by the court
qadi (pl. *qudah*)	judge (*Qadi al-Qudah*: Chief Justice)
qiwama	authority, supervision, guardianship; used in the debates examined in this study as the principle of the husband's authority in the family
rushd	legal majority
sulh	reconciliation
sunna	the practice or precedent of the Prophet Muhammad recorded in the *hadith*
ta'a	obedience
tafriq	judicial divorce

talaq	unilateral divorce by the husband of his wife; sometimes translated as 'repudiation'
tamlik	delegation of *talaq*, where the husband 'possesses' his wife of his own power of unilateral *talaq*
tatliq	judicial divorce
ta'wid	compensation due to a divorcée from the man who divorced her (see also *mut'a*)
thayyib	a woman who has been married before (see *bikr* above)
'ulama'	scholars of Islamic law and religion
'urfi	'customary', used in some countries (Egypt, Palestine) to refer to unregistered marriages concluded outside official procedures
wakil	representative, agent
wali	guardian
wasi	legal guardian for children appointed by their father at his death
wilaya	guardianship
zifaf	part of customary wedding celebrations in which a procession takes the wife to her new home with her husband
zina	unlawful (i.e. in *fiqh*, pre- or extra-marital) sexual intercourse

Bibliography

Abdo, Nahla, 'Muslim family law: articulating gender, class and the state', *International Review of Comparative Public Policy,* 9 (1997), pp.169-193.

Abu-Odeh, Lama, 'Egyptian feminism: trapped in the identity debate', in Yvonne Yazbeck Haddad and Barbara Freyer Stowasser (eds), *Islamic law and the challenges of modernity,* (Walnut Creek, 2004) pp.183-211.

— 'Modernizing Muslim family law: the case of Egypt', 37 *Vanderbilt Journal of Transnational Law* (2004), 1043.

— 'Modern family law, 1800-present. Arab states', *Encyclopaedia of Women in Islamic Cultures* Vol. 2, (2005), pp. 459-462.

Abu Zahra, Muhammad, *Al-ahwal al-shakhsiya.* (Cairo, 1957).

Ahmed, Leila, *Women and gender in Islam.* (New Haven, 1992).

el-Alami, Dawoud, *The marriage contract in Islamic law.* (London, 1992).

— 'Remedy or device? The system of *khul'* and the effects of its incorporation into Egyptian personal status law,' 6 *Yearbook of Islamic and Middle Eastern Law* (2000), 134-139.

el-Alami, Dawoud and Doreen Hinchcliffe, *Islamic marriage and divorce laws of the Arab world* (London, 1996).

El-Alem, 'Libya,' I *Yearbook of Islamic and Middle Eastern Law* (1994), 225-236.

American Bar Association / Iraq Legal Development Project (ABA ILDP), 'The status of women in Iraq: an assessment of Iraq's *de jure* and *de facto* compliance with international legal standards' ABA July 2005.

Amnesty International, 'Gulf Cooperation Council (GCC) countries: women deserve dignity and respect.'(Amnesty International, AI Index: MDE 04/004, 2005).

'Amr,'Abd al-Fattah, *Al-qararat al-qada'iyya fi'l-ahwal al-shakhsiyya,* (Amman 1990).

Anderson, J.N.D., 'Recent developments in *shari'a* law II: matters of competence, organization and procedure,' 41 *Muslim World* (1951) pp.34-48.

— 'The contract of marriage', 41 *Muslim World* (1951) pp.113-126.

— 'The Jordanian Law of Family Rights', 42 *Muslim World* (1952), pp.190-206.

— 'The Syrian Law of Personal Status' *Bulletin of the School of Oriental and African Studies* 17/1 (1955) pp.34-49.

— 'The Tunisian Law of Personal Status' 7 *International and Comparative Law Quarterly* (1958) 263-279.

— 'Reforms in Family Law in Morocco', 2/3 *Journal of African Law* (1958).

— 'A Law of Personal Status for Iraq'. 9 *International and Comparative Law Quarterly* (1960) pp.542-563.

— *Law reform in the Muslim world.* (London, 1976).

An-Nai'm, Abdullahi (ed), *Islamic family law in a changing world. A global resource book.* (London, 2002).
— *'Shari'a* and Islamic family law: transition and transformation' 1-22 in an-Na'im (ed) (2002)
— (ed) *Inter-religious marriages among Muslims – Negotiating religion and social identity in family and community*, (New Delhi 2005).
Al-'Arabi, M. *Al-mabadi' al-qada'iyya li mahkamat al-isti'naf al-shar'iyya* Volume II. (Amman, 1984).
Arabi, Oussama, 'The dawning of the third millenium on shari'a: Egypt's Law no.1 of 2000, or women may divorce at will', *Arab Law Quarterly* 16:1 (2001) pp. 2-21.
— *Studies in modern Islamic law and jurisprudence.* (The Hague, 2001).
'Atari, Mamduh (ed), *Qanun al-ahwal al-shakhsiyya.* (Damascus, 2002).

Badran, B.A., *Huquq al-awlad fi al-shari'a al-islamiyya wa'l-qanun.* (Alexandria, 1981).
Badran, Margot, *Feminists, Islam and nation: gender and the making of modern Egypt.* (Princeton, 1995).
Bargach, Jamila 'Orphans of Islam: family, abandonment and secret adoption in Morocco' (Boulder, 2002);
— (2002 a) 'Orphans of Islam: family, abandonment and secret adoption in Morocco,' *ISIM Review* 11 (2002).
Barger, John, 'Gender law in the Jamahiriyya: an application to Libya of Mounira Charrad's theory of state development to women's rights,' *Journal of Libyan Studies* Vol. 3/1 (2002), 30-41.
Bennani, Farida Taqsim *al-'amal bayn al-zawjayn fi daw' al-qanun al-maghribi wa'l-fiqh al-islami.* (Marrakesh 1993)
— *Haqq tasarruf al-zawja fi maliha.* (Marrakesh, 1995).
Bennoune, Karima, 'Between betrayal and betrayal: fundamentalism, family law and feminist struggle in Algeria', *Arab Studies Quarterly* 17 (1995), pp.51-76.
Benyahya, Muhammad (ed), *Al-Mudawwana al-jadida li-al-usra.* (Rabat, 2004).
Bernard-Maugiron, 'Dissolution du marriage et persistance non juridictionnelle des conflits conjugaux en Égypte', in Dupret and Burgat (eds), *Le shaykh et le procurer*, pp.73-100.
Bourdieu, Pierre, *Outline of a theory of practice.* (Cambridge, 1979).
Brand, Laurie, *Women, the state and political liberalization: Middle Eastern and North African experiences.* (New York 1998).
Brown, Nathan J., *Constitutions in a nonconstitutional world. Arab basic laws and the prospects for accountable government.* (New York, 2002).
Bruch, Carol S., 'Religious law, secular practices, and children's human rights in child abduction cases under the Hague Child Abduction Convention,' 33 *New York University Journal of International Law and Policy* (2000-2001), 49-58.
Buskens, Léon, 'Islamic commentaries and French codes: The confrontation and accommodation of two forms of textualization of family law in the Morocco', in

Hank Driesen (ed), *The Politics of ethnograhic reading and writing. Confrontations of western and indigenous views.* (Fort Lauderdale, 1993), pp.65-100.

— *Islamitisch rechten en familiebetrekkingen in Morokko.* (Amsterdam, 1999).

— 'Recent debates on family law reform in Morocco: Islamic law as politics in an emerging public sphere', *Islamic Law and Society* 10,1 (2003), pp.70-131.

Chamari, Alya Chérif, *La Femme et la loi en Tunisie.* (Casablanca, 1991).

Charrad, Mounira, *States and women's rights. The making of postcolonial Tunisia, Algeria and Morocco.*(Berkeley, 2001).

El-Cheikh, Nadia, 'The 1998 proposed civil marriage law in Lebanon: the reaction of the Muslim communities', *Yearbook of Islamic and Middle Eastern Law*, 5 (1998-1999), 147-161.

Chekir, Hafidha, *Le statut des femmes entre les texts et les résistances. Le cas de la Tunisie.* (Tunis, 2000).

Chemais, Amina, 'Obstacles to divorce for Muslim women in Egypt', in Hoodfar, *Shifting Boundaries.*

Chiba, Masaji, 'Introduction' in Chiba (ed) *Asian indigenous law in interaction with received law.* (London and New York, 1986) pp.1-9.

Cole, Juan, 'Struggles over personal status and family law in post-Baath Iraq', in Cuno (ed), *Family, Gender and Law* (forthcoming 2007).

Connors, Jane, 'The Woman's Convention in the Muslim world', in Yamani (ed) (1996), pp. 351-371.

Coulson, Noel and Doreen Hinchcliffe, 'Women and law reform in contemporary Islam', in Lois Beck and Nikki Keddie (eds), *Women in the Muslim world* (Cambridge, Mass., 1978), pp.37-51.

Cuno, Kenneth, 'Disobedient wives and neglectful husbands: marital relations and the first phase of reform of family law in Egypt', in Cuno (ed), *Family, Gender and Law* (forthcoming 2007).

Cuno, Kenneth (ed) *Family, Gender and Law in a Globalizing Middle East and South Asia* (forthcoming 2007).

Dahi, 'Izzat, *al-mabadi' al-qanuniyya allati qararatha al-ghuruf al-qada'iyya fi'l-ahwal al-shakhsiyya* 1953-1976. (Damascus, 1978).

Dahlgren, Susanne,'Women's *adah* versus 'women's law': the contesting issue of *mahr* in Aden, Yemen', in Dupret and Burgat (eds), *Le shaykh et le procurer*, pp.125-144.

Darghouth-Medimegh, Aziza, *Droits et vécu de la femme en tunisie.* (Lyon, 1992).

Daoud, Zakya, 'En marge de la Conférence mondiale des femmes de Pékin; la strategie des feministes maghrébines', *Monde Arabe MaghrebMachrek* 150 (1995), 105-121.

Dennerlein, Bettina, 'Islam, Recht under gesellschaflicher Transformation. Zur Entwicklung des algerischen Personalstatus seit 1962', Ph.D. thesis, Free University of Berlin (1996).

- 'Changing conceptions of marriage in Algerian personal status law,' in R.S. Khare (ed), *Perspectives on Islamic law, justice and society*. (Lanham, 1999).

Al-Dimashqi, Irfan Bin Salim, *Nikah al-masyar*. (Sidon, 2002).

Dupret, Baudouin, 'Legal pluralism, normative plurality and the Arab world', in Dupret, Berger and al-Zwaini (eds), *Legal pluralism in the Arab world*. (The Hague, 1999), pp.29-40.

- 'Sexuality at the Egyptian bar. Female circumcision, sex change operations and motives for suing', 9,1 *Islamic Law and Society* (2002), 42-69.

- 'The practice of judging: the Egyptian judiciary at work in a personal status case,' in Khalid Masud, Rudolph Peters and David Powers (eds), *Dispensing justice in Islam. Qadis and their judgments*. (Leiden, 2006), 143-168.

Dupret, Baudouin and Francois Burgat (eds), Le shaykh et le procurer. Systèmes coutumiers et pratiques juridiques au Yémen et en Égypte. CEDEJ: *Égypte/Monde Arabe* no.1 – 3ᵉ série (2005).

Eickelman, Dale F. and Jon W. Anderson, *New media in the Muslim world. The emerging public sphere*. (Bloomington and Indianapolis, [1999] 2003).

Esposito, John L., *Women in Muslim family law*. (Syracuse, 2001), second edition with Natana J. DeLong-Bas.

Fahmi, Hoda, *Divorcer en Egypte: Etude de l'application des lois du statut personnel*. (Cairo,1987).

Fakhro, Munira, 'Gulf Women and Islamic Law', in Yamani (ed., 1996), 251-261.

Fawzy, Essam, 'Muslim personal status law in Egypt: the current situation and possibilities of reform through internal initiatives', in Welchman (ed), *Women's rights and Islamic family law. Perspectives on reform*. (London, 2004), pp.17-94.

Foblets, Marie-Claire and Jean-Yves Carlier, *Le code marocain de la famille. Incidences au regard du droit international privé en Europe*. (Brussels, 2005).

al-Gabali, Tahani 'Al-Khulʿ bayn al-qanun wa'l tatbiq,' in al-Sawi (ed.) *Al-hisad*, (2003), pp. 39-44.

Hafez, Sherine, 'The terms of empowerment. Islamic women activists in Egypt', *Cairo Papers in Social Science* 24, 4, (2001).

Hajjar, Lisa, 'Domestic violence and *shariʿa*: a comparative study of Muslim societies in the Middle East, Africa and Asia', in Welchman (ed) *Women's rights and Islamic family law* (2004), pp.233-272.

Hamadeh, Naila, 'Islamic family legislation. The authoritarian discourse of silence', in Mai Yamani *Feminism and Islam* (ed., 1996), pp.331-349.

Hammami, Rema, 'NGOs: the professionalisation of politics', *Race and Class* 37,2 (1995), 51-64.

- 'Attitudes towards legal reform of personal status law in Palestine', in Welchman (ed), *Women's rights and Islamic family law* (2004), pp.125-143.

Hammami, Rema and Penny Johnson, 'Equality with a difference: gender and citizenship in transitional Palestine', *Social Politics* 6/3 (1999), 315-343.

Al-Haq, *Al-mar'a wa al-'adala wa al-qanun.* (Ramallah, 1995).

Hatem, Mervat, 'Economic and political liberalisation in Egypt and the demise of state feminism', *International Journal of Middle East Studies* 24 (1992), 231-251.

Hélie-Lucas, Marie-Aimée, 'The preferential symbol for Islamic identity: women in Muslim personal status laws', in Valentine Moghadam (ed), *Identity politics and women. Cultural reassertions and feminisms in international perspective.* (Boulder, 1994), pp.391-407.

Hijab, Nadia, *Womanpower: the Arab debate on women at work.* (Cambridge, 1988).

Hinz, Almut, 'The development of matrimonial law in Libya', *Journal of Libyan Studies* no.3/1 (2002), 13-29

Hoodfar, Homa, 'Circumventing legal limitation: mahr and marriage negotiation in Egyptian low-income communities', in Homa Hoodfar (ed), *Shifting boundaries in marriage and divorce in Muslim communities,* (Grabels, 1996), pp.120-141.

Hooper, C.A., *The civil law of Palestine and Transjordan.* (Jerusalem, 1933).

Human Rights Watch, *Divorced from justice: women's unequal access to divorce in Egypt,* Human Rights Watch, Vol. 16, No. 8(E), (2004).

el-Imam, Noor, 'Experience of the Jordanian Women's Movement in Amending the Personal Status Law', paper at the Regional Conference on Personal Status Laws in the Arab World: Theory, Practice and Chances for Reform (Amman, 2000).

Imber, Colin, *Ebu's-Su'ud, The Islamic legal tradition.* (Edinburgh, 1997).

Inhorn, Marcia C., 'Gender, religion and in vitro fertilization', *ISIM Review* 11 (2002).

Jacobson, Heather, 'The marriage dower: essential guarantor of women's rights in the West Bank and Gaza Strip', 10 *Michigan Journal of Gender and Law*, (2003), 143-167.

Jad, Islah, 'The NGOization of the Arab women's movements', *Review of Women's Studies* 2 (2004), 42-56.

Jamshir, Ghada Yusuf (ed), *Al-jallad wa al-dahiya fi al-mahakim al-shar'iyya.* (Beirut, 2005).

Jansen, W., 'Sleeping in the womb: protracted pregnancies in the Maghrib', 90 *Muslim World* (2000), 218-237.

Kandiyoti, Deniz, 'Bargaining with patriarchy', *Gender and Society* 2.3 (1988), 274-290.
— 'Introduction' in Deniz Kandiyoti (ed), *Women, Islam and the state.* (Philadelphia, 1991), pp.1-21.

Al-Kashbur, Muhammad, *Qanun al-ahwal al-shakhsiya.* (Casablanca, 1996).

Keddie, Nikki R., *Women in the Middle East. Past and present.* (Princeton 2007).

Khadr, Asma, *Al-qanun wa mustaqbil al-mar'a al-filastiniya.* (Jerusalem 1998).

Layish, Aharon, *Women and Islamic law in a non-Muslim state.* (Jerusalem, 1975).

— *Divorce in the Libyan family. A study based on the sijills of the shari'a courts of Ajdabiyya and Kufra.* (New York/Jerusalem, 1991).
— 'The transformation of the *shari'a* from jurists' law to statutory law in the contemporary Muslim world', 44/1 *Die Welt des Islams* (2004), 85-113.
Lazreg, Marnia, *The eloquence of silence: Algerian women in question.* (London, 1994).
Loukili, Mohamed and Michèle Zirari-Devif, 'Le nouveau code marocain de la famille: une reforme dans la continuité,' 11 *Yearbook of Islamic and Middle Eastern Law* (2004-2005) pp.205-218.
Ltaief, Wassila, 'International law, mixed marriage, and the law of succession in North Africa: "...but some are more equal than others"', 184 *International Social Science Journal* (June 2005), 331-350.

Maddy-Weitzman, Bruce, 'Women, Islam and the Moroccan state: the struggle over the personal status law', *Middle East Journal* 59/3 (2005), 393-410.
Mahmood, Tahir, *Family law reform in the Muslim world.* (Bombay, 1972).
— *Statutes of personal law in Islamic countries – history, texts and analysis*, second edition (New Delhi, 1995).
Mallat, Chibli, 'Shi'ism and Sunnism in Iraq: revisiting the codes', in Mallat and Connors (ed), *Islamic family law* (London, 1990), pp.71-91.
Mayer, Ann Elizabeth, 'Libyan legislation in defence of Arabo-Islamic sexual mores', 28 *American Journal of Comparative Law* (1980), 287-313.
— 'Rhetorical strategies and official policies on women's rights: the merits and drawbacks of the new world hypocrisy,' in Mahnaz Afkhami (ed) *Faith and freedom: women's human rights in the Muslim world.* (Reading, 1995), pp.104-132
— 'Islamic reservations to human rights conventions' 15 *recht van der Islam* (1998)
— 'Internationalizing the conversation on Arab women's rights: Arab countries face the CEDAW Committee', in Yvonne Yazbeck Haddad and Barbara Freyer Stowasser (eds), *Islamic law and the challenges of modernity*, (Walnut Creek, 2004) pp.133-160.
Meriwether, Margaret L., 'The rights of children and the responsibilities of women. Women as *wasis* in Aleppo, 1770-1840', in Sonbol (ed) *Women, the family and divorce laws in Islamic history.* (1996) pp. 219-235
Messick, Brinkley, *The calligraphic state. Textual domination and history in a Muslim society.* (Berkeley, 1993).
Ministry of Justice, Morocco, *Dalil 'amali li-mudawwanat al-'usra* (Practical guide to the Code of the Family) (Rabat, 2004).
Mir-Hosseini, Ziba, *Marriage on trial. A study of Islamic family law, Iran and Morocco compared.* (London, 1993; second edition 2000).
— 'Tamkin: stories from a family court in Iran,' in Bowen and Early (eds), *Everyday life in the Muslim Middle East*, second edition (Indiana, 2002), pp.136-150.
— 'The construction of gender in Islamic legal thought and strategies for reform,' *Hawwa: Journal of Women of the Middle East and the Islamic World* 1,1 (2003), 1-28

Mitchell, Ruth, 'Family law in Algeria before and after the 1404/1984 Family Code,' in Robert Gleave (ed.), *Islamic law, theory and practice*. (London 1997) pp.194-204.

Moghadam, Valentine (ed), *Gender and national identity. Women and politics in Muslim societies*. (London, 1994).

Molyneux, Maxine, 'Women's rights and political contingency: the case of Yemen, 1990-1994', *Middle East Journal* 49.3 (1995), 418-431.

Moors, Annelies, *Women, Property and Islam. Palestinian Experiences 1920-1990*. (Cambridge, 1995).

— 'Debating Islamic family law: legal texts and social practices,' in Margaret C. Meriwether and Judith E. Tucker (eds), *A social history of gender in the modern Muslim Middle East*. (Boulder, 1999), pp.141-175.

— 'Public debates on family law reform: participants, positions and styles of argumentation in the 1990s', *Islamic Law and Society* 10,1 (2003), 1-11.

Moosa, Ebrahim, 'The poetics and politics of law after empire: reading women's rights in the contestation of law', *UCLA Journal of Near Eastern Law* 1 (2001-2002), 1-46.

Mordizadeh, Naz K., 'Taking Islamic law seriously: INGOs and the battle for Muslim hearts and minds', 19 *Harvard Human Rights Journal* (2006), 193-235.

Motzki, Harold, 'Child marriage in seventeenth century Palestine', in Muhammad Khalid Masud, Brinkley Messick and David Powers (eds), *Islamic legal Interpretation: muftis and their fatwas*. (Cambridge, Mass., 1996).

Najjar, Fawzi, 'Egypt's laws of personal status', *Arab Studies Quarterly* 10 (1988), 319-344.

Nasir, Jamal J., *The Islamic law of personal status*, second edition (London, 1986).

— *The status of women under Islamic law*. (London, 1990, second edition 1994).

Paradelle, Muriel 'Legal pluralism and public international law: an analysis based on the International Convention on the Rights of the Child', in Dupret, Berger and al-Zwaini (eds), *Legal Pluralism in the Arab World*. (The Hague, 1999), pp. 97-112

al-Qassim, Ragheb, 'Qanun al-ahwal al-shakhsiyya al-urduni bayn al-nazhariyya wa'l-tatbiq,' paper for the Regional Conference on Personal Status Laws in the Arab World: Theory, Practice and Chances for Reform. (Amman, 2000).

Raafat, Hassan, 'Marriage without approval of bride's guardian illegal', *Khaleej Times* 26 January 2001.

Rahman, Fazlur, 'A survey of the modernization of Muslim family law', *International Journal of Middle East Studies* 11 (1980), 451-465.

Rosen, Lawrence, 'Equity and discretion in a modern Islamic legal system', 15 *Law and Society Review* (1980-1), 217-245.

Rouhana, Hoda, 'Practices in the *Shari'a* Court of Appeal in Israel; gendered reading of arbitration decisions', Women Living under Muslim Laws Dossier 25 (2003), pp. 49-70.

Sanders, Paula, 'Gendering the ungendered body: hermaphrodites in medieval Islamic law', in Nicki Keddie and Beth Baron (eds), *Women in Middle Eastern History*. (Yale, 1991), pp.74-95.

al-Sawi, Muhammad Ahmad (ed.), *Al-hisad: 'aman 'ala al-khul'* (Cairo, 2003).

al-Sawi, Muhammad Ahmad and Mervat Ahmad Abu Taj, *Sahafat min daftar ahwal al-usra al-misriyya.* (Cairo, 2000).

Sen, Purna, '"Crimes of honour", value and meaning', in Lynn Welchman and Sara Hossain (eds), *'Honour': crimes, paradigms and violence against women.* (London, 2005), pp.47-63.

Shaham, Ron, *Family and the courts in modern Egypt. A study based on decisions by the shari'a courts 1900-1955* (Leiden, 1997).

— 'State, feminists and islamists – the debate over stipulations in marriage contracts in Egypt', *BSOAS* 62 (1999), 462-483.

Shahd, Laila S., 'An investigation of the phenomenon of polygyny in rural Egypt, *Cairo Papers in Social Science* 24,3 (2001).

al-Sharif, Muhammad al-Habib, *Majallat al-ahwal al-shakhsiyya; juma' wa ta'liq,* (Soussa, 1997).

Shehada, Nahda, 'Women's experience in the *shari'a* court of Gaza City. The multiple meanings of maintenance', *Review of Women's Studies,* 2 (2004), 57-71.

— 'Justice without drama: enacting family law in Gaza City *shari'a* court', Ph.D. Thesis, Institute of Social Sciences (The Hague, 2005).

Shehadeh, Lamia Rustum, 'The legal status of married women in Lebanon', *International Journal of Middle East Studies* 30 (1998), 501-519.

Sidahmed, Abdel Salam, 'Problems in contemporary applications of Islamic criminal sanctions: the penalty for adultery in relation to women', 28/2 *British Journal of Middle Eastern Studies* (2001), 187-204.

Singerman, Diane, 'Rewriting divorce in Egypt: reclaiming Islam, legal activism and coalition politics', in Robert Hefner (ed), *Remaking Muslim politics. Pluralism, contestation, democratization.* (Princeton, 2005), pp. 161-188.

Skovgaard-Petersen, J., 'Never change your sex in Cairo', in *Defining Islam for the Egyptian State.* (Leiden, 1997), pp.319-334

Soliman, Azza and Azza Salah, ''al-khul' qanunan wa tatbiqan', in al-Sawi (ed) *al-Hisad* (2003), pp. 13-38.

Somerset, Carron, *Early marriage: whose right to choose?* (London, 2000).

Sonbol, Amira El Azhary (ed), *Women, the family, and divorce laws in Islamic history.* (Syracuse, 1996).

— 'Ta'a and modern legal reform: a rereading', *Islam and Christian-Muslim Relations* 9.3 (1998), 285-294.

— 'Women in shari'ah courts: A historical and methodological discussion', 27 *Fordham International Law Journal* (2003), 225-253.

— '"The woman follows the nationality of her husband": guardianship, citizenship and gender,' *Hawwa: Journal of Women of the Middle East and the Islamic World* 1,1 (2003), 86-117.

— 'Muslim women and legal reform: the case of Jordan and women's work', in Yvonne Yazbeck Haddad and Barbara Freyer Stowasser (eds), *Islamic law and the challenges of modernity.* (Walnut Creek, 2004), pp. 213-232.

Sonneveld, Nadia, 'If only there was *khul'...'* *ISIM Review* 17 (2006), 51-52.

Stowasser, Barbara 'Gender Issues and Contemporary Qur'an Interpretation', in Yvonne Haddad and John Esposito (eds), *Islam, gender and social change.* (Oxford, 1998), pp. 30-44.

Stowasser, Barbara Freyer and Zeinab Abul-Magd, *'Tahlil* marriage in *shari'a,* legal codes, and the contemporary *fatwa* literature,' in Yvonne Yazbeck Haddad and Barbara Freyer Stowasser (eds), *Islamic law and the challenges of modernity.* (Walnut Creek, 2004), pp.161-181.

Tadrus, Marlene, 'Qanun al-khul' fi al-sahafa al-misriya', in al-Sawi (ed), *al-Hisad* (2003), pp.83-100.

Al-Thani, Alya, 'The realization of the rights of the girl child in Qatar: towards ending the traditional practice of early marriage,' MA dissertation (SOAS, 2006).

Tucker, Judith, 'Revisiting reform: women and the Ottoman Law of Family Rights, 1917', *Arab Studies Journal* 1 (1996), 4-17.

— *In the house of the law. gender and Islamic law in Syria and Palestine, 17th-18th centuries.* (Berkeley, 1998).

UNICEF, Early Marriage: Child Spouses,': *Innocenti Digest* 7 (Florence, 2001).

— 'Early marriage: A harmful traditional practice. A statistical exploration' (UNICEF, 2005).

Welchman, Lynn, *Beyond the code. Muslim family law and the shar'i judiciary in the Palestinian West Bank.* (The Hague, 2000).

— 'Jordan: capacity, consent and under-age marriage in Muslim family law', *International Survey of Family Law* (2001), 243-265.

— 'In the interim: civil society, the *shar'i* judiciary and Palestinian personal status law in the transitional period', *Islamic Law and Society* 10,1 (2003), 34-69.

— (ed) *Women's rights and Islamic family law: perspectives on reform.* (London, 2004).

— 'Egypt: new deal on divorce,' *International Survey of Family Law* (2004), 123-142.

— 'Family, gender and law in Palestine and Jordan', in Cuno (ed) *Family, Gender and Law* (forthcoming 2007)

White, Elizabeth H., 'Legal reform as an indicator of women's status in Muslim nations', in Lois Beck and Nikki Keddie (eds), *Women in the Muslim world,* (Cambridge, Mass., 1978), pp.52-68.

Wing, Adrien Catherine, 'Custom, religion and rights: the future legal status of Palestinian women,' 35 *Harvard International Law Journal* (1994) pp.149-200.

Women Living Under Muslim Laws, *Knowing our rights: women, family, laws and customs in the Muslim world.* (Lahore, 2003; and with 2003-2006 update, London, 2006).

Women's Leadership Institute Iraq, 'The Constitution and the international obligations of Iraq under CEDAW with special concern to article 39 of the Constitution' 2006 (at http://www.wluml.org retrieved 2 August 2006.)

Wurth, Anna, 'A Sana'a court: the family and the ability to negotiate', 2,3 *Islamic Law and Society* (1995), 320-340.

— *al-shari'a fi Bab al-Yaman: Recht, Richter und Rechtspraxis an der familien-rechtlicher Kammer des Gerichtes Sud-Sanaa* 1983-1995. (Berlin, 2000).

— 'Stalled reform: family law in post-unification Yemen', *Islamic Law and Society* 10,1 (2003), 12-33

— 'Mobilising Islam and custom against statutory reform: *bayt al-ta'a* in Yemen', in Dupret and Burgat (eds), *Le shaykh et le procurer.* (2005), pp. 289-308.

Wynn, Lisa, 'Marriage contracts and women's rights in Saudi Arabia', in Hoodfar, *Shifting boundaries*, pp.106-120.

Yamani, Mai (ed) *Feminism and Islam: legal and literary perspectives.* (Reading, 1996).

Yilmaz, Ihsan, 'Secular law and the emergence of unofficial Turkish Islamic law', 58/ 1 *Middle East Journal* (2002).

Zakariya, Huda, 'Al-khul': dirasa fi 'ilm al-ijtima' al-qanuni', in al-Sawi (ed), *Al-hisad* (2003), pp.45-81.

Zubaida, Sami, *Law and power in the Islamic world.* (London, 2003).

Zulficar, Mona and Hoda al-Sadda, 'Hawl mashru' tatawwir namudhij 'aqd al-zawaj', *Hagar* 3-4 (1996).

Al-Zulmi, Mustafa Ibrahim, and Ali Ahmad Salih al-Mahdawi, *Usul al-fiqh fi nasijihi al-jadid wa tatbiqatuhu fi al-tashri'at al-qanuniya wa khassatan al-qanun al-madani al-urduni* (Irbid, 1999).

Index